Rwanda
a country study

Foreign Area Studies
The American University
Coauthors
Richard F. Nyrop, Lyle E. Brenneman,
Roy V. Hibbs, Charlene A. James,
Susan MacKnight, Gordon C. McDonald
Research Completed April 1969

On the cover: Hoe and sickle, bow and arrow symbolize
 peaceful agricultural work and Rwanda's readiness
 to defend its liberties. Illustration by Paul T. Angel.

First Edition, 1974; Fifth Printing, 1985

Library of Congress Catalog Card Number: 72-606089

Headquarters, Department of the Army
DA Pam 550–84

FOREWORD

This volume is one of a continuing series of books written by Foreign Area Studies, The American University, under the Area Handbook Program. The last page of this book provides a listing of other country studies published. Each book in the series deals with a particular foreign country, describing and analyzing the economic, national security, political, and social systems and institutions and examining the interrelationships of those systems and institutions and the ways that they are shaped by cultural factors. Each study is written by a multidisciplinary team of social scientists. The authors seek to provide a basic insight and understanding of the society under observation, striving for a dynamic rather than a static portrayal of it. The study focuses on historical antecedents and on the cultural, political, and socioeconomic characteristics that contribute to cohesion and cleavage within the society. Particular attention is given to the origins and traditions of the people who make up the society, their dominant beliefs and values, their community of interests and the issues on which they are divided, the nature and extent of their involvement with the national institutions, and their attitudes toward each other and toward the social system and political order within which they live.

The contents of the book represent the work of Foreign Area Studies and are not set forth as the official view of the United States government. The authors have sought to adhere to accepted standards of scholarly objectivity. Such corrections, additions, and suggestions for factual or other change that readers may have will be welcomed for use in future revisions.

William Evans-Smith, Director
Foreign Area Studies
The American University
5010 Wisconsin Ave., NW
Washington, D.C. 20016

PREFACE

Rwanda, a small, landlocked country in east-central Africa that gained independence from Belgium in 1962, is engaged in the process of nation building and economic development. As of early 1969, the Government, under the leadership of President Grégoire Kayibanda and the only political party, was endeavoring to promote social and political unity and economic development.

This book is an attempt to provide in a compact, convenient, balanced, and objective form an integrated exposition and analysis of the dominant social, political, and economic aspects of the society. It is designed to give readers an understanding of the dynamics of the component elements of the society and an insight into the ideas and feelings of its people.

Sources of information used included scholarly studies, official reports and publications, reports by missionary organizations, and current newspapers and periodicals. The economic data available were subject to varying degrees of error, and most available ethnographic studies were based on field work completed before the social and political revolution that occurred immediately before independence.

The spelling of proper names conforms to the current usage in the country. Prefixes, which are used in Bantu languages to indicate categories—e.g., Ba for people, Mu for man—have not been used. The ethnic groups are referred to simply as Hutu, Tutsi, and Twa, and no indication of the plural is made. Throughout the book, Rwanda as opposed to the preindependence spelling of Ruanda is used. Place names are given as established by the United States Board on Geographic Names as of November 1964. A brief glossary of acronyms, economic terms, and foreign words is included for the convenience of the reader.

COUNTRY SUMMARY

1. COUNTRY: Republic of Rwanda.

2. GOVERNMENT: Secured independence from Belgium on July 1, 1962. Constitution of November 24, 1962 provides for a unitary republic with executive, legislative, and judicial branches of government.

3. POPULATION: Approximately 3.6 million in early 1969 with estimated growth rate of 3 percent per annum. Hutu ethnic group constitutes about 88 percent; Tutsi about 11 percent; Twa less than 1 percent. Europeans and Asians about .02 percent.

4. SIZE: Area 10,186 square miles.

5. TOPOGRAPHY: Mostly hilly but with some swamps and extensive mountainous areas. Most of land at least 3,000 feet above sea level; average altitude of densely populated central plateau region 4,700 feet and average for country 5,200 feet.

6. LANGUAGES: Kinyarwanda, a Bantu language spoken by all Rwandans, and French the official languages. Limited commercial use of Swahili, an East African trade language. Very limited English.

7. RELIGION: Over 40 percent Christian, mostly Roman Catholic. Remainder observe traditional animist religions. The few Asians are Hindus or Muslims.

8. EDUCATION: Rapidly expanding school system in 1967–68 had about 372,000 students in 6-grade primary system; about 8,800 in secondary system. National University of Rwanda had about 160 students and National Pedagogical Institute about 70. There is instruction in French from the 4th primary grade.

9. HEALTH: Principal diseases: *kwashiorkor*; bronchial and lobar pneumonia; infectious hepatitis; bacillic and amoebic dysentery; malaria, and tuberculosis, many of which are endemic. Approximately one doctor per 70,000 persons.

10. CLIMATE: Pleasant tropical highland climate, with daily temperature range as much as 25°. Two wet, and two relatively dry seasons. Kigali, the capital and largest city, is located on central plateau with average temperature of 66° and 40 inches rain.

11. JUSTICE: Formal legal structure headed by Supreme Court. Despite expanding body of written law, overwhelming majority of civil and criminal cases resolved in customary courts pursuant to customary law.

12. ADMINISTRATIVE DIVISIONS: Ten administrative divisions (prefectures) and 141 sub-divisions (communes).

13. ECONOMY: Predominantly subsistence agriculture, supplemented by a small amount of cash-crop production for export of coffee, tea, and pyrethrum. Major food crops bananas, sweet potatoes, cassava, sorghum, and legumes. Food-crop production generally failed to keep pace with expansion in population. *Industry:* Extremely small manufacturing sector, limited to processing of agricultural produce. Construction industry small but growing. Main mineral production tin ore. *Labor Force:* About 90 percent of population engaged in subsistence agriculture. In 1966 about 84,000 persons employed temporarily or permanently for wages. Many skilled positions filled by foreigners.

14. FOREIGN ECONOMIC RELATIONS: *Exports:* In 1967 coffee accounted for 56 percent of export earnings and tin ore for 30 percent. Small but increasing amounts of tea and pyrethrum also exported. About 90 percent of coffee exports sold to United States; Belgium main purchaser of tin ore. *Imports:* Heavily dependent on imports. In 1967 textiles and semifinished products each accounted for one-quarter of total value of imports. Belgium main supplier, followed by Uganda and Japan. *Aid Agreements:* Belgium main source of project aid and technical assistance. European Economic Community second largest donor. Aid also received from United Nations, United States, Republic of China, Switzerland, Canada, and Federal Republic of Germany.

15. FINANCE: *Currency:* Rwandan franc, valued at approximately U.S.$0.01. Currency devalued from 50 to 100 Rwandan francs per United States dollar in April 1966. *Banking:* Central bank, National Bank of Rwanda, issues currency and acts as banker to Government and to 2 commercial banks. Has considerable influence in economy. *Public Finance:* Large deficit, financed mainly by advances from central bank. Defense and education together absorb one-half of current expenditures. Import, export, and excise taxes main sources of Government current receipts. Virtually no public savings.

16. COMMUNICATIONS: *Radio:* Government owned and operated. One 50 kw transmitter, an estimated 20,000 receivers. No television. Very small telephone system. *Newspapers:* 3 monthly, low circulation.

17. ROADS: 3,090 route miles, about 1,360 of which central Government has responsibility for maintenance. Few bridges; many routes washed out in rainy seasons.

18. AIRFIELDS: Main airport at Kigali capable of receiving 4-engine jet aircraft; 10 other, smaller airfields.

19. PRINCIPAL AIRLINES: Served by Sabena, Air Congo and East African Airways.

20. INTERNATIONAL ORGANIZATIONS AND MEMBERSHIPS: United Nations; Organization of African Unity, and UAM (African and Malagasy Union). Associate members of European Economic Community.

21. SECURITY FORCES: *National Guard:* over 2,500, mainly infantry. *Police:* Over 1,000 men.

RWANDA

TABLE OF CONTENTS

Economy—Public Order and Internal Security—Incidence of Crime—Control of Firearms

LIST OF ILLUSTRATIONS

Figure

LIST OF TABLES

Table

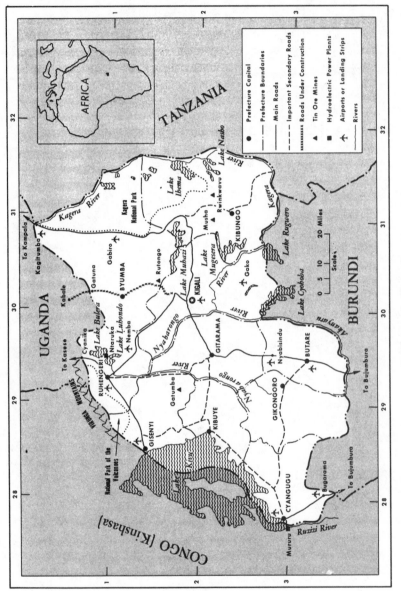

Figure 1. Rwanda

CHAPTER 1

GENERAL CHARACTER OF THE SOCIETY

Rwanda regained independence on July 1, 1962, after over half a century of foreign rule, first by the Germans and then, after World War I, by the Belgians. Both colonial powers ruled indirectly through the traditional hierarchical system in which the Tutsi, an ethnic minority constituting about 14 percent of the population, had for over 400 years maintained social, political, and economic dominance over the Hutu, the ethnic majority with about 85 percent of the population. By the 1950's, however, the democratic and Christian concepts of equality and freedom, which were taught in the missionary schools, prompted the Hutu leaders to challenge, and eventually to overthrow, the ancient feudal regime. As a result of extensive rioting in 1959 and 1960 and an election in 1961, the Hutu majority wrested power from the Tutsi and abolished the Tutsi monarchy, and Rwanda regained independence not as a feudal kingdom, but as a democratic republic (see Historical Setting, ch. 2).

The country is landlocked, located just south of the equator in east-central Africa, about 700 miles from the Indian Ocean (see fig. 1). Much of the terrain of 10,186 square miles is covered by grasslands and small hillside farms, but there are also swamplands and mountains, including volcanic peaks north of Lake Kivu in the northeastern corner.

Most of the land is at least 3,000 feet above sea level, and the heaviest concentrations of people are in the central uplands at 5,000- to 7,000-foot levels. There are few towns or villages, and the overwhelming majority of the people live in small kin-group clusters along the hillsides. In early 1969 Kigali, the capital and, with a population of about 15,000, the largest city, was the only urban area (see Physical Environment, ch. 3).

In early 1969 there were an estimated 3.6 million Rwandans, of whom about 88 percent were Hutu; 11 percent, Tutsi; and less than 1 percent, Twa, a small tribe of pygmoid people. The population growth rate was believed to be between 3 and 3.6 percent annually. There were, in 1969, an estimated 8,000 Europeans and Asians, few of whom were Rwandan citizens (see Ethnic Groups, ch. 4).

1

All Rwandans speak Kinyarwanda, a Bantu language, Kinyarwanda, is the language of instruction for the first 4 years of school, but from that point on all instruction is in French, which is, with Kinyarwanda, an official language. In 1968 Government expenditures on education took over 27 percent of the budget, as compared to about 23 percent for the security forces and about 9 percent for health, the other two large items in the budget. With minor exceptions, education is compulsory until a person is 16 years of age, but in 1969 only an estimated 60 percent of the school-age children were in school, and only about 25 percent of those who started remained in school past the 4th grade. In early 1969 estimates of literacy in either Kinyarwanda or French ranged from 10 to 25 percent (see Education, ch. 7; Public Finance, ch. 8).

The nation's economy is almost totally dependent on agriculture. An estimated 90 percent of the population is directly engaged in subsistence or cash-crop farming, and additional persons are employed in industries and commercial firms closely linked to agriculture. Although most farming is subsistence food-crop production, exports of coffee, tea, and pyrethrum (a flower used in the production of insecticides) account for about 60 percent of foreign exchange earnings (see Agriculture, ch. 9).

The major food crops are bananas, sweet potatoes, cassava, sorghum, and legumes. Most of the banana crop is used to make beer, the extensive consumption of which is socially important since most adults and virtually all men drink large quantities on all social occasions (see Social Values, ch. 5). Food production has generally failed to keep pace with the high population growth rate, and the agricultural economy has on occasion, because of bad weather, experienced sharp production declines, resulting in famine (see Physical Environment, ch. 3).

The limited industrial sector consists of a few agricultural-products processing plants and simple manufacturing at the artisan and workshop level. Industrial expansion is hampered by limited domestic investment capital, the lack of skilled labor, the absence of a Rwandan entrepreneurial class, and the small domestic demand for industrial goods (see Industry, ch. 9).

An estimated two-thirds of the paid labor force of about 80,000 persons are employed in private industry, principally in agriculture, the processing plants, and mining. The Government, however, is the largest single employer (see Labor Force, ch. 9).

In early 1969, although approximately 55 percent of the population adhered to traditional, animistic beliefs, Christianity, particularly Roman Catholicism, continued to be of paramount importance. An estimated 80 percent of the primary schools and almost all of the secondary schools are operated by Catholic missions. Many of the country's leaders, including President Grégoire Kayibanda and many of his senior associates, are former seminarians. In addition, Catholic concepts of natural law form an important part of the Constitution (see Religion, ch. 5).

It was in the Catholic mission schools that egalitarian concepts were first heard by the oppressed Hutu. Until shortly before independence, most of the students in the schools were Tutsi, particularly the sons of Tutsi nobles. By the 1950's, however, numerous Hutu who had studied in the mission schools began to question the "premise of inequality" that had centered all power not held by the Belgians in the hands of the Tutsi minority. In 1958 these young Hutu leaders founded a political party, the Party of the Hutu Emancipation Movement (Parti du mouvement de l'emancipation Hutu—PARMEHUTU), and published a manifesto demanding equal rights. By 1961 the Tutsi monarchy had been deposed, and the PARMEHUTU had formed a preindependence government which negotiated and concluded the terms of independence with the Belgians and the Trusteeship Council (see Historical Setting, ch. 2).

Under the leadership of its president, President Kayibanda, PARMEHUTU has dominated political events since independence. In early 1969 all key elected and appointed officials of the Government belonged to and were active in PARMEHUTU, the only active political party.

The Constitution, which was approved on November 24, 1962, provides for a unitary republic with executive, legislative, and judicial branches. Tradition and constitutional prerogatives combine to make the President a powerful chief executive. The President has extensive appointive powers, and he and his government share legislative power with the National Assembly (see Political and Governmental Systems, ch. 6).

Under Kayibanda's leadership and direction, Rwanda has adhered to an independent but generally pro-Western foreign policy. A primary concern has been the procurement of foreign economic aid and assistance, a large percentage of which, in 1969, continued to come from Belgium.

In both the United Nations and the Organization of African Unity, Rwanda has acted in harmony with other newly independent African states in opposition to Portuguese rule in Angola and Mozambique, and to the white minority governments of Rhodesia and South Africa. Rwanda has been equally outspoken and specific in its criticism of Communist activity in Africa, particularly of the People's Republic of China (see Foreign Relations, ch. 6).

In early 1969, because of the diminished threat of any attempt by Tutsi refugees to invade the country, the authorities were not confronted with any threats to the nation's security. The security forces are largely Belgian equipped and trained and have a number of Belgian advisers. In early 1969 the Minister of Police and National Guard, Lieutenant Colonel Juvenal Habyarimana, who was responsible directly to the President, was in operational control of both forces (see The Armed Forces, ch. 10).

CHAPTER 2

HISTORICAL SETTING

The Republic of Rwanda became an independent member of the world community of nations as recently as 1962, but its existence as a social and political entity can be traced back through several centuries with two distinct periods, precolonial and colonial. In the precolonial period, dating from the 14th or 15th century to the close of the 19th century, most of the present area of the country was gradually brought under the centralized control of the Tutsi monarchy and was developed into a cohesive social and political system. During a colonial period that covered slightly more than a half-century, the area was administered successively by Germany and Belgium. The Belgian Administration was instituted officially in 1919 under a mandate of the League of Nations and, after 1946, was continued under a Trusteeship Agreement of the United Nations (UN).

Rwanda shared its colonial history with Burundi because the two kingdoms were administratively joined by Germany into a single territory. Historically, they had been separate, and the two administrations were unable to develop them into a political union.

The single most important fact in the preindependence history was the domination of the Hutu majority by the Tutsi minority. Two periods of colonial rule did not basically alter the traditional structure; in fact, for reasons of expediency, the colonial administrations served to reinforce Tutsi control.

The colonial era did, however, foster a gradual political, social, and economic evolution of the Hutu. Restrictions placed on the arbitrary powers of the monarch, the introduction of a money economy, and the access of a growing number of Hutu to some degree of education were among the factors that contributed to the eventual dissolution of Tutsi dominance. An awakening Hutu political consciousness during the 1950's created a momentum that resulted in the collapse of the Tutsi monarchy in 1959 and led to political independence as a republic on July 1, 1962.

5

BEFORE COLONIALISM

The Period Covered by Tradition

Little is known of the origins of the present-day inhabitants. Since there were no written histories before the arrival of the Europeans, information on the pre-European period is derived from investigations of popular traditions and the oral records of the chroniclers of the royal court.

The population is made up of three distinct ethnic groups: Twa, Hutu, and Tutsi (see Ethnic Groups and Languages, ch. 4). The Hutu and Tutsi came into the mountainous regions of central Africa in widely separated phases. The Twa, the first inhabitants, are a pygmoid people believed to be related to the pygmies of the Congo forest. Most of them live in the northern regions where they have existed mainly as hunters and food gatherers. In 1969 they constituted less than 1 percent of the total population.

Hutu origins are obscure, though it is clear that they were the principal occupants of the region at the time of the Tutsi arrival. Hutu life centered about small-scale agriculture, and social organization was based on the clan, with petty kings ruling over limited domains. These kings were called Bahinza "those who cause things to grow," and their strength was based on the popular belief that they controlled fertility. The Bahinza were believed to be endowed with magical powers by which they could cause rain to fall and seeds to germinate and could protect crops from insects and cattle from disease.

The Tutsi are believed to have first penetrated the area in the 14th or 15th century, entering from the northeast. Nomadic pastoralists, they came not in a sudden invasion but, rather, through the process of a slow and largely peaceful infiltration. Although far fewer in number, the Tutsi used their possession of cattle and their more advanced knowledge of warfare as sources of power and prestige and, in time, achieved economic, social, and political dominance over the Hutu. Their striking physical size and aristocratic bearing lent credibility to their claims of being divinely ordained to rule. Over a period of time the ownership of the land was taken from the Hutu, becoming the property of the Tutsi king, the Mwami (see Ethnic Groups and Languages, ch. 4).

The relationship between the Tutsi and Hutu came to be expressed in the form of a patron-client contract called *ubuhake*, an agreement by which the Hutu obtained the use of Tutsi cattle and, in return, rendered personal and military service to the owners of the cattle.

This agreement probably began as a simple, small-scale exchange of a cow for land and labor, but eventually it crystallized into a feudal-type class system in which land, cattle, and power were in the hands of the Tutsi. Hutu peasants bound themselves to individual Tutsi lords, giving agricultural goods and personal services in exchange for the lord's protection and use of his cattle. The *ubuhake* between the ruling Tutsi minority and the subject Hutu majority became the dominant factor in the political and social organization.

The Mwami, who stood at the apex of the pyramid-like political structure, was considered to be of divine origin and was said to be "the eye through which God looks upon Rwanda." The royal symbol of the power of the Mwami was the *kalinga*, or sacred drum, on which the genitals of vanquished enemies were hung.

The myth of divine origin was elaborated and preserved by the royal chroniclers of the Mwami's court. According to this myth, three children—Kigwa, his brother Mututsi, and their sister Nyampundu—were born in the heavens but, by accident, fell to the earth, bringing with them fire, iron, the forge, and cattle. Kigwa married his sister and founded the dominant Tutsi clan of the Abanyiginya. The line of descent is traced through a series of legendary ancestors, who are called *ibimanuka*, "those fallen from the heavens," to Gihanga, whose name means "founder."

According to Tutsi tradition, Gihanga led the migration of his people into the area of present-day Rwanda and established them in the region between Lake Muhazi and Lake Mugesera. The area was first divided into a number of hereditary chieftaincies, and the Mwami was only first among equals. Gihanga is said to have designated his son Kanyaruanda as his heir and commanded that all other descendants submit to his rule. The fact that the other descendants were not submissive to the chosen heir is cited in the royal mythology as the justification for the expansion, by force, of what was at first only a small chieftaincy, centering in the region of Lake Muhazi.

Tradition relates that, after Gihanga, there were several other Bami (plural of Mwami), but the expansionist period was most fully initiated by Mwami Ruganzu I Bwimba who, according to oral historians, began his reign in the last decade of the 15th century.

The history from the 15th through the late 19th centuries is one of conflict and expansion. Mwami Mibambwe I Mutabazi of the mid-16th century is credited with centralizing the monarchy and reducing neighboring chiefs to vassalage. During this 400-year period there were frequent conflicts between Rwanda and Burundi, creating a historical enmity which later caused the leaders of Rwanda and Burundi to resist all attempts by the UN to unite them politically.

By the late 19th century Mwami Kigeri IV had established the borders much as they existed when the Germans arrived in 1894. The Mwami's control was strongest in the immediate areas surrounding the capital, Nyanza, and in areas of easy access, but his control decreased in proportion to the distance vassal chiefs were located from the Mwami's power center. In the Hutu-controlled areas of the northwest there was a continuing struggle for hegemony throughout the history of the kindom. This area was never brought under the complete control of the Mwami's government, and it is from here that the strongest Hutu influences emanated in the decade preceding independence.

The Basis of Tutsi Rule

The structure of the Tutsi monarchial system as it existed toward the close of the 19th century was organized by Mwami Yuhi IV Gahindiro, who reigned about 1830. The Mwami dominated a complex hierarchy of chiefs and subchiefs structured into a delicate balance of power and allegiance based on self-interest.

Below the Mwami were the members of Council of Great Chiefs who served as the monarch's advisers on important matters and as chiefs of the more important of the districts into which the kingdom was divided. In each of these districts there were two administrative chiefs, a cattle chief and a land chief, who collected tribute in livestock or agricultural produce, respectively. Tribute made the offices profitable, and the Mwami used it to reward loyal service as well as to assure continued fealty on the part of those in office.

Districts, in turn, were divided into *umusozi*, or hills, under hill chiefs. These were again divided into neighborhoods, each division having a type of subchief. Over 95 percent of these administrative posts were held by Tutsi.

Critically important in the Mwami-dominated system were the military chiefs, who were given full control over the frontier districts. Their functions were both offensive and defensive, carrying out cattle raids on neighboring groups, as well as protecting the frontiers. It frequently occurred that the great chief was also named an army chief.

Another important institution in the system was that of the *biru*, or council of guardians of traditions. These honored persons advised the Mwami of those special duties of his office which were ordained by supernatural forces. They were entrusted with the memorization of the court rituals and with the selection of the Mwami's successor.

The entire structure was designed to reinforce the powers and position of the Mwami. On the one hand, the most powerful families were in competition with each other for royal favor and continually sought to secure one of the powerful chieftaincies at the expense of another family; on the other hand, each chief in the system was either directly responsible to the monarch or was controlled by a higher chief who owed allegiance to the monarch. Thus, the Mwami was able to reign over the entire hierarchical system as the lord of feudal lords.

Legitimacy of Tutsi rule was derived both from conquest and an appeal to divine origins. According to Tutsi traditional belief, the science and mystery of governing were reserved to the elite of their lineages. History was seen as both predestined and cyclic in nature. As a result, the Bami were given names which recurred in sequence; kings having similar names were believed to have similar fortunes. A king with the name Kigeri, for example, was expected to be victorious in war, whereas a Ruganzu was not expected to be and thus would not be an expansionist ruler. In this way, historical precedent was of a sacred nature to the Tutsi. Therefore, the *biru*, who interpreted history and established traditions, were men of great importance to the system.

European Exploration and Annexation

Remoteness and difficulty of access caused the area of Rwanda-Burundi to be one of the last regions of Africa to be penetrated by Europeans. The perimeters of the area had been traversed by the British explorers Sir Richard Burton and John Hanning Speke as early as 1855 in their search for the source of the Nile, but they did not enter Rwanda. In 1861 Speke again passed along the northeastern frontier on his journey to Lake Victoria. Henry Morton Stanley, who came into this same frontier region in 1876, did not penetrate into Rwanda, but started a long controversy between European powers when he claimed to have acquired treaties with several chiefs to a "Mont Mfumbiro" in north-western Rwanda.

The Conference of Berlin in 1885 designated the Kingdoms of Rwanda and Burundi as a German sphere of interest, although it was not until 9 years after the conference that the first European traversed Rwanda. He was the German explorer Count von Götzen, who later became governor of German East Africa. Before his explorations, the European political debates concerning the frontiers of the several spheres of interest in Africa were merely conjectural. Lack of accurate geographical information, vague boundaries, Stanley's claims on behalf of Great Britain to an unknown "Mount Mfumbiro," and overlapping territorial claims formed the basis for a border controversy among Belgium, Germany, and Great Britain that lasted for over a decade.

The area of Rwanda-Burundi was located at the strategic junction of three empires. Belgium's King Leopold II, who held personal dominion over the Congo Free State, wanted the region for its access to Lake Victoria and as a link to the east coast of Africa. Germany desired the area as a part of the formation of a great Mittelafrika, a German central African empire. The British saw the territory as a necessary link in the proposed Cape-to-Cairo railroad, uniting British possessions in the north with those in the south.

During the first decade of the 20th century there was extensive European diplomatic maneuvering in regard to the exact location of the borders of the African territories. The death of King Leopold II in 1909 cleared the way for a 1910 agreement whereby representatives of the three powers settled on the natural frontiers as the boundaries between their possessions, and the territories known today as Rwanda and Burundi officially became possessions of Germany.

During the period of the European diplomatic struggle over colonial boundaries, there were other important forces at work in the region of central Africa. As early as 1898 the Roman Catholic order of the Missionaries of Africa (White Fathers) founded missions in Burundi and, in 1900, the first stations were founded in Rwanda. Protestant missions established their first posts in Rwanda in 1907 and 1908. With their emphasis on education and implicit egalitarianism, the missions had a significant influence on the history of Rwanda during the colonial period (see Religion, ch. 5).

THE COLONIAL PERIOD

German Rule

Although the Council of Berlin designated Rwanda-Burundi as a German sphere of interest in 1885, it was not until the 1890's that the German Government extended its authority in East Africa to cover the region of Rwanda-Burundi. In 1896 a military station was founded in Usumbura in Burundi and, by 1907, a post was established at Kigali in Rwanda with Richard Kandt, a prominent explorer and scientist, as the first Resident.

The Germans, in general, used the existing structure of the Mwami's government. This indirect rule, in fact, characterized the German Administration, and such a system was considered mutually advantageous to both the Germans and the Mwami. Because of the limited size of the German presence in Rwanda, they ruled through the Mwami, and the Mwami, in turn, utilized German force to strengthen his own position. It was during the German period that the Mwami came closer to absolute rule over his entire territory than at any other time.

The most significant aspects of German Administration were the punitive expeditions carried out against rebellious Hutu chiefs in the northern region, who had long proved difficult for the Mwami to control, a phenomenon which continued throughout both the German and Belgian periods. In 1912 Germany sent an expedition into this northern region to supress a revolutionary movement and to punish the murderers of a Catholic missionary. The village of the rebellious chief was attacked and burned and the captured leaders executed. The separatist-minded Hutu leaders of the north were forced to submit to German-backed Tutsi authority.

The German Administration made serious attempts at economic planning, but was able to initiate few of its plans before the outbreak of World War I in 1914. Rwanda-Burundi's economic potential was extremely limited compared with the diamonds, gold, and copper which had been discovered in some of the Belgian and British territories. Cattle were numerous but of limited economic potential, and the agricultural productivity barely supported the population.

In 1913 Richard Kandt, as the German Resident, declared that Rwanda and Burundi must be turned into coffee lands, and shortly thereafter the German Administration initiated the development of coffee as a cash crop. The project, which the Belgians later developed more extensively, introduced the money economy and had far-reaching influence. In time the Hutu came to look upon money as a substitute for cattle as a symbol of wealth and, to the extent that this occurred, Tutsi domination was correspondingly weakened.

Early in 1914 the colonial administration instituted a general head tax. Mwami Musinga opposed this move, concerned that the Hutu, if taxed, might look upon the Germans as their protectors and no longer feel indentured to their Tutsi lords. This fear turned out to be justified, and Tutsi domination was further weakened.

Attempts were made by the German Administration to complete a census, but the difficulty of communications and the limited number of colonial officials made a precise head count impossible. Instead, each chief was required to report the number of huts in his area. The resulting estimate, considered reasonably accurate, was, that in 1911, the African population was approximately 2 million (see Population, ch. 4).

German colonial policy toward the missions provided for mission education of the Tutsi to equip them for a variety of tasks in the administration. Tutsi rule was looked upon as preferential, and the intention was to develop a sizable number of Tutsi civil servants to work under German direction. The missions, however, were permitted to educate a few Hutu, and this became another significant factor in the eventual Hutu emancipation. Through education, the Hutu secured access to new positions and to a status which had previously been denied them. The religious teaching that all men are equal before God was a revolutionary concept in a society with such a rigid class structure.

The German Administration was carried out by a handful of Europeans; the total European population of both Rwanda and Burundi in 1914 was approximately 190, of whom some 130 were missionaries. The remaining 60 included a few traders and about 40 soldiers. In 1914 there were reportedly only five civilian officials in Rwanda.

Some senior German officials viewed World War I as the opportunity to create a great German empire in central Africa by linking the territories of German East Africa to both the Cameroons and South West Africa. Such high ambitions proved illusory, however, for the German forces in East Africa were far inferior to those of her enemies, particularly in the territories of Rwanda-Burundi.

Belgian strength in the area was placed at 7,700 troops, 52 pieces of artillery, and 52 machineguns. In January 1916 German military forces were cited at a total of 1,407 African troops, 166 Germans, 3 cannon, and 12 machineguns in the entire territory of Rwanda-Burundi. In April one-third of this force was withdrawn, so that there was only token German resistance to Belgian occupation of Rwanda-Burundi. German forces were withdrawn from Rwanda-Burundi without a major battle with the advancing Belgian troops. By May 21, 1916, the area was under Belgian control.

Belgian plans for the conquered territories involved their use as a pawn in postwar negotiations. Belgium's hopes were for a three-way exchange: Belgium would cede Rwanda-Burundi to Great Britain; the British would cede a portion of German East Africa to Portugal; and the Portuguese would cede the southern bank of the lower Congo River to be joined to the Congo colony. Belgium's first task, however, was to have its claims to the possession of the conquered territories recognized by the four-power allied council, which consisted of the United States, Great Britain, France, and Italy.

The negotiations were long, and the Portuguese were not amenable to the proposed exchange but, on August 7, 1919, the Council of Four finally recognized Belgium's claims to Rwanda-Burundi. The United States was more hesitant in approving the claims than were the other three members of the council, withholding its vote for 2 weeks.

On August 23, 1923, with the decision of the Council of Four and subsequent approval by the League of Nations, Rwanda-Burundi became a mandated territory of the League under the supervision of Belgium.

Belgian Administration Under the Mandate

Under the Mandate the responsibilities of the Belgian Government were to maintain peace, order, and good administration; to work toward the emancipation of all slaves; to protect the African population from fraud, arms traffic, and the sale of alcoholic beverages; and to promote both social progress and moral well-being. In 1924 the Belgian Parliament formally accepted responsibility for Rwanda-Burundi under the conditions established by the League.

Belgium's administration of the territories followed a pattern similar to that employed by Germany. Confronted with a multitude of problems such as famine, endemic diseases, difficulties of communication, and a scattered population, the Belgians decided to use the political system of the Tutsi aristocracy who still dominated the political-social-economic structure. The colonial administration turned to the existing Tutsi organization in order to be able to concentrate administrative personnel on the more pressing social and economic problems.

The Belgians concluded, however, that, although it was expedient to respect and utilize the traditional political organization, the abuses of the system would have to be eliminated. As early as 1917 the occupying Belgian military forces had placed limits on the arbitrary power of the Mwami and, in order to fulfill the requirements of the League's Mandate, other changes also became necessary.

In 1923 the Administration issued the first of a series of ordinances greatly modifying the system of *ubuhake* and eliminating the payment of tribute to anyone other than the Mwami. In 1926 a number of changes were made in the administrative structure, and the three offices of land chief, cattle chief, and army chief were replaced by a single authority.

Mwami Musinga proved an obstacle to Belgian development plans; thus, the administration deposed him in 1931, sending him into exile in the Congo, where he remained until his death in 1940. Ignoring tradition, the Belgians bypassed the *biru* in the selection of the new Mwami, naming the 18-year-old son of Musinga, Charles Mutara III Rudahigwa, as the new monarch.

Although the terms of the Mandate required that Rwanda-Burundi be maintained as a separate and distinct territory, the League permitted Belgium to administer it as a part of the Congo colony. A law joining Rwanda-Burundi in an administrative union with the Congo was passed by the Belgian Parliament in August 1925. A separate budget was maintained for each colony, but the administrations, customs, and monetary systems were combined into one.

The major colonial policy decisions were made in Brussels in the Ministry of Colonies. The chain of command then passed to the Governor General in Leopoldville and on to the Vice Governor General in Usumbura (Bujumbura), the administrative center for Rwanda-Burundi. Kigali was subordinate to Usumbura in the administrative system, and Rwanda was considered, both in administration and in development, an appendage to Burundi. Many in Brussels considered the territory of Rwanda-Burundi merely another province of the Belgian Congo.

Efforts to make Rwanda-Burundi economically self-sufficient were concentrated on the development of agriculture. After a severe famine in 1928-29 necessitated a large-scale emergency relief program, the Administration tried to ensure the production of a food surplus in good harvest years and to encourage the production of cash crops. The cultivation of coffee as a cash crop, initiated during the German Administration was developed more fully. For the most part, the production of coffee was a European-guided enterprise, with the African farmers being assigned production quotas (see Agriculture, ch. 9).

Government educational policy during the early years of this period concentrated on training the sons of Tutsi chiefs and sub-chiefs. The intent was to enable them to fill positions in the administration and the civil service. For the remainder of the population, emphasis was placed on mass primary education and was carried out mainly through subsidizing the Catholic mission schools. A 1930 report indicated a total of slightly more than 44,000 primary school students attending 552 schools (see Education, ch. 7).

During the period of the Mandate, Belgian policy was focused on goals of gradual social and economic progress. In giving emphasis to these ends, the administration declared that

> . . . the Government should endeavor to maintain and consolidate traditional cadre composed of the Tutsi ruling class, because of its important qualities, its undeniable intellectual superiority and its ruling potential. However, the mentality of this class must gradually

alter. A way must be sought gradually to modify its conception of authority, which must be changed from one of domination exercised solely for the benefit of its holders, to one of a more humane power to be exercised in the interests of the people.

Belgian Administration Under the United Nations

With the formation of the UN, Rwanda-Burundi was made a Trust Territory, and the period of the Mandate was ended. On December 3, 1946, the General Assembly approved the Trusteeship Agreement and made Rwanda-Burundi the charge of Belgium. The Belgian Parliament did not ratify the Trusteeship Agreement until April 1949.

The UN was more explicit than the League in delineating the responsibilities of the Administering Authority. A significant addition to the Trusteeship Agreement, which was not found in the Mandate, involved the political development of the inhabitants. The agreement stated that Belgium was to

> . . . promote the development of free political institutions suited to Rwanda-Burundi. To this end the Administrating Authority shall assure to the inhabitants of Rwanda-Burundi an increasing share in the administration and services . . . of the territory; it shall further such participation of the inhabitants in the representative organs of the people as may be appropriate to the particular conditions of the Territory . . . the Administering Authority shall take all measures conducive to the political advancement of the people of Rwanda-Burundi in accordance with Article 76(b) of the Charter of the United Nations.

The UN's Trusteeship Council sent a number of Visiting Missions to the Trust Territory to review and report on the implementation of the agreement. The first mission visited Rwanda-Burundi in 1948, a second in 1951, and others followed at 3-year intervals. In essence, the views of the first two missions were that social and political advances were proceeding at too slow a pace. They further insisted that the administrative union with the Congo should not be allowed to impede the political development of Rwanda-Burundi.

In response to the conclusions of the 1948 and 1951 Visiting Missions, Belgium implemented a series of reforms in the economic structure, in education, and in the administrative organization. In 1952 proposals for economic and social development were embodied in the Ten-Year Development Plan. In the field of education, important curriculum changes were made in which studies based on African languages and culture were replaced by a program very similar to that practiced in Belgium. The proposed political reforms involved some significant changes in the organization of indigenous political structures and instituted a limited degree of representative government.

The Ten-Year Development Plan was based on extensive research and analysis of the existing situation with regard to natural resources, population pressures, labor, economic development, health, education, and projects of the infrastructure. It was considered necessary to concentrate first on these areas of economic and social advancement before it would be possible to bring about significant political progress.

Although it was the Administration's intention to give precedence to social and economic development, the Decree of July 14, 1952, represented an attempt to broaden participation in Government. By the law of 1943 a limited system of councils had been established to advise the Mwami and the great chiefs in matters of budget and taxation. The 1952 Decree broadened the functions of these councils and allowed for some degree of elected representation. Through a complicated system, part of the membership of each council was chosen by the members of the council below it.

At the bottom of the scale each subchief compiled a list of notables, ". . . taking into account the preferences of the inhabitants." Those named on this list then elected, from among their own number, five to nine members of the "Sub-Chiefdom Advisory Councils." The next higher level was the "Chiefdom Council," composed of the presiding chief; five to nine subchiefs, chosen by their peers; and an equal number of notables, elected by their peers from the membership of the Sub-Chiefdom Councils. This process was repeated again at the level of the Territorial Council, with the notables elected from among members of the Chiefdom Councils. The High Council of State, presided over by the Mwami, was made up of appointed members and notables elected by and from the membership of the Territorial Councils. The implementation of this system in 1953 resulted in the preponderance of Tutsi representation on the councils of Rwanda-Burundi (see table 1).

While the 1954 Visiting Mission was in Rwanda-Burundi, the High Council of Rwanda decided upon the gradual suppression of *ubuhake*. In implementing this decision over the next 4 years, a series of acts brought about the redistribution of ownership of some 200,000 head of cattle. Although the Administration looked upon this as a sign of progress, the Hutu leadership maintained that giving over cattle to the Hutu peasants did little good because the control of the pasturelands was left in the hands of Tutsi lords.The abolition of *ubuhake*, however, had an important psychological impact on the Hutu, who believed that, if the Tutsi control of cattle could be broken, so could the Tutsi control of the land.

A further change in the system of electing members of the advisory councils was made in 1956 when the governor of

16

Table 1. Members of the Rwanda-Burundi Councils, 1953

	Tutsi	Hutu	Twa	Total
Sub-chiefdom electoral colleges (electors appointed)	5,442 (41.4%)	7,674 (58.38%)	29 (0.22%)	13,145
Sub-chiefdom councils (members elected)	2,190 (52.3%)	1,995 (47.65%)	2 (0.05%)	4,187
Chiefdom councils (members)	613 (88.6%)	79 (11.4%)	----------	692
District councils (members)	185 (90.7%)	19 (9.3%)	----------	204
High councils of the state (members)	29 (90.6%)	3 (9.4%)	----------	32

Source: Adapted from United Nations Visiting Mission to Trust Territories in East Africa, 1960, *Report on Ruanda-Urundi*, T/1551, p. 14.

Rwanda-Burundi decided to interpret the Decree of 1952 to allow the notables of the subchiefdom electoral colleges to be chosen by secret ballot of all adult males. This resulted in some Hutu gains on the lower councils. The gains were made mainly in the northern districts of Ruhengeri and Gisenyi, regions which the Mwami's Government had never been able to control fully without direct German or Belgian aid.

A number of Hutu electors, however, whether for reasons of tradition or as a result of intimidation, voted for Tutsi so that Tutsi losses on the lower councils were offset by gains on the High Council of State. (see table 2.)

Events Leading to Independence

In February 1957 the High Council of Rwanda, composed entirely of Tutsi, released its "Statement of Views" calling for definite action leading toward self-government through rapid preparation of the élite. Because of its emphasis on the training of the élite to prepare them for greater responsibilities and participation in Government, the document brought an immediate response from Hutu leaders who saw, in the ideas expressed, a Tutsi attempt to perpetuate their dominant status.

The following month a counterdocument, "The Manifesto of the Bahutu," signed by Grégoire Kayibanda and eight other Hutu leaders, was made public. Although agreeing that Africans should be allowed greater participation in Government, the Manifesto declared that the basic problem of the country was the political, economic, and social domination of the Hutu majority by a Tutsi minority. The Manifesto demanded a continuation of Belgian Trusteeship until such time as this situation could be corrected.

17

Table 2. Results of 1956 Elections in Rwanda-Burundi

	Tutsi	Hutu	Twa	Swahili and Congolese	Total
Sub-chiefdom electoral colleges (electors elected)	3,223 (33.08%)	6,501 (66.72%)	1 (0.01%)	18 (0.19%)	9,743
Sub-chiefdom councils (members elected)	1,895 (45.56%)	2,261 (54.35%)	1 (0.02%)	3 (0.07%)	4,160
Chiefdom councils (members)	597 (84.8%)	107 (15.2%)	----------	----------	704
District councils (members)	163 (88.6%)	21 (11.4%)	----------	----------	184
High councils of the state (members)	31 (96.9%)	1 (3.1%)	----------	----------	32

Source: Adapted from United Nations, Trusteeship Council, Visiting Mission to Trust Territories in East Africa, 1960, *Report on Ruanda-Urundi*, T/1551, p. 15.

The Manifesto of the Bahutu was the first indication of organized Hutu opposition; a further step was taken in June 1957 when the nine signers joined in the formation of the Hutu Social Movement ". . . to promote democratization of institutions and to combat abuses." Together, the Manifesto and the Statement articulated the conflicting principles which promoted the continuing alienation of the Hutu and Tutsi. The 1960 Visiting Mission reported that it was greeted by two contradictory slogans: "Immediate independence. Get rid of the Belgians for us" and "Down with Tutsi feudalism. Long Live Belgian Trusteeship."

A second Hutu organization was formed in November 1957. This was the Association for the Social Betterment of the Masses (Association pour la promotion sociale de la masse—APROSOMA), founded by Joseph Habyarimana Gitera. Through its newspaper, *Ijwa rya rubanda rugafi* (The Voice of the Common People), APROSOMA launched strong attacks on the entire system of Tutsi domination.

Throughout 1958 the Hutu leaders attempted to convince the Mwami and the High Council of the gravity of the problem of Hutu-Tutsi relations. In June a Hutu delegation presented the Hutu case before the High Council. Its views were not accepted, and the APROSOMA newspaper declared that there was reason "to honestly wonder if the Bahutu still have anything to hope for from the Batutsi for their emancipation."

Political activity gained momentum in 1959. Riots in Leopoldville in January caused the Belgian Government to announce its intention to accelerate the program for Congo independence. The possibility of similar action for Rwanda-Burundi motivated both Hutu and Tutsi to attempt to strengthen their positions.

The sudden, unexpected, and mysterious death of Mwami Mutara III on July 24, 1959 initiated a period of intense political activity. Mutara was reported to have died after an injection of an antibiotic, and the Tutsi *biru* acted quickly to name a successor, Jean-Baptiste Ndahindurwa, a son of Musinga and half-brother to Mutara. The Belgian Vice Governor learned of the selection only after the fact, but felt compelled to accept the choice of the *biru*, and the new Mwami was later invested as Kigeri V Ndahindurwa.

The rising tempo of political activity was manifested in the formation of a number of political parties during the next few months. APROSOMA had already been transformed into a political party in January. On September 3 the Rwanda National Union Party (Union nationale ruandaise—UNAR) was founded with the goals of immediate self-government and total independence in 1962 under a hereditary constitutional monarchy Appealing for the unity of all Rwandans, UNAR accused Belgian administrators and missionaries of having divided the country.

Another party, the Rwanda Democratic Rally (Rassemblement Démocratique Ruandaise—RADER), was established on September 14. Advocating an "authentic democracy in harmonious relationship with the various constituent groupings of the Rwandese people," RADER proposed a constitutional monarchy and the election of chiefs through universal suffrage. In addition, the party listed among its purposes the maintenance of good relations with Belgium, the spreading of the Gospel, internal autonomy in 1964, and independence in 1968. The UNAR group charged that RADER was nothing more than a tool of the Belgian administration. RADER played little part in the agitations leading to the subsequent civil disorders.

On October 9, 1959, the Hutu Social Movement was transformed into a fourth political party, the Party of the Hutu Emancipation Movement (Parti du mouvement de l'émancipation Hutu—PARMEHUTU). The declared goals of this party were the termination of Tutsi hegemony and the ending of the feudal system. It called for sweeping land reforms and for ready access by the Hutu to all levels of education. Kayibanda emerged as the leader of the party and, in keeping with the Manifesto of the Hutu published some 2 years earlier, rejected the concept of internal autonomy as another means of perpetuating Tutsi domination. Independence, according to PARMEHUTU, would be possible only after there were guarantees of genuine democracy.

The day after the formation of PARMEHUTU, the Governor of Rwanda-Burundi prohibited all political meetings. Tensions had been increasing daily during October, and the Governor's order was issued with a view to the restoration of calm.

Tensions continued to mount, however, principally because of what was seen as a UNAR-sponsored campaign of intimidation of members of opposition parties through threats and assaults. There was also an attempt by the Belgian Administration to discipline three highly placed Tutsi chiefs for alleged UNAR political activities which were detrimental to the Government. Mwami Kigeri allied himself with the chiefs and declared the action of the administration illegel. The conflict led to a break between the administration and UNAR.

In November the tensions culminated in a series of attacks and counterattacks between Hutu and Tutsi groups. On November 3 a group of Tutsi youths attacked a leader of PARMEHUTU, who was also one of the few Hutu subchiefs. The following day, when it was falsely reported that the Hutu chief had died, Hutu and Tutsi groups clashed and two Tutsi notables were killed. These incidents touched off a wave of violence in which the Hutu pillaged and burned thousands of Tutsi huts, and Tutsi commando bands attacked and killed several PARMEHUTU and APRO-SOMA leaders.

By November 14 the Administration was able to restore order by declaring a state emergency, calling in troops from the Congo, and bringing in two companies of Belgian paratroopers. A number of UNAR leaders were arrested and subsequently convicted by a military court. Several other UNAR leaders fled to Tanganyika or Uganda to avoid prosecution.

One immediate result of the civil disorders was a serious refugee problem. Nearly 5,000 Tutsi huts had been burned, and the number of Tutsi refugees unable to return to their homes reached 7,000. Two more incidents of burning in March and April of 1960 added substantially to the number of refugees. The matter of refugees was made a strong political issue by Tutsi leaders, and the administration charged them with impeding solution of the problem because of political motivations. By the end of April 1960 the number of refugees living in Government refugee centers in Rwanda had grown to 22,000. Others had fled in large numbers to Burundi, Uganda, and the Congo.

At the height of the civil disturbances in November 1959, the Belgian Administration issued a statement of its plans for the political future of Rwanda-Burundi. Earlier that year a special Working Group had been established to visit Rwanda-Burundi, study the political situations, and make recommendations. The proposals made by this Working Group formed the basis for the administration's plans, the main features of which provided for the transformation of the subchiefdoms into communes with a burgomaster and an elected council, and the formation of a new State council, with the Mwami as a figurehead ". . . outside the government and above parties."

In February 1960 the first of the proposed communes was formed and in March, it was announced that communal elections would be held in June. The 1960 Visiting Mission of the UN Trusteeship Commission expressed opposition to the holding of elections at that time, believing that it was first necessary to bring about a measure of reconciliation between the opposing groups. Belgium, however, decided to go ahead with the proposed schedule, and the elections for communal councils were held between June 26 and July 30, 1960. The results were heavily in favor of the Hutu parties. UNAR officially boycotted the elections, although their lists were not withdrawn in some areas, and a few UNAR candidaes were elected (see table 3). Mwami Kigeri went to Leopoldville in July, intending to meet there with the Secretary General of the UN to protest the elections. The Belgian Administration decided not to permit him to return to Rwanda.

On October 26 the administration proclaimed the establishment of a Provisional Government for Rwanda. Gitera was elected President of the Legislative Council by its 48 appointed members. Kayibanda, the head of PARMEHUTU, was appointed Head of the Provisional Government.

Discussion of the Rwanda-Burundi situation at the 15th (1960) Session of the UN's General Assembly resulted in a call for Belgium to hold a conference of all political parties before the proposed general election of 1961 in order to ". . . compose the differences between the parties and to bring about national harmony." The General Assembly also registered regret that the Mwami had been arbitrarily suspended by the Administering Authority and had not been allowed to return to Rwanda. In addition, the General Assembly endorsed the Trusteeship Council's views that the "best future for Rwanda-Burundi lies in the evolution of a single, united and composite State, with such arrangements for the internal autonomy of Ruanda and Urundi as may be agreed upon by their representatives."

In December 1960 the Permanent Representative of Belgium to the UN informed the Secretary General that a conference of political parties of Rwanda-Burundi would be held in Ostend, Belgium, beginning on January 6, 1961. The UN was invited to send observers. At the conference the representatives of the political parties simply restated their views, and no decision was

Table 3. Results of Elections for Communal Councils in Rwanda-Burundi, 1960*

District	PARMEHUTU	APROSOMA	PARMEHUTU/APROSOMA (coalition)	RADER	UNAR	Independents and various other groups	Total seats
Kigali	280	--	--	87	--	11	378
Astrida	237	223	--	28	--	49	537
Nyanza	257	10	--	5	4	45	321
Gitarama	233	--	--	13	1	12	259
Shangugu	--	--	190	11	12	24	237
Kibuye	158	--	--	13	--	19	190
Ruhengeri	359	--	--	4	--	4	367
Kisenyi	257	--	--	6	--	36	299
Kibungu	160	--	--	38	39	33	270
Biumba	259	--	--	4	--	4	267
TOTAL	2,200	233	190	209	56	237	3,125
Percentages	70.4	7.4	6	6.6	1.7	7.9	100

*The names and boundaries of several of these prefectures were changed following independence.

Source: Adapted from United Nations, General Assembly, Interim Report of the United Nations Commission for Ruanda-Urundi, 1961, p. 4.

taken on the future relationship of Rwanda and Burundi. An election date for Rwanda was fixed for January 23, 1961.

Two days before the scheduled election date, however, the Belgian Government announced that it had agreed to follow the recommendations of the UN General Assembly and that the elections would be postponed until such time as it would be possible to arrange a referendum on the question of the Mwami. On January 25 Belgium granted self-government to the Provisional Government of Rwanda, asserting that the measure was necessary to offset the Hutu unrest caused by the decision to postpone elections.

On January 28 a meeting of all burgomasters and communal councilors was convened at Gitarama by the Minister of the Interior, Jean-Baptiste Rwasibo, ostensibly for the purpose of taking steps to ". . . facilitate pacification and the maintenance of order in view of the tense situation resulting from the news concerning the postponement of the elections." Rwasibo declared that Tutsi feudalism and its symbols, especially the *biru* and the Kalinga, were offensive to the people of Rwanda and must be eliminated. Gitera, President of the Council of Rwanda, and Kayibanda, the Prime Minister of the Provisional Government, then introduced a new flag and proclaimed the Republic.

The assembled burgomasters and councilors then chose Dominique Mbonyumutwa, the same Hutu chief whose reported death as the result of an attack of Tutsi youth had sparked the incidents of November 1959, as President of the Republic and elected 44 members of the Legislative Assembly. Of these, 40 were members of PARMEHUTU and four, of APROSOMA. Kayibanda was again named Prime Minister and charged with setting up the Cabinet of the Provisional Government.

Two days later, on February 1, the Belgian Administration declared, that in order to avoid provoking serious disorders in Rwanda, it had decided to grant de facto recognition to the Republican regime. Strong objections came from the UN, and the Trusteeship Commission charged collusion between the PARMEHUTU and Belgian authorities in staging the Gitarama coup. By a vote of 86 to one, the General Assembly passed a resolution declaring that "exclusive responsibility" had been given to Belgium for the administration of Rwanda-Burundi and that Belgium was accountable to the UN for fulfilling the Trusteeship Agreement. In addition, the General Assembly asked Belgium to establish broad-based caretaker governments in both Rwanda and Burundi.

A period of negotiations ensued between Belgium and the Rwanda leadership. On August 4, unable to reach an agreement, the Belgian Government withdrew the de facto recognition of the Hutu Republican regime and resumed administrative powers. Elections, however, were set for September 18.

UN teams attempted to supervise the election preparations as well as the voting and tabulation. In addition to the selection of members of the Legislative Assembly, the electorate voted on questions concerning the future of the monarchy. In the balloting PARMEHUTU received 77.7 percent of the vote; UNAR, 16.8 percent; APROSOMA 3.5 percent; and other parties totaled 2 percent. On the basis of this tabulation, the 44 seats in the Legislative Assembly were distributed as follows: 35 for PARMEHUTU, seven for UNAR, and two for APROSOMA. As to the question of continuing the monarchy, the vote was 80 percent negative, a figure corresponding to the total vote of the two Hutu parties.

After being installed on October 2, 1961, the Legislative Assembly voted to abolish the monarchy, divest the Mwami of all authority, and set up a Republic. On October 26, with the UNAR representative abstaining Kayibanda was elected President of the Republic.

A protocol concluded between Belgium and Rwanda in December 1961 granted Rwanda powers of internal autonomy and paved the way for independence. The 16th Session of the General Assembly requested that representatives of Belgium, Rwanda, and Burundi meet with a five-member UN Commission in Addis Ababa in April 1962 to explore the possibilities of affecting the "closest possible form of political, economic and administrative union" between the two territories. At the meeting there was agreement on the formation of a monetary and customs union and a joint coffee board, but both Rwanda and Burundi felt that, because of ancient antagonisms and because the political developments in the two countries had progressed in different directions, no form of political union was possible.

The final act leading to the close of Belgian Administration came on June 27, 1962, when the General Assembly voted to terminate the Trusteeship Agreement. Three days later, on July 1, 1962, Rwanda attained independence.

CHAPTER 3

PHYSICAL ENVIRONMENT, SETTLEMENT PATTERNS AND LIVING CONDITIONS

The country is landlocked, covering 10,186 square miles, located south of the Equator in east-central Africa, 700 miles from the Indian Ocean (see fig. 1). It borders Uganda to the north, Tanzania to the east, Burundi (previously called Urundi) to the south, and the Democratic Republic of the Congo and Lake Kivu to the west.

The geologic base is an irregularly shaped area of the Great East African Plateau. Much of the countryside is covered by grasslands and small farms extending over rolling hills, but there are also areas of swamps and rugged mountains, including volcanic peaks north of Lake Kivu, in the northwest border area. The divide between two of Africa's great watersheds, the Congo and Nile Basins, extends from north to south through western Rwanda at an average elevation of almost 9,000 feet. On the western slopes of this Congo-Nile ridgeline, the land slopes abruptly toward Lake Kivu in the Great Rift Valley on the western border of the country. The eastern slopes are more moderate, with rolling hills extending across the central uplands, at gradually reduced altitudes, to the plains, swamps, and lakes of the eastern border region.

Except for the eastern and western border areas, high altitudes are common. Most of the land is at least 3,000 feet above sea level; much of the central plateau has an average altitude of 4,700 feet, and the average for the entire country is about 5,200 feet. The heaviest concentrations of people are located in these central uplands, in the 5,000- to 7,500-foot-altitude levels. Trade winds from the Indian Ocean tend to hold temperatures down, providing the plateaus and rolling hills with a climate that is more healthful for human beings than the higher altitudes of the Congo-Nile Crest, the lower altitudes in the Rift Valley, or the areas along the eastern border.

The capital at Kigali, which had grown rapidly to a population of more than 15,000 by 1969, was the only settlement in the nation to have developed the communal organization and exchange of services usually associated with urbanization. Other areas of concentrated population, such as Gitarama or Cyangugu, were enlarged settlements that had only begun to develop the characteristics of organized towns.

Most Rwandans live by subsistence agriculture. Perhaps 5 percent of the population derive a part of their income from occupations such as mining, trade, or labor on commercial plantations. Even among this group or among the relatively few who are nominally town dwellers, most families produce a large part of their food by subsistence farming. Rural families prefer to live on or near the hilltops, above the humidity, floods, and insects that affect the valleys. In many cases, a family will work several small scattered tracts of land, each at different elevations or having different characteristics, in order to reduce the risk of food shortages. Soils in the farming and grazing areas—about 60 percent of the total land area—remain moderately productive, despite intensive farming and damage from erosion.

The country has an extensive road network, consisting almost exclusively of natural materials, and many routes are useful only during dry seasons. There are no railroads and very few useful waterways except for Lake Kivu.

Malnutrition and disease are major problems throughout Rwanda. Kwashiorkor, a shortage of protein in the diet, predisposes the population, especially children, toward debilitating or fatal diseases such as whooping cough, pneumonia, dysentery, and various other illnesses. Recognizing the need, in 1968 the Government allocated 7 percent of the national budget to health programs making such services the third largest item in the budget, exceeded only by education and defense. Missionary organizations maintain some medical facilities, as they have for half a century, and cooperate with the Government in its health programs.

NATURAL REGIONS

There are six regions, from west to east: the narrow Great Rift Valley region along or near Lake Kivu; the volcanic Virunga Mountains and high lava plains of northwestern Rwanda; the steep western slopes of the Congo-Nile Divide, which extends generally north-south in western Rwanda; the high-altitude area near the ridgeline of this mountain range; the rolling hills and valleys of the central plateaus, which slope eastward from the Congo-Nile Ridge; and the savannas and marshlands of the eastern and southeastern border areas, which are lower in altitude, warmer, and drier than the central upland plateaus (see fig. 2).

Lake Kivu and the Rift Valley

In this westernmost region altitudes range from 2,600 to 6,000 feet. Volcanic soils, usually richer than the granite-based soil of the central Rwanda plateaus, are found south and north of Lake Kivu. These have been farmed extensively in the north, and some recent agricultural development and resettlement improvement projects were established in the Ruzizi Valley south of the lake. The climate is fairly regular and humid in this southwestern area, and rainfall averages about 50 inches per year. The northeastern lakeshore areas near Gisenyi include both volcanic and granite-based soils. The climate is temperate and humid, becoming cooler within a few dozen miles of the lakeshore as elevation increases in the Virunga Mountains to the northwest and the Congo-Nile Divide to the east.

The Virunga Mountains

Lava plains in the northwest constitute one of the most productive areas. Above these lava plains five volcanic peaks stand within Rwanda or on the Congo (Kinshasa) border; three more are within the Congo. Two of these former volcanoes still emit steam and smoke. Trade winds moving against these lofty slopes are forced upward into cooler strata, causing an almost constant mist. This moisture fosters a high-altitude rain forest, which includes a great variety of trees, shrubs, and lichens, varying according to altitude. Upper elevations are too cold for trees, despite the proximity to the Equator, and Mt. Karisimbi, at 14,870 feet, is snowcapped.

The Western Slope

East of Lake Kivu a belt averaging 25 miles in width makes up the western face of the Congo-Nile Crest. Within this short horizontal distance the land rises in sharply cut ridges from 4,700 feet at the lakes shore to an average of 9,000 feet at the crest of the divide. The rivers are swift torrents that erode deeply during the rainy months and dry up quickly during the two annual dry seasons. Although the percentage of slope on much of this land makes cultivation difficult, food crops and coffee are produced. Where it has not been removed, the natural cover consists of either bushy savanna or forest trees that tend to form a top cover over open aisles (gallery forests).

The Congo-Nile Crest

Most of the few remaining forests are located on the granite soils of the upper levels of the Nile-Congo Divide, running north-

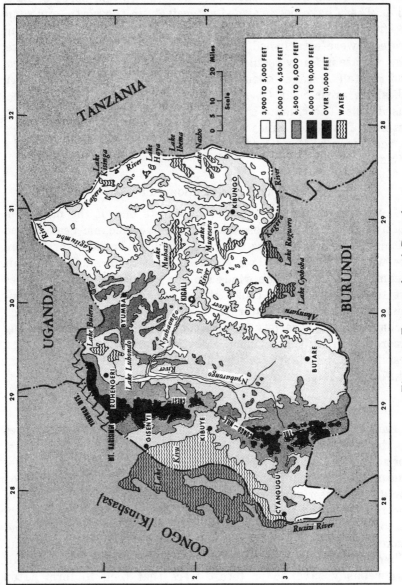

Figure 2. Topography of Rwanda.

south in western Rwanda. The average elevation is about 9,000 feet, but some peaks are 800 feet higher. The mass of peaks is from 12 to 30 miles wide. Rainfall is heavy, averaging 58 inches annually in much of the chain and is especially heavy in the south near the Burundi border, where more than 70 inches is normal. In general, the climate is cooler, more variable, and less comfortable than that of the lower altitudes nearby, and the area has never been densely settled.

The Central Plateaus

East of the mountains lie the central plateaus, covered by rolling hills, becoming progressively lower in altitude as they extend toward the eastern border. Population densities run in the hundreds per square mile over most of these central uplands. The ancient forests, from which the typical soils of this area were derived, have long since disappeared, and the land has been intensively farmed or grazed. One result has been considerable erosion and soil depletion. Under Belgian guidance thousands of miles of hedges and small dikes were established through erosion control projects, and many rows of trees and shrubs remain as visible features of an intensively farmed landscape. Average annual temperatures are near 65° F., and annual rainfall about 50 inches, both figures varying considerably according to altitude. By comparison with most tropical locations, the climate of these plateaus is pleasant and is suitable for the cultivation of a wide variety of subsistence crops.

Eastern Swamps and Savannas

Below the farmlands of the central plateaus lie the savannas and swamps of eastern and southeastern Rwanda, at altitudes averaging 4,200 feet. The weather is hotter and drier than that of the upper plateaus. These low hills and broad valleys may receive no precipitation for up to 6 months of the year in some areas, becoming desert-like, although the rainy months may bring as much as 30 inches of rain per year.

Kagera National Park (Parc National de la Kagera), along the northeastern border, encloses about 1,000 square miles—one-tenth of the nation's territory—of protected homeland for large and small African wildlife species. Low, scrubby trees and thorny bushes dot these grasslands. Between its many lakes and marshes, southeastern Rwanda (south of Kigali), also has a semidesert landscape, despite its 30 to 40 inches of rain annually. As everywhere in the country, particularly in the east, precipitation is irregular. Centuries ago this was a pastoral region, which has since been damaged by overgrazing and brush fires. Small numbers of cattle are still kept here, in spite of diseases such as nagana, the cattle disease related to sleeping sickness. This has been a project area for the resettlement programs of recent years. As tsetse fly infestation is reduced, the area offers two possibilities —draining swamplands and irrigating areas previously too dry for most crops.

NATIONAL AND INTERNAL BOUNDARIES

The national boundaries remain essentially as they were during the colonial period, from 1899 to World War I, and during the subsequent periods of the League of Nations Mandate and the United Nations Trusteeship.

The northern boundary, with Uganda, extends due eastward for 105 miles from a tripoint with Congo (Kinshasa), located on Sabinio Peak in the Virunga Mountains. In its western sections the border area is above 10,000 feet altitude, dropping to 5,000 feet at Rwanda's northeastern point. In some segments, especially in the east, the midlines of each of several streams are the border markers. From Congo (Kinshasa) to the eastern (Tanzania) tripoint, at the juncture of the Kakitumba and Kagera Rivers, the boundary is clearly marked by either streams or pillars.

This dividing line has remained essentially unchanged since it was formalized by agreements between colonial powers in 1910. Relatively heavy populations of from 100 to 250 persons per square mile live on both sides, except in the western mountains. Several roads join the two countries. For several decades and probably for several centuries, there has been considerable temporary and permanent migration in both directions across this border.

In the east the Rwanda-Tanzania boundary originally marked an internal administrative division in German East Africa. The line has continued through the period of Belgium's League of Nations Mandate and United Nations Trusteeships for Ruanda-Urundi, becoming a national boundary when Ruandi-Urundi and Tanganyika achieved independence between 1961 and 1962 as Rwanda, Burundi, and Tanganyika (now Tanzania).

From northeastern Rwanda the boundary extends southward through the swamps and lakes of the Kagera River Valley. In some areas the median line (thalweg) of the river is the boundary. Elsewhere, straight-line segments are marked by pillars. This 135-mile boundary was partially established in 1920, when the former German East Africa was divided into separate mandates. Details were reviewed several times, particularly in 1924, 1934, and 1949. Much of this border area is sparsely populated swampland. Practically no important roads cross this boundary.

A de facto boundary existed between Rwanda and Burundi during the period of German control before World War I. The division of the area of Ruanda-Urundi and the establishment of the present boundary moved through a series of steps taken under Belgian administration during the period of the League of Nations Mandate and, after World War II, the United Nations Trusteeship. On August 14, 1949, the Vice Governor General of the Trusteeship published an ordinance that formally recognized the boundary. When Rwanda and Burundi became independent states in 1962, they accepted the border defined in the statute. There were no active disputes in 1968 concerning the Rwanda-Burundi boundary.

Much of this 180-mile boundary follows rivers, including, from east to west, the Kagera, Akanyaru, and Luhwa. In the eastern area it also traverses Lakes Rugwero and Cyohoha. Segments between river sources are connected by artificial lines. The western tripoint at the junction with Congo (Kinshasa) is at the confluence of the Luhwa and Ruzizi Rivers.

Like the eastern boundary, this southern border traverses many swamps. In other areas, especially in the west, the dividing line crosses sharply eroded ridges and valleys. The west central section crosses the Nile-Congo Divide at an elevation of 8,700 feet. From this forested mountain area the land slopes eastward to the 5,000-foot level in the plateau and lake area of the southeast. Westward there is a drop of 5,000 feet in the 25 mile distance to the Congo (Kinshasa) border at 3,200-foot elevation in the Great Rift Valley. Except in the areas of very poor drainage or high-altitude forest, population density is from 100 to 250 per square mile.

An important road crosses the boundary east of the mountains, connecting Kigali and central Rwanda market towns with Bujumbura, capital of Burundi, commercial center, and port on Lake Tanganyika. Another road crosses the border inside the Great Rift Valley in extreme southwestern Rwanda, connecting the population centers near Lake Kivu in western Rwanda with Lake Tanganyika. Trails also cross this relatively open border in many places. There is little ethnic or linguistic difference between the people on opposite sides of the boundary.

The present boundary with the Congo, now a part of Congo (Kinshasa), was defined by the same 1910 agreements between colonial powers that established the northern border. It remained essentially unchanged as Congo (Kinshasa), Uganda, Rwanda, and Burundi became independent states between 1960 and 1962. Since independence Congo (Kinshasa) has unofficially questioned Rwanda ownership of three small islands in Lake Kivu, but there is at present no active dispute concerning this 135-mile border.

For 71 miles the boundary passes through Lake Kivu. South of the lake the Ruzizi River, in the bottom of the Great Rift Valley, marks the border. From Lake Kivu northward for 37 miles to the Congo-Uganda tripoint on Mt. Sabinio, the separation line passes between high volcanic mountains, rising to the north from Lake Kivu to 4,788 feet. Roads cross into Congo (Kinshasa) at both ends of the lake, which is itself a route for local commerce.

In past centuries, Rwanda's most numerous tribal group, the Hutu, probably migrated through the Great Rift Valley region from the Congo Basin. In recent years, a number of Tutsi refugees, under attack by the Hutu, have moved westward across this boundary.

Some internal governmental matters are administered through the 10 provinces, or prefectures, which are further divided into a total of 141 communes. These 10 provinces are named for their administrative centers: Ruhengeri, Byumba, Gisenyi, Kibuye, Gitarama, Kigali, Cyangugu, Gikongoro, Kibungo, and Butare.

The scope and activities of these prefectural governments are limited. Governmental installations are small, and the expanded settlements in which they are located have not yet developed into fully organized or urbanized centers. Most administrative matters are handled directly from the centrally located capital city of Kigali.

CLIMATE

Altitude, averaging 5,600 feet in the central plateau uplands, accounts for a relatively pleasant tropical highland climate, with daily temperature ranges of as much as 25 degrees, despite the nation's proximity to the Equator. Kigali, centrally located and at an average elevation, has an average temperature of approximately 66°F. from March through July and during November and December, with slightly higher averages at other times. Annual rainfall in this area is about 40 inches, slightly below that of the higher plateaus. Eastward, temperatures increase, and rainfall decreases, becoming sporadic and less dependable in the lower elevations. Daytime temperatures rise to 90°F. and slightly above. Westward and upward from the densely populated central plateau farmlands, the Congo-Nile Crest area is much cooler. Night-time temperatures above the 9,000-foot level may drop below freezing, and annual rainfall may be as much as 70 inches.

Although normally no month of the year is completely dry, there are two wet and two relatively dry seasons annually. In terms of its importance to the subsistence farmer, the climatic year begins with a short dry season, lasting through January and

February, followed by the long rainy season from March to May. June through September are relatively dry months, and rainfall increases again during the last quarter of the year. Heavy downpours are common during this wet season, interspersed with periods of bright sunshine.

Rainfall is derived from moisture-bearing winds moving westward and northwestward from the Indian Ocean. It may result from the clash of these airmasses with equatorial fronts, or from condensation caused by the upward movement of these relatively wet airmasses as they strike the hills and mountains of Rwanda and neighboring areas. As wet air is pushed upward into cooler strata, condensation brings on either local or regional rains. These may be either violent storms that wash away topsoil and hillside terraces, gentle local showers, or prolonged general rains. Since local influences determine at least part of the total, the weekly, monthly, or annual precipitation in a particular commune or province may be erratic. Food surpluses or stored reserves are rare in this heavily populated nation, and local droughts sometimes cause serious food shortages or outright famine in a particular area.

Some of the highest elevations above 8,000 feet in the Congo-Nile Divide may receive more than 70 inches of rain per year, but the average in the heavily populated central uplands is between 40 and 55 inches, depending upon altitude and varying considerably from year to year and from region to region (see fig. 3). In the lower altitudes, such as northeastern and eastern Rwanda, the annual total is lower and less dependable, varying upward or downward from about 30 inches per year.

DRAINAGE

The areas east of the main mountain range, sometimes called the Kagera Basin, drain eventually into the Nile River system. The central uplands and the eastern lakes and swamps are drained by the Nyabarongo River and its main tributaries: the Lukarara, Mwogo, Biruruma, Mukungwa, Base, Nyabugogo, and Akanyaru Rivers. The generalized direction of flow is eastward. Collected runoff moves northward via the Kagera River, which forms much of the eastern boundary, eventually flowing into Lake Victoria.

In these central highlands, east of the Congo-Nile Crest, erosion is a serious problem, although the average slopes are less steep than those of the west. This is an area of small farms and grazing lands spread over rounded hills between eroded gullies. The various plateaus descend eastward in successive

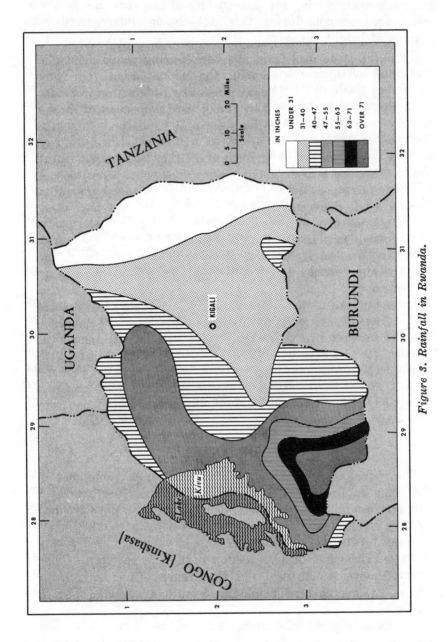

Figure 3. Rainfall in Rwanda.

34

tiers, ending abruptly in central and eastern Rwanda in a series
of escarpments. Below, at approximately 3,000 to 5,000 feet above
sea level, is an irregular basin containing minor elongated valleys, lakes, and swamplands. This basin, less densely populated
than the plateaus that border it on three sides, extends from the
capital city of Kigali to Lake Rugwero on the southeastern border.
Similar swamps and relatively flat lands less desirable for human
habitation than the central highlands, extend over hundreds of
square miles in eastern and southeastern border areas.

The Lake Kivu region west of the mountains is part of the
large Congo drainage basin. The western slopes of the Congo-Nile
Divide form a narrow, steep belt of rugged hills and ravines
between the mountain crests and the lake, sharply eroded by
runoff waters moving swiftly into Lake Kivu or the Ruzizi River
Valley. Kivu, with a 4,700-foot altitude, drains southward into
Lake Tanganyika via the Ruzizi, a swift river that descends
2,300 feet in less than 75 miles.

The upper reaches of most rivers in the mountains of the
Congo-Nile Ridge tend to be steep. They become torrents during
the rainy season and may be completely dry at other times.

VEGETATION AND SOILS

Most of the surviving forests, probably covering less than 3
percent of the nation's land, are at the top of the Congo-Nile
Ridge, on the volcanic mountains of the northwest, or on Wahu
Island in Lake Kivu. Only small vestiges of the ancient forests
remain in other areas, although there are some scattered savanna
woodlands in the eastern provinces. The high-altitude forests,
now controlled by law, tend to be mixed forests in inaccessible
areas, and exploitation is difficult. Although used locally for both
fuel and construction, none of the forests are very important to
the national economy.

Shrubs and trees, such as eucalyptus, grow among the farms
of the central highlands. Many of these were planted during the
past 20 years as part of an erosion control program. Thus, although the original forests have long since been removed from
the heavily populated plateaus, the landscape is not entirely tree-
less. Depending upon altitude, natural tree cover once included a
wide variety of temperate and tropical zone trees, shrubs and
bushes, both evergreen and deciduous.

Most soils contain many of the metal compounds found in
laterite soils, but are generally lighter, more fertile, more work-
able, and less troublesome to agriculturalists than the true
laterites. In some areas, especially in the northwest, soils are

of volcanic origin and are quite fertile. Approximately 30 percent of the land is suitable for farming, and another 30 percent for grazing (see ch. 9, Agriculture).

Most of the farming and grazing areas were derived from the forests that covered the area until they were removed by Hutu farmers during the last 500 years. Except where seriously eroded or leached by heavy farming, humus content and fertility are good, comparing favorably with the soils of many African areas. Soil quality and productivity are usually excellent in the alluvial valleys and the volcanic soils in the northwestern provinces of Gisenyi and Ruhengeri. Tillable soils throughout the country are heavily cropped, producing a large variety of cereals, legumes, grasses, tubers, shrubs, and trees.

Intensive food crop production, often on steep slopes, has led to serious soil erosion. Pastureland has been overgrazed in many areas. Erosion control measures, such as the planting of hedges in appropriate areas to control runoff, were established by the Belgians during the Trusteeship period. Population pressure on the better lands is so intense that soil damage, through leaching, erosion, and intensive farming without adequate fertilizing continues to be a serious problem.

CONSERVATION AREAS AND WILDLIFE

Ruhengeri and Gisenyi Provinces in the northwest are areas of dramatic scenery and rich lava soils, producing both food and commercial crops. Karisimbi, the volcanic peak north of Lake Kivu, rises to 14,870 feet above sea level, almost 2 miles above the average elevation of the Rwanda plateaus. Although located within 100 miles of the Equator, the mountain is snowcapped. Above 7,800 feet, a near-permanent mist prevails, fostering a specialized forest that thrives on such conditions. Fast-growing tropical and semitropical forests laced with old buffalo and elephant trails, cover the slopes of the middle elevations. A game preserve and conservation region, the Parc National des Volcans (National Park of the Volcanoes), has been established here in order to preserve special plant and animal species, including the few remaining gorillas. The preserve is adjacent to the border and is contiguous to Albert National Park, maintained on the west side of this border by Congo (Kinshasa).

Southwest, and far below the rain forests, lies Lake Kivu, at approximately 4,700 feet in altitude. The Gisenyi area on the northeastern edge of the lake has been described in Government publications as one of the most beautiful shorelines in the world, combining pleasant beaches, islands, and luxuriant vegetation against a background of high mountains. It attracts a small number of tourists in spite of its distance from main travel routes.

In the northeast, adjacent to the Tanzania border, Kagera National Park, one of Africa's major game preserves, encloses more than 1,000 square miles—one-tenth of the nation's entire land area.

Most of the well-known African animal species are native to Rwanda. Lion, elephant, buffalo, zebra, various kinds of gazelles and related grazing and browsing species, rhinoceros, hippopotamus, warthog, gorilla, and other animals are found in Rwanda. Many thrive especially well in the savannas, swamps and meadowlands of Kagera National Park. There are also pythons, cobras, and other snakes, as well as crocodiles. A variety of fishes, including local species of pike and perch, are found in the various waters except Lake Kivu, where methane-producing organisms discourage fish life. Many types of tropic and temperate zone aquatic and land birds are found in Rwanda.

MINERALS

Known mineral resources include columbo-tantalite, beryllium ore, amblygonite (phosphate of lithium), cassiterite (tin ore), wolframite (tungsten ore), and small quantities of gold and the rare earths (uranium ores). Large quantities of methane are dissolved in the waters of Lake Kivu. Certain lava beds in the west and northwest contain potassium compounds that can be used for fertilizers.

None of the metallic ores has proved to be rich enough to have a major effect on the economy (see Industry, ch. 9). The most heavily mineralized area extends from the Congo-Nile Crest eastward across the plateaus to the capital at Kigali. Small amounts of various ores have been recorded in most areas except the northeast.

TRANSPORTATION AND COMMUNICATIONS

The road network is extensive, but only a few miles have been hard-surfaced. Many routes are impassable during the rainy months. The system was developed by the Belgians, primarily to link the administrative and commercial centers that they had initiated. Unsurfaced dirt roads, typically constructed of laterite, connect the capital at Kigali with all 10 prefectures. Counting local routes and unfinished tracks, the system includes about 3,090 route miles, among the densest networks in Africa. There are few bridges; many river crossings are simple fords, passable only during dry seasons. About 1,360 miles of this network may be considered main roads, maintained by the national Government. The remaining 1,730 miles includes secondary roads, trails, and tracks, maintained to some degree by local authorities (see Domestic Trade, ch. 8).

The road northeastward from Kigali to the border settlement of Kagitumba is the most important route for external trade, providing a road connection with the railhead at Kampala, Uganda, some 235 miles from Kagitumba and 350 miles from central Rwanda. This railhead is an important connection with outside trade centers, including the Indian Ocean port of Mombasa, about 800 miles southeast of Kampala. Another important road route extends from Kigali to the southern border and on through Burundi to Bujumbura, trade center and port on Lake Tanganyika, a water route to towns and road connections farther south. A second road route to Bujumbura extends southward through the Great Rift Valley from Lake Kivu.

There are no railroads within the country, and no foreign railroads penetrate to the borders. Thus, although their carrying capacity is limited, roads are almost the only means of moving the nation's limited tonnages of internal and external trade.

None of the rivers is navigable for any significant distance. Local water freight movement is limited to Lake Kivu and to short stretches of other lakes and rivers that have only negligible importance. Lake steamers from Congo (Kinshasa) serve the settlements of Kibuye, Cyangugu, and Gisenyi. In 1968 these lakeside settlements had only very small docks and warehouse facilities.

By early 1969 the most important airfield, at Kigali, was adequate to permit landing and limited servicing of four-engine jet aircraft. There were smaller airfields of limited capability at Bugarama, Butare, Cyangugu, Gabiro (near Kagera National Park), Gako, Gisenyi, Kagitumba, Nemba, Nyabisindu, and Ruhengeri.

A Government Post Office, under the Ministry of Postal Services, Telecommunications and Transport, distributes mail twice a week. Some additional services are provided to prefecture officials and burgomasters in the communes.

In 1967 a telephone system serving 300 subscribers in Kigali was replaced by a system for 600, which could be expanded to 2,000. Five other settlements have limited telephone services—Butare, Cyangugu, Gisenyi, Gitarama, and Nyabisindu (Nyanza). Small radio transmitters and receivers provide telephone connections with the administrative center of each prefecture. A 1-kilowatt transmitter connects Kigali with Bujumbura, and a 5-kilowatt unit reaches Nairobi, Kenya, and Brussels, Belgium.

With assistance from the Netherlands, a telecommunications systems connecting Kigali with Kampala, Uganda, was expected to become operational during 1969. A public radio transmitter of 50-kilowatts power broadcasts from Kigali, distributing instruction, news, and entertainment (see Public Information, ch. 7).

LIVING PATTERNS AND CONDITIONS

The pattern of life is overwhelmingly rural, 95 percent of the population being engaged in agriculture. Despite the high density of the population, estimated at 360 per square mile in 1969, there is a very limited degree of urbanization. The few existing villages are products of European rule that were established primarily as administrative centers. In recent years there has been a moderate degree of migration to the few existing towns, which are in fact enlarged settlements. Kigali, the capital and the only center with a population greater than 5,000, has grown from 4,800 in 1959 to an estimated 15,000 in 1968.

In the rural areas the traditional ways of life remain the dominant pattern. Each family occupies a self-contained homestead on its own plot of land. Family units, spread over the summits and slopes of the hills, consist of a small beehive-shaped hut, an *inzu*, and a courtyard within a circular enclosure. Hut size is reduced to the minimum since most activities, including cooking, are carried on in the open air. The dwellings of wealthy landowners are generally larger, the size depending on the wealth and status of the owner, and may include several courtyards. Even a poor family may farm several small plots of land, preferably at different altitudes or on different types of slope or soil, to reduce the risk of crop failure. The hut itself may be burned after several years of use, when its grass roof has rotted and vermin have infested the entire structure. The soil of the hut area, enriched by the ashes, is soon producing crops while a new hut is built elsewhere.

Surrounding the enclosed compound is the family banana plantation, the produce of which is used in the making of beer, a drink important in social functions. Around the banana plantation are several plots used for growing beans, sorghum, corn, and other crops. A family may also work other small pieces of land, separate from the compound, on the lower slopes and in the valleys.

The rhythm of rural life follows the agricultural calendar. Since storage is limited and difficult, it is necessary that one or several food crops be maturing throughout the year. September, which marks the end of the principal dry season, is a time of tilling the soil in preparation for planting. Corn, beans, peas, and millet are generally planted during October and early November in order to gain the maximum benefit from the principal rainy season. Beans and peas are ready for harvest in January, and then sorghum is planted. The principal root crops, cassava (manioc), and sweet potatoes, are planted in the lowlands during February and on the hills in March. The cassava matures beginning in May, whereas corn and sorghum, along with the second bean crop, are ready for harvest during June and July (see Agriculture, ch. 9).

Each crop is harvested with great selectivity. Sweet potatoes large enough to eat are extracted from the earth without disturbing the rest of the plant. Green vegetables and beans are individually collected. By planting a variety of crops the subsistence farmer seeks to insure against disastrous losses resulting from drought, insects, blight, and roving warthogs or antelope.

Settlement is concentrated on the crests and slopes of the hills; the lower lands have been avoided because of higher temperatures and the health hazards posed by the tsetse fly. The preference for living on the upper slopes is deeply ingrained, and the pattern prevails even though the family water supply must be carried up from the valleys. The heaviest concentrations of population are found in the areas where the soil is most fertile, the central plateau regions of Butare (Astrida) and Ruhengeri.

Because of the high population density, reaching a high of 678 per square mile in Ruhengeri Prefecture in 1966, all available land is used for either crops or pasture. Terracing is employed on the hillsides. The amount of arable land available is only 3¼ acres per family. Considering the generally poor soil, absence of fertilizer, and low level of technology, this amount is insufficient. There are also about 3¼ acres of pastureland per head of cattle, but these animals are kept primarily for prestige rather than for food (see Agriculture, ch. 9).

With the implementation in 1952 of the Ten-Year Development Plan for the Economic and Social Development of Ruanda-Urundi, the Belgian Administration carried out a program of tsetse-fly and mosquito eradication in the lowlands and initiated the resettlement of some of the population from the overcrowded regions. It proved difficult, however, to persuade residents of the densely populated uplands to move to these new developments in the southeast and in the Ruzizi Valley of the southwest.

The per capita annual income is one of the lowest in Africa, $40 in 1961. The average Rwandan buys few consumer goods, and the industrial sector is very limited. The Government considers the improvement of living conditions to be of first priority and an important part of the current Five-Year Plan (1967-1972). Its goals include general economic progress, the increased production of food crops, and more adequate means of distribution (see Agriculture, ch. 9; Economic and Financial Systems, ch. 8).

Nutrition and Health

The diet varies with the agricultural season, although some crops, such as cassava, sweet potatoes, and bananas, are usually available all year. Seasonal foods such as corn, peas, beans, and millet are commonly used. Foods of vegetable origin make up most of the meals. Despite the abundance of cattle, meat consumption is minimal. An investigation of the eating habits of a representative cross-section of Rwandans revealed that 56 percent of the meals included sweet potatoes and 50 percent included beans.

Few people eat meat more than once or twice a month, and many even less frequently since for most, it is a luxury they cannot afford. To some, particularly to Tutsi women, meat is taboo. Also, for reasons of tradition, when meat is eaten it is always from a cow, never from a bull or ox. Fish is eaten by only a small portion of the population and is almost unknown in the upland areas.

The average diet is inadequate and unbalanced nutritionally, running heavily to starch and deficient in fats and proteins. Many of the health problems are directly related to deficiencies in diet. Even though the prevalent nutritional diseases are not usually fatal, they are debilitating, breaking down resistance to a long and varied list of other diseases that affect much of the population, especially the children.

Kwashiorkor, a serious form of malnutrition caused by a shortage of protein, is particularly prevalent and damaging among young children. It is frequently caused by the sudden changeover from a protein to a predominantly carbohydrate diet when the child is weaned. It results in the death of many children and a high rate of incidence of liver disorders among older people who have survived it. A government study states that protein and related deficiency conditions account for 11 percent of hospital deaths. In addition, the physical weaknesses brought about by kwashiorkor play an important role in deaths attributed to pneumonia, tuberculosis, whooping cough, and some types of dysentery. The investigation report concludes that malnutrition is the greatest single health problem.

Of the infectious diseases, those presenting the most serious problems are bronchial and lobar pneumonia. Together these are cited as accounting for 25 percent of all hospital deaths. Intestinal illnesses constitute another major health problem, and 11 percent of recorded hospital deaths are attributed to various types of dysentery. In 1968 there were 20,600 cases of whooping cough reported, 22,600 cases of measles, and an estimated 50,000 cases of tuberculosis. An epidemic of infectious hepatitis in 1965 was attributed to contaminated drinking water. Poor sanitation and water pollution also contribute to the spread of bacillic and amoebic dysentery and intestinal parasites.

By 1968 Government planners were placing heavy emphasis on preventive health measures, such as the improvement of nutrition levels and sanitation, as well as the extension of facilities for medical treatment. Implementation of the plan, however, has been limited by lack of sufficient financing and adequately trained personnel.

Both preventive health programs and medical treatment services are included under the responsibilities of the Ministry of Public Health. The Government considers the improvement of health conditions a matter of great importance and has directed a sizable portion of the national budget to health services. The funds allocated to the Ministry of Public Health amounted to about 7 percent of the annual national budget between 1966–68 (see Economic and Financial Systems, ch. 8).

In 1968 the ratio of medical doctors was 1 to each 95,000 inhabitants although there was a medical assistant, having less training than a doctor, for every 70,000 inhabitants. There were 20 hospitals, 82 dispensaries, 14 maternity wards, 1 sanatorium and 1 leprosarium. Of the hospitals, 11 were under direct Government administration, 7 were administered by missionary societies, and 2 by the private mining companies. Missionary organizations sponsored 19 dispensaries, and the Government administered 68. Medical personnel, including nurses, nurses' aides and accredited midwives, totaled 538.

Under the Belgian technical assistance program an agreement was signed in October 1967 by which Belgium agreed to place 15 doctors at the disposal of Rwanda and to provide medicines and medical equipment. The agreement also included plans for Belgium to build a new hospital center in Kigali, in 1968, which was to include a 60-bed clinic and an 80-bed hospitalization unit, at an estimated cost of RF72 million (1 Rwandan franc equals approximately U.S.$0.01). Another hospital was projected for Ruhengeri, to be built with the aid of French funds, and the United States agreed to assist with the building of a water purification plant in Kigali.

CHAPTER 4

POPULATION, INCLUDING ETHNIC GROUPS AND LANGUAGES

In early 1969 the population was estimated to be about 3.6 million, with the highest population density in Africa, averaging nearly 360 inhabitants per square mile. The population growth rate exceeded 3 percent per year and may be as high as 3.6 percent. In 1969 over half the population was under 20 years of age.

The country is also overwhelmingly rural, with small family groups dispersed in clusters throughout its hilly terrain. Urban centers and villages are few, although small settlements have developed near the several Christian mission stations.

The African population is composed primarily of three distinct, hereditary ethnic groups: the Twa, representing approximately 1 percent of the population; the Hutu, about 88 percent of the population; and the Tutsi, less than 10 percent of the population. These three groups are considered the people of Rwanda, or Rwandans.

A small number of Hima pastoral nomads wander throughout the country, and there are an estimated 15,000 Congolese refugees. In addition, there are approximately 5,000 Europeans and 3,000 Asians. The former are mostly missionaries, teachers, and administrators in business or Government; the latter are either small businessmen and traders or perform clerical and technical tasks in business or Government.

Population trends before independence in 1962 were heavily influenced by periodic famines and by the migration of workers to the Belgian Congo (now the Democratic Republic of the Congo —Kinshasa), Tanganyika (now Tanzania), or Uganda. Since independence the emigration of Tutsi political refugees, the growing pressure on the land because of a rapidly growing population, the increasing land erosion, and the Government-sponsored programs for rural and urban development and resettlement have altered the population distribution somewhat.

The national language is Kinyarwanda, a Bantu language. There are minor regional variations in dialect and some differences in pronunciation among the three ethnic groups, but the variations and differences do not prevent mutual intelligibility. French, which was introduced by the Belgian administrators and missionaries, is used in official documents, newspapers, and radio broadcasts. The Rwandan Constitution designates both French and Kinyarwanda as the country's official languages.

ETHNIC GROUP CHARACTERISTICS

Although the three ethnic groups—the Twa, Hutu, and Tutsi—differ markedly in physical characteristics and adhere to general dividing lines in social relationships, they do share a common language. The Hutu and Tutsi are organized in similar kinship and clan systems, agree on a common set of social values, and share either animistic or Christian religious beliefs. Positioning within the social structure for the Hutu and Tutsi was reversed by the social and political events between 1959 and 1962, but many of the essential features of their cultures have been retained.

It is difficult to distinguish which cultural features were principally Tutsi from those which were originally Hutu. Clan membership probably began with the Tutsi, and the focus on cattle, which became the basis of the society, evolved from the pastoral Tutsi tradition. On the other hand, the common language, Kinyarwanda, is the Bantu language of the Hutu.

For several centuries the Tutsi functioned as feudal lords, granting cattle and land usage to Hutu cultivators in exchange for services and goods. As part of the agreement, the Tutsi provided protection for their Hutu clients against other feudal lords. The clientship agreement, *ubuhake*, could be terminated at any time by either party, but it generally was continued by the descendants of both the patron and the client. The relationship was transferred to the deceased's patrilineal descendant. This feudal *ubuhake* relationship was the dominant one in a whole system of dominant-subordinate roles which existed throughout the society (see Social Structure, ch. 5).

The Tutsi and Hutu share essentially the same kinship system and reckon their descent patrilineally. The smallest unit in the patrilineal line is called the *inzu*, or house. It includes all persons, both male and female, who can trace their descent through four or five generations to one ancestor who was the original forefather of the group. The *inzu*, after reaching approximately seven generations, would segment, or subdivide, to form new *inzus* (see Social Structure, ch. 5).

The *ubwoko* is the largest kin group or patriclan organization. Persons in this group recognize a common descent in a paternal

44

line, but are unable to identify a specific ancestor. In some cases the ancestor is a mythical figure. Both Tutsi and Hutu can belong to the same clan. There are 13 *ubwoko* in Rwanda. The Abanyiginya was the most important in that it was the royal clan from which the Bami (plural of Mwami—king) were selected. The queens usually came from the Abega *ubwoko*.

Marriages between Tutsi and Hutu occasionally occur, but marriages of Tutsi or Hutu to Twa are very rare. Intermixing of the ethnic groups in the past was most frequent when Tutsi males acquired Hutu concubines. It was rare for a Hutu male to marry a Tutsi female but, when this occurred, the Hutu's social and political status was elevated. A substantial brideprice of livestock or a substitute was generally required for a marriage; local exogamy, or out-group marriage, was most prevalent (see Family, ch. 5).

The Hutu and Tutsi who have not been converted to Christianity share a common, traditional, animistic religious belief. The dominant spirit or creator-god is Imana, who is described as essentially good and very powerful. Although he is referred to frequently, there are no rites of worship to him. The term *imana* also refers to the force of good, a pervasive power which causes fecundity, prosperity, joy, and peace.

The spirit world also includes *bazimu*, or the spirits of dead ancestors. They cause evil and difficulties for humans. Among the *bazimu* is a small number of ancestors, the *imandwa*, who are very powerful and might be helpful to an individual if he is initiated into the sect of Ryangombe. Apart from the *imandwa*, all other spirits are malevolent toward human beings (see Religion, ch. 5).

The Twa

The Twa are a pygmoid subgroup of the larger group of Twide pygmies who were the first known inhabitants of East and Central Africa. The Twa closely resemble the pygmy type, but are larger in stature. The average male is 5 feet 1 inch in height and weighs 106 pounds. The Twa have wide noses, peppercorn hair, and yellowish-colored body hair.

The Twa are, by preference, forest dwellers with an economy based on food gathering and hunting. Before the arrival of the Tutsi, the Twa retreated before the agrarian Hutu, who systematically reduced the forest area. When the Tutsi achieved political, economic, and social dominance, the Twa settled near the courts of the Tutsi nobility, although small bands remained in the forest areas along the western mountain ridges. During the several centuries of Tutsi monarchy, the Twa served in the Tutsi courts as dancers, buffoons, guards, and concubines and, on occasion, acted as spies and executioners.

The Twa occupy an inferior social position, and many of their dietary and hygenic customs are considered reprehensible by both the Tutsi and Hutu. With the loss of power by the Tutsi and the disappearance of the Tutsi courts, the Twa are even further outside the social structure. A few manage to subsist in the remote forest regions, whereas those who have settled near the Hutu and Tutsi work as potters and artisans.

The Hutu

The Hutu are identified as the Rwandan cluster of the Bantu tribes of the East and Central African lake region. This group also includes tribes in Burundi, parts of Tanzania, Uganda, and Congo (Kinshasa). Little is definitely known of their origin other than that they came from the northern equatorial region.

The average male is 5 feet 5 inches tall and weighs 131 pounds. The Hutu are generally stocky with muscular frames, but because of considerable intermixing with the Tutsi over the past 4 or 5 centuries, many of them have the lighter skin and more slender body structure characteristic of the Tutsi.

Traditionally, the Hutu are hoe cultivators, with little division of labor by sex. Their principal crops include beans, peas, sorghum, cassava, and maize (corn), and almost every household has a banana grove (see Agriculture, ch. 9). Work is highly valued, and the ideal man is one who is prosperous, hardworking, and proud of his reputation, although he may not hold an important position in the social structure (see Social Values, ch. 5).

Before independence the Hutu were the social inferiors of the Tutsi rulers and, in addition to forced contributions of agricultural produce, were obligated to perform numerous menial services for the Tutsi overlords (see Social Structure, ch. 5). Since the political uprising of 1959–61, however, the Hutu have assumed control of the social and political systems. They are still primarily agriculturalists, but they are beginning to develop trades and skills and, with increased educational opportunities, have taken over more significant positions throughout the Government and the economy (see Political Dynamics and Values, ch. 6).

The Tutsi

The Tutsi are fairly tall, angular, small-boned, and relatively light-skinned Nilotic people. Their average height is 5 feet 9 inches and average weight is 126 pounds. Occasionally, a member of the court or a royal dancer exceeded 6 feet 3 inches in height, but this was an exception.

The Tutsi were pastoralists and filled the ranks of the warrior caste. Before independence they regulated and controlled the society, which was composed of Tutsi royalty and nobility and Hutu commoners, by means of a clientship structure (see Social Structure, ch. 5). They occupied the dominant positions in the sharply stratified society and constituted the ruling aristocracy. This form of control was based upon the hierarchical arrangement of Tutsi endogamous clans.

The Tutsi preoccupation with cattle and herding was transmitted to the Hutu agriculturalists. The skills of milking and caring for cattle were spread, and livestock became an integral part of the society and took on importance in the value system.

The Hima

The Hima, a small tribe of Nilotic nomads, travel through the northern and northeastern portions of Rwanda. They are considered bad omens by Rwandans. Legend states that their ancestors lost the land because of illness and evil behavior, and the settled inhabitants have little to do with them.

LANGUAGE AND COMMUNICATIONS

The language of the people is Kinyarwanda, part of the Bantu subgroup of the central branch of the Niger-Congo language family. Kinyarwanda is closely related to Kirundi, the language of Burundi; Kinyarwanda-Kirundi speakers comprise the third largest group of all the Bantu languages.

Kinyarwanda is noted for its great complexities. The language uses five vowels, each having a long and short form. Intonation and tonality pervade both the grammar and vocabulary. There are seven schemes of intonation in addition to one low and three high forms of tonality.

All Rwandans speak Kinyarwanda, but there is some variation in pronunciation. The forms spoken by the Tutsi and Hutu are very similar, whereas the variation used by the Twa has certain peculiarities. There are also dialectical differences between regions. The modes of pronunciation differentiating central and northern Rwanda can be distinguished easily.

The focal points around which much of the vocabulary is built are children and cattle, the latter predominating. Individual characteristics of the cattle, their beauty, and the herds themselves are denoted by numerous words. Much of the oral tradition revolves around their virtues (see Artistic and Intellectual Expression, ch. 7). Metaphors and symbols are also drawn from pastoral activities. The language is rich in nuances and double meanings. The same term is used, for example, for a polygamous family and for jealousy.

In addition to Kinyarwanda, a small number of persons have adopted French as a second language. The monthly periodical *Rwanda Carrefour d'Afrique* (Crossroads of Africa) is published in French, and the country's one radio station broadcasts in French (see Public Information, ch. 7). In some areas Swahili is spoken.

POPULATION STRUCTURE

The figures on population are informed estimates. According to one Government publication, the population increased from 2,988,509 in 1964 to 3,321,706 in 1966, an increase of over 5 percent annually. Other estimates are that the population of approximately 3.6 million is increasing at a rate of about 3.3 percent per year.

Demographic Factors

In 1966, the most recent year for which estimates were available in early 1969, 56 percent of the population was under 20 years of age, and less than 8 percent was over 55 years of age. Those within the 5 to 14 age category accounted for 28.8 percent of the total population. The sex ratio for the total population is approximately 48 percent male and 52 percent female, with sex ratios of all age categories relatively even (see table 4).

Births registered for the year 1965 totaled 82,705. The rate indicated by this figure is 26.6 per 1,000, but the estimated birth rate was 52 per 1,000. Failure to register births and high infant mortality account for the discrepancy.

Deaths registered during the same year totaled 14,822, a rate of 4.8 per 1,000. The estimated death rate, however, is higher at 13.7 per 1,000. Comparative statistics of the constantly under-

Table 4. Population of Rwanda by Sex and Age Groups, 1966 Estimates

Age groups	Male	Percent of total	Female	Percent of total	Age total	Percent of total
Under 20	883,092	26.59	976,860	29.41	1,859,952	56
20 to 55	567,173	17.06	642,263	19.33	1,209,436	36.39
55 and Older	119,635	3.61	132,683	4	252,318	7.61
TOTAL	1,569,900	47.26	1,751,806	52.74	3,321,706	100.00

Source: Adapted from Rwanda, Ministère de la Coopération Internationale et du Plan, Direction de l'Office Général des Statistiques, *Bulletin de Statistique*, No. 16, Janvier 1968, p. 4.

stated figures over several years indicate, however, that the mortality rate has been declining. The estimated crude death rate for 1952–53 was 19 per, 1,000 but had dropped by 1957 to 14 per 1,000. Treatment of disease in hospitals and increased dispensary care presumably account for most of the decrease in deaths. In 1969 there were no official figures available on average life expectancy. Forty years of age is a reasonable estimate.

Population Distribution

The population density was estimated in early 1969 to be about 360 persons per square mile, the highest population density of any African nation and one of the highest in the world. The density varies from a high of 678 per square mile in Ruhengeri Prefecture in the northwest to a low of 141 persons per square mile in Kibungo Prefecture in the southeast (see table 5).

A generally hilly to mountainous terrain, increasing land erosion, a seriously excessive cattle population, and a lack of readily exploitable mineral and other natural resources aggravate the problem of population density. In 1969 it was estimated that there were about 1,140 persons per square mile of arable land, one of the highest population densities in the world (see Settlement Patterns and Living Conditions, ch. 3; Agriculture, ch. 9).

Although a few urban centers are developing, less than 2 percent of the people live in small towns or larger villages. Extended families settle in groups on the hills, with no direct relationship to a larger neighborhood or village group. The pattern is one of rural dispersion with little or no concentration.

Table 5. Prefecture Population by Sex and Population Density in Rwanda, 1966 Estimates

Prefectures	Male	Female	Total	Population density (per square mile)
Ruhengeri	210,940	250,117	461,057	678
Butare	211,660	242,362	454,022	642
Gitarama	203,121	228,762	431,883	499
Kibuye	103,428	103,814	207,242	406
Gisenyi	167,495	177,039	344,534	373
Gikongoro	138,074	156,396	294,470	348
Cyangugu	125,535	132,961	258,496	301
Kigali	146,742	163,201	309,943	247
Byumba	155,831	180,025	335,856	175
Kibungo	107,073	117,130	224,203	141
				Average Density
TOTAL	1,569,899	1,751,807	8,321,706	327

Source: Adapted from Rwanda, Ministère de la Coopération Internationale et du Plan, Direction de l'Office Général des Statistiques, Bulletin de Statistique, No. 16, Janvier 1968, p. 4.

The population is concentrated on hilltops and in plateau regions which are between 4,900 and 6,500 feet in altitude. The lowest population density occurs in areas which are below 4,900 feet. The climate below this height is hot and humid, and the incidence of human and animal diseases is much greater than at the higher altitudes.

Ethnic Group Statistics

There has been no recent census of ethnic groups, Tutsi migration rates are undetermined, and there are discrepancies in the estimates of the number of Tutsi who were killed or who fled during the preindependence revolution.

The Hutu outnumber other Rwandans in all regions. The regional percentages of Tutsi vary from less than 5 percent to as much as 40 percent. The central portion of the country near Nyanza, the traditional residence of the former Mwami, has a large Tutsi population, with approximately 45 percent of all Tutsi residing there.

Non-Rwandan Population Statistics

The non-Rwandan inhabitants account for less than 1 percent of the total population. Approximately 15,000 Africans, mostly Congolese, live in the country. Europeans, mostly Belgians, account for 5,000 of the non-indigenous population. There are about 3,000 Asians, including Pakistanis, Indians, and Arabs, who round out the non-Rwandan population.

Indians and Pakistanis constitute 34 percent of the non-African, non-European population; Arabs, 20 percent; and other Asians, 2 percent. The remaining 44 percent are descendants of mixed Asian, African, or European ancestry, most of whom are of Asian-African descent. In general, the Indian and Pakistani populations have grown rapidly, whereas the Arab population has remained static. Arabs, Pakistanis, and Indians engage almost exclusively in trade.

POPULATION DYNAMICS

Historically, the population has been greatly influenced by periodic famines and by seasonal and permanent migration. In 1968 there had not been a famine in the country for over 25 years. There had been a large exodus of Tutsi between 1959 and 1965. The population increase since independence is attributed primarily to an absence of famine, a sharp decrease in permanent migration, and a notable increase in the availability of medical facilities.

Famines

Between 1897 and 1943 famines occurred in several sections of the country, partly because of the irregular distribution of food and population. In 1928 central and western Rwanda had the worst famine recorded to that date: deaths exceeded 300,000 and migration reached 100,000. During the famine of 1943–44, which was caused by severe drought and subsequent crop failure, approximately 300,000 persons died or migrated.

The Government's efforts to expand its transportation facilities and roads so that food from other areas can be made available to a stricken area and to resettle people from overpopulated areas have seemingly reduced the dangers of extensive famine. In addition, the Agricultural Service is inaugurating studies of microclimates in an effort to develop a general approach to the lacks and inadequacies of the country.

Migration Patterns

In the past both seasonal and permanent migrations have been extensive. The 1957 British East African census figures listed 35,000 migrants to Tanganyika, and Uganda's 1966 Statistical Abstract listed 378,656 Rwandans as permanent residents in 1959.

Migration to neighboring countries before 1959 was economically motivated. Periodic famines and chronic underemployment prompted numerous Rwandans to leave, to become either contract workers in mines in the Belgian Congo or agricultural workers in Uganda. Between 1959 and 1964, however, an estimated 150,000 Tutsi political refugees fled to Burundi, Tanzania, Uganda, and Congo (Kinshasa) (see Foreign Relations, ch. 6). Few have returned, and each year an unknown number of Tutsi join friends and relatives outside the country, usually on a permanent basis. Most of the estimated 15,000 Congolese residing in Rwanda are political refugees from Congo (Kinshasa).

Development Programs and Population Changes

A five-year plan, the Interim Emergency Plan adopted in 1967, focused on the related needs of coping with the population growth, increasing agricultural production, and developing stronger social and communal ties among the rural population. The plan provides for an intensification of the resettlement programs instituted by the Belgian Government in 1953 (see Agriculture, ch. 9). Several thousand families have been moved from overpopulated, badly eroded areas to those less densely populated. In early 1969 it was not possible to determine how successful the

Government's attempts had been to create new social and communal systems among the transferees.

In 1968 Dr. Sixte Butera, Minister of Public Health, suggested that the problem of population increase can be met only through a combination of methods: eliminating polygamy, encouraging later marriages, augmenting food production, and encouraging emigration. The religious, social, and economic aspects of artificial birth control are under official consideration.

Urban and Village Centers

The number of persons living in urban or village areas is less than 2 percent. The urban populations are largely composed of Europeans, Indians, Pakistanis, and Arabs. Before 1962 there were only six principal urban centers with a total population of less than 15,000. By 1969, however, the capital city of Kigali had an estimated population of 15,000. It is estimated that, by 1987, its population will have exceeded 70,000.

Other larger centers include Gisenyi, a residential and tourist center; Butare; Nyabisindu; and Gitarama. For the most part, towns were located, planned, and built by the Belgians.

CHAPTER 5

SOCIAL STRUCTURE, FAMILY, RELIGION, AND SOCIAL VALUES

Although the Hutu revolution of 1959 and 1960 against the Tutsi feudal system resulted in the termination of Tutsi dominance and in a drastic realignment of the social structure, the traditional concept of a hierarchically structured social system centered on the family provides meaning and guidance for most Rwandans. Although the Tutsi no longer enjoy almost exclusive ownership of cattle and land, some form of patron-client relationship continues to exist; however, the relationship is much less rigid and less all-encompassing in nature. In early 1969 there was little information available on the nature and extent of change in the traditional values as a result of the revolution and of European and Christian modernization. There were indications, however, that local kin groups were replacing in importance the traditional clan and bloodline groupings.

Family, clan, and local kin group affiliations continue to be the focal points of societal unity. Close-knit family units are maintained under unquestioned paternal authority. Most persons can associate themselves with large clans of ancient origin, but these have been subdivided into smaller lineages, or groups of persons claiming descent from common ancestors through the male line. Bloodlines continue to be important, but it is the local, loosely defined residential kin group, clustered together on the hilltops, which provides the most support to the maturing individual. The individual seeks happiness through adherence to rigid family and clan traditions. Few nonfamilial social groupings or clubs exist.

The traditional marriage system includes polygyny which, although now illegal, continues in a limited way. Incest taboos preclude marriages between close relatives, but cross-cousin (children of a brother and a sister) marriages are socially approved. In customary law the transfer of the bridewealth from the family of the bridegroom to that of the bride validates the marriage. In 1969 most young men depended upon family cooperation as a means of accumulating the gifts necessary for the bridewealth. It was only in this way that the husband's clan could claim the issue of the marriage.

Christianity, especially Roman Catholicism, has attracted many converts. More than 40 percent of the population was at least nominally Christian in 1967. Many of the existing medical and educational programs were established by missionaries, with financial subsidies from the colonial authority. The Christian schools were instrumental in forming the thoughts of many of the social and political leaders who rose to power in the 1950's and 1960's. President Grégoire Kayibanda and several of his closest political associates were educated in Catholic seminaries. The influence of mission schools continues to be strong but, as a result of increased governmental interest in the educational system, church officials are relinquishing some of their administrative authority (see Education, ch. 7). Many converts vacillate between the teachings of the Christian church and traditional beliefs, but apparently see little contradiction in holding to both religious systems.

According to the traditional value system, the individual must totally resign himself to the will of Imana. This outlook accounts for pronounced fatalistic tendencies and for the widely held belief that neither natural phenomena nor personal fate can be humanly controlled. This conviction, along with strong family ties and the desire for fertility, is the most pervasive social value.

Parents in the tradition-bound society play the major role in teaching their children socially approved traits. Successful men are dignified, eloquent, and constantly cognizant of their parental duties. Collectively, women are respected as the embodiment of fertility, but individual women rarely have any authority. They are trained to be silent and content with their submissive status in the hierarchical society.

Rwandans have a strong emotional attachment to cattle, which are used primarily as media of exchange, indices of wealth and prestige, and symbols of interpersonal contracts. Considerable emphasis is also placed upon beer, made from bananas or sorghum. It is an indispensable factor in social life and is consumed during ritual events and minor occasions of everyday hospitality.

FAMILY

The traditional family is characterized by the orientation of all members to the welfare of the entire group. Family cohesion and stability are founded upon the father's authority. The homestead, or *kraal*, provides a residential base for the nuclear family, which consists of the spouses (at times more than one wife) and their children. On occasion the family may be extended to include other relatives, such as an elderly parent, aunt, or uncle.

Reinforcing the traditional family structure, the Constitution states that the "Family, in its three constituent elements, man, woman, and children is the primary basis of Rwandan society" and that "The father and mother have the natural right to raise their children." Polygyny, originally prohibited by the Roman Catholic church and now outlawed by the Constitution, still occurs to a limited degree, but obtaining more than one wife is generally difficult. In 1969 an estimated 75 percent of the marriages were monogamous; 24 percent, bigamous; and 1 percent, polygamous.

In recent decades the traditional family structure and activities have been influenced by missionary activity. In families that have received some Christian teaching, the members recite psalms taught to them by catechists, but they often pay homage to ancestral gods as well. The discrepancy between the two belief systems does not appear to cause undue concern.

Interfamilial Relations

The male head of the household, exercising the prerogative of authority derived from the clan ancestors, governs all family affairs, and the Constitution declares that "Men and women are legally equal but the man is the natural head of the family." The husband's responsibilities go beyond the immediate affairs of presiding over discussions, allocating family duties, and leading the rites of worship, but also include the responsibility of maintaining the dignity of the family and insuring the future of the clan. Historically, the family head had the right to kill any member of the family who was insubordinate or to punish any member whose actions violated his dignity or detracted from his personal prestige. Respect is so important and behavior so tightly controlled that a child is not allowed to say the father's name.

The father is rewarded for successfully caring for the family by its lifelong loyalty. He can expect propitiation of his spirit after death and vengeance by his heirs if his death results from violence through either physical attack or witchcraft

Although a close and familiar relationship exists between a man and his sons, there is an element of servitude in the sons' role since it is necessary for them to pay a great deal of respect to the father. They may be treated severely, forced to beg for assistance in raising the bridewealth, and then expected to continue serving the father even after establishing their own families. Sons are not emancipated as long as their father is alive.

A strong taboo prohibits the father from entering the huts of his daughters from the time they have reached puberty. After they marry and have a child, he is allowed to resume paternal contact with them. The mother visits the daughters frequently, showing her affection by bringing small gifts. After marriage a daughter is expected to divide her sentiments and loyalties between her own blood relatives and her husband's kin.

Jealousy between brothers is proverbial, but the relationship between brothers and sisters is usually amicable. A male and his sister's children form a special relationship in that he is expected to help provide for and nurture them and is respected as a second father. The father's sisters are also given a great deal of respect by the children.

A strict avoidance taboo separates a male from his mother-in-law and a female from her father-in-law. A bridegroom, desiring respect and friendship, will give the wife's family beer and other gifts periodically. He fears them and is always on guard against any misunderstandings that might occur in the relationship between the two families. The birth of children lessens the requirement for avoidance, and an attitude of distant respect is adopted by both parties.

Family ties are generally so strong and inclusive that there are no unattached persons; all relatives are taken care of by clan members regardless of the actual degree of blood relationship. The elderly, especially grandparents, are provided for within the homestead and are treated with deference, for they will soon join the ancestral spirits. An orphaned child is taken into another nuclear family of his father's clan without formal arrangement. Little notice is taken of the actual parentage; the child is treated as a natural member of the adoptive family.

The death of the family head changes the living pattern within the homestead. Although the various members continue to live in close residential proximity, the original family land is divided among the heirs. The chosen heir, generally the eldest son of the first wife, receives leadership authority, religious amulets, and the personal property and tools of the father. If there are no heirs, the brothers of the deceased divide the property, and the childless widow returns to her family. The property of an individual who dies and leaves no immediate family is traditionally taken over by the clan.

Fictive or Blood Brotherhood

Occasionally, when a member of one clan establishes a strong friendship with a member of another, they enter into a unique type of social relationship, the blood brotherhood. Having decided to share their clan identity, the two parties perform a ceremony to formalize the relationship. Blood from skin incisions on the chest of each man is mixed and drunk by both parties. As part of the ritual, they pledge eternal loyalty and mutual assistance.

Aside from the family there are few units of organization in the society. The *inzu*, or loosely organized patrilineal (male line) group of four or five generations, lives in close proximity either on one or on adjoining *kraals* and is the basis of whatever traditional social organization extends beyond the nuclear family.

The *inzu* provides a limited amount of communal sharing and the necessary hierarchy for superior-inferior relationships. Its functioning is directed by the *umukungu*, or head, who is chosen by all the male members. He presides at all occasions of collective activity, judging disputes, representing the family, if necessary, in governmental affairs, punishing wrongdoings, and assigning tax amounts. When the *inzu* becomes too large, some of its members move elsewhere.

When the relationships of the household are extended to include a larger group of blood kin, members of the *inzu* acknowledge their affinity with other households who share a common ancestor in a lineage group known as the *umuryango*. Although the organization and corporateness of the *umuryango* varies from lineage to lineage, it generally extends to over six generations of persons and enforces a rule of exogamous marriage. Members constitute a residential, politically autonomous group. Traditionally, the *umuryango* was more important to the Tutsi than to the Hutu. Through the lineages, the Tutsi chiefs could recognize their relatives and give them land and cattle to tend. It was also the lineage designation that was historically significant in dividing the sides in a blood feud. In recent years the *umuryango* has lost much of its importance, because the non-kin residential groups are emphasized as the source of societal unity.

The largest kin group, composed of several lineages, is the patriclan (relationship through the male line), or *ubwoko*. As a nonresidential group, the members do not have constant interaction with one another, nor can they trace their vague kinship bonds back to common ancestor. It is not an ethnically pure kin group because it includes Hutu, Tutsi, and Twa (see Ethnic Groups, ch. 4). Each *ubwoko* has its own totem, a symbol which unites it to nature, but these are not held to be very important. The most prestigious clans boast of primordial ancestral founders; generally, their membership was predominantly Tutsi. Among the clans in this group were the Abayiginya (royal clan), Abega (clan of the queens), Abasinga, Abasigaba, Abagesera, and Ababanda. Most Hutu belonged to the then less important clans such as the Abatsoba, Abacyaba, Abatira, Abakono, Abaniakarama, Abaha, and Abashambo.

Changing Family Patterns

In 1969 the *inzu, umuryango,* and *ubwoko* were losing their previous strength, and the *umuhana,* or local kin group, similar to a neighborhood, was replacing the traditional social groupings. The *umuhana,* which may consist of as few as several nuclear families or as many as several lineages, is a group whose members have lost track of their actual lines of blood relationship. It is a cooperative unit which assists the individual members and unites them in the performance of religious rites. It presents its views to the governmental authorities more as a residential entity than as a family group, but it takes collective responsibility for the crimes involving its members. Individuals within the group regularly exchange food, beer, and other commodities. They assist one another in farming, herding, constructing huts, and setting up transactions.

As the effects of political and social change of recent decades have reached more Rwandans, the traditional emphasis on family and clan affiliation has been reduced. Land shortage has made it difficult for sons to settle on or near their father's *kraal,* as had been traditional. New families are forced to migrate to other areas. For some, migration is made more tolerable by the promise of available land in the governmental *paysannats* (planned agricultural settlements) (see Agriculture, ch. 9). Although the young married couples who migrate lack communication facilities, and the interwoven patterns of social relationships fortified by geographical proximity are breaking down, their familial ties continue to be strong as evidenced by their attempts to visit their home area frequently. The material dependency of young people on blood ties has also been reduced. For example, since a marriage without the exchange of bridewealth is recognized by the State and church authorities, a young man need not look to the family to arrange a marriage, although most continue to do so.

Youth societies sponsored by Catholic missions provide new social opportunities. Government-subsidized mutual aid societies, such as the Christian Mutual Society of Butare (La Mutualité Chrétienne d'Butare) and the Christian Mutual Society of Nyundo (La Mutualité Chrétienne de Nyundo), encourage memberships by providing birth and death allowances. As the younger generation is freed from total dependence upon the benefits derived from family membership, they also become less concerned with traditional beliefs and customs.

LIFE CYCLE OF THE INDIVIDUAL

The stages in the life of an individual are observed through elaborate rituals and exchanges of gifts; the rituals of birth, naming, marriage, and death are particularly important. Numerous taboos and rituals are designed to insure the close ties of the family and to intensify cooperation within the group.

Birth and Naming

The birth of a child, preferably a male, is considered a joyful occasion for both civil and religious reasons. Procreation assures the perpetuation of the clan. Male children are highly prized because they contribute to the power of their clan, whereas female children are welcomed because they will bring in bridewealth, although they eventually pass out of their clan and into their husband's clan. It is not uncommon for a Hutu woman to have as many as 8 to 12 children. The Tutsi birth rate is somewhat lower. Many infants die at birth or in early childhood, but there is always an abundance of children.

A woman desires children and, on occasion, takes herbal juices to increase her fecundity. When pregnancy occurs she consults a diviner, who gives her amulets, or *ibiheko,* to protect the embryo against evil spirits. She receives instructions in food taboos. As an added precaution, her husband sometimes blows tobacco smoke at her to insure the birth of a healthy baby. In recent years there has been a great stress on prenatal care, and women are encouraged to visit a missionary or Government clinic when they realize they are pregnant.

Available medical facilities are limited, and most children are born in the home. When labor begins, the woman calls in her female neighbors, including some who are experienced midwives, to assist her in giving birth. As soon as the child is born, it is washed in cold water and rubbed with butter. This practice is continued until the child reaches 6 months of age. As protection against harmful spirits, the placenta is buried under the bed, and the umbilical cord is kept as an amulet. The infant's limbs are massaged so that they will take the proper shape. After 6 days of seclusion the mother and child are presented to relatives. The mother is honored with a crown symbolizing maternity, and she and the child are given gifts of beer and possibly money.

Twins, or *impanga,* are believed to have been conceived through intercourse with the spirits. They are the favorites of the gods and will be called to the spirit world unless the parents perform special sacrifices. Their birth is also thought to be an omen of disaster and creates apprehension for the entire community.

Traditionally, children born of marriages in which bridewealth has not been paid or whose birth has not been legally or religiously sanctioned through marriage are in an unfortunate position. Their bloodline has not been consecrated by a paternal clan, and the kin of the mother have no way of accepting the child into their clan. Generally, the mother and child are hidden or sent away so that they will not defile the ancestral lands. The mother may eventually marry, whereupon her husband, although not necessarily the biological father, will accept the child into his clan.

On rare occasions an unmarried woman may resort to artificial abortion, induced by intensive massage and the infusion of herbs. Although there appears to be no formal law against it, abortion is usually treated as a criminal offense. Infanticide is also very rare and occurs only if a women does not want the work involved in child rearing. This is considered a crime in customary law, and the woman generally is treated as a deviant.

The naming ceremony takes place about 3 or 4 months after birth, when the danger of infant mortality is decreasing. As the creator, the father assumes the privilege of choosing the name, since it must correspond with personality traits he wishes to see in the child. Names may relate to events during birth, familiar incidents, or attributes of Imana. In instances where a man and woman have lost several children in infancy, they may guard against further mortality by naming the child "mouse excrement" or "prostitute" in the hopes that the unsavory name will be unattractive to the spirits and they will not snatch the child away.

The paternal grandfather presides over the rite at which the child receives a personal name and his clan name. One or more nicknames are also given, since calling a person by his proper name may bring him harm. The baby's feet and hands are anointed, and the families are told the reason for its name. Among Rwandans who have accepted Christian teachings, the ceremony may be supplemented by baptism and legal birth registration, followed by a celebration at which the family and friends come to see the baby and bring gifts.

Childhood and Puberty

Education by the family begins almost immediately after birth with the inculcation of oral tradition, myths, rituals, and the codes of proper behavior, encouraging the virtues of respect, generosity, sacrifice, and cooperation. The mother is responsible for feeding and caring for the child. They are inseparable until the child is at least 2 years of age. Breast feeding persists as long as the mother has milk, sometimes until the child is 3 or 4 years of age or when the woman discovers she is pregnant again. The child is carried in a sling on the mother's back; older children ride astride the mother's hip. Although sex distinctions are made immediately—boys are unclad, whereas girls are given a string of beads to wear around their hips—little attention is paid to the difference.

Children are expected to obey and respect their superiors. Under the tutelage of the mother, girls are introduced to woman's work early in their development. The father instructs the young boys in their manly duties, beginning to teach them to herd when they are 5 or 6 years of age. Both boys and girls play a game with nuts, hiding them in the sand. Playthings for boys include swords, spears, and bows and arrows. Since the 1960's football has become a popular sport. Boys are taught the importance of politeness as well as athletic prowess.

There are few rituals or organized social activities for the transition from childhood to puberty. Instruction of children in sexual matters is done primarily through the segregated, informal peer groups that meet while young men are tending the herds and young girls are weaving baskets.

Marriage and Divorce

Generally, by his late teens or early twenties a young man will wish to marry. Males do not voluntarily remain bachelors, and celibacy is practically nonexistent. Since the bridewealth is still a necessity for most young men, they seek family assistance in accumulating the gifts for the transaction. A woman usually demands the legitimacy and insurance provided to her by the transfer of the bridewealth.

A father is instrumental in obtaining a first wife for his son. Before the marriage a series of visits takes place between the parents of the young couple. During this time they discuss the economic arrangements and the desirability of a union between the two families. They invoke the tutelary ancestral spirits, since their approval is necessary for an extension of the family through marriage. As part of the marriage negotiations, a pot of beer is blessed by his parents in the name of the young man's paternal ancestors, and a sacrifice to Lyangombe, the spirit of fecundity, is performed by the future bride's family. It is not until the last visit that the young man accompanies his family. This visit completes the arrangements for the union, but the marriage is not valid until after the exchange of gifts takes place and the bride leaves her homestead to take up residence at the *kraal* of the bridegroom's father.

On the wedding day, or *bukwe*, a cortege leaves the bridegroom's home bearing gifts and the bridewealth. The girl is taken from her home, crying and resisting, but gifts appease her sorrow. At the *kurongora* ceremony, which symbolizes future maternity, she is blessed and crowned with flowers and then goes to her new home to be introduced to the family and ancestors. The newlyweds will temporarily take up residence in or near the *kraal* of the bridegroom's father. During the feast that follows, the girl and her relatives sing, dance, and drink beer. Traditionally, her parents are excluded from the festivities. The young couple receive gifts from members of both families. At the first menstrual period after her marriage, the bride will go through a final ceremony. She is given a cowhide, and her head is shaved, indicating that she now has the status of a married woman.

The bridewealth, a compensation to the girl's clan, is generally in cattle, hoes, and goats, but sometimes a young bull, ewe, or a pledge of 1 or 2 years' service will suffice if the young man cannot afford other gifts. The girl's reputation is important in determining the size of the bridewealth, since a great value is placed on her virginity. Premarital relations between the betrothed are strictly prohibited. Gifts in the form of utensils, wearing apparel, and beer are given to the bridegroom's family by relatives of the bride. The exchange symbolizes a new alliance between families and legitimizes the children. The transfer of bridewealth also makes divorce more difficult, since the bride's family would have to reimburse the man's family. Marriage without bridewealth is still thought to be precarious and unwise.

In the minority of cases in which the bridewealth custom is no longer observed, marriage is an individual arrangement rather than the union of families. In recent years a few Rwandan students have married non-Rwandan mates, but most young men of marriageable age in 1969 still followed the traditional marriage customs.

Customary law prohibits certain marriages, specifically those between members of the same immediate, nuclear family and between persons who belong to the same clan. This taboo fosters exogamy, or marriage outside the group. It applies to any two persons who can trace their parents back to a common ancestor. The rule against marriage within the nuclear family is strongly enforced, but an exception is a marriage between cross-cousins who, although not preferred mates, would be entering into a marriage that is highly approved of socially. Such arrangements between a male and his father's sister's daughter or his mother's brother's daughter or between a female and her father's sister's son or her mother's brother's son are not included in the taboo because the two parties actually belong to different clans. Their common affiliations and previous close, joking relationship keep the family and its wealth closely united.

Traditionally, it was uncommon for a Hutu man to marry a Tutsi woman because of caste distinctions. This normally occurred only when, through special favor, the Mwami raised a Hutu's status and verified it by the bestowal of a Tutsi wife. Tutsi men sometimes took Hutu women, usually, daughters of their clients, as wives or concubines. In 1969 interethnic group marriages were more prevalent.

The language, Kinyarwanda, includes numerous phrases to identify various aspects of extramarital relations. Among the names applied to women involved in illegitimate unions are *abaja*, or servant or concubine; *inshoreka*, or woman taken on a long trip with a chief or lord; *abapfakazi*, or woman who will live with a man even though he is poor; *inzorezi*, or woman who will have sexual relations for presents; and *nyamuraza*, or roaming girls who live temporarily with one man and then with another.

Gutana, or the termination of a marriage without elaborate formal procedures, is relatively common. The husband sends the wife away, and she returns to her parents, who generally attempt to reconcile the marriage so that the bridewealth will not have to be returned. If arbitration is not successful, the marriage is dissolved. Although not a legal divorce, *gutana* has the same effect in that it makes public the dissatisfaction of the marriage partners. The Constitution legalizes divorce by stating that, "Divorce may be authorized by competent jurisdiction and according to the forms provided by law." Divorce is forbidden among Catholics, but even converted women occasionally leave their husbands and return to their fathers' compounds.

The husband expects total fidelity from his wife, and if she is unfaithful he has the right to dismiss her. He may do the same if she has borne no children, because sterility is always considered the fault of the woman. Idleness or neglect of wifely duties also leads to divorce and the return of the bridewealth. Rules of fidelity do not apply as stringently to the male, but ill treatment or reluctance to provide the necessities of life constitutes grounds upon which the wife can divorce the husband. Verbal humiliation, desertion, physical incompatibility, and refusal to have sexual relations are also legal grounds for divorce. Young children accompany the mother, but the father is obligated to help support them. The male children are returned to him when they are old enough.

Any time after a divorce, another marriage can be arranged. Generally, it does not take long for the woman to remarry because her childbearing potential is always in demand. Four or five marriages and separations for one woman are not uncommon.

Death, Burial, and Mourning

Rituals connected with death, *urupfu*, and mourning are significant in that they attempt to solidify the family and society which have lost a member. The family of the deceased suspends all daily activity. Their subsistence needs are taken care of by friends or relatives, and their sorrow is shared by the extended family and communal group.

Because of the belief that the dead live on as ancestral spirits, they are buried near the dwelling of the deceased's kin. A family head is placed in a grave near the cattle*kraal*. The soul is said to leave the body to find a new residence. This does not imply reincarnation or reward or punishment after death, but indicates belief in a continuity of the spirit's participation in family life. The corpse is rubbed with butter, placed in a crouched position, then wrapped in a mat with the limbs tied to prevent the spirit from returning. During the funeral female relatives shave their heads, remove their bracelets, wail, and attempt to prevent the body from being buried. At the end of the ceremony the family goes to the river and performs a purification ritual. During the time of mourning, which may last for as long as 2 months, family members are not allowed to eat salt, cut their hair, or have sexual relations. To emphasize their sorrow, immediate relatives may rub their bodies with kaolin, a chalky mineral.

A widow becomes the ward of her dead husband's brother or, in some cases, marries either the husband's brother (levirate) or a member of his family. If none of these is possible, she returns to her family, since she and her daughters are excluded from any inheritance.

RELIGION

The Constitution assures freedom of religion, subject to respect for public order and security. More than 40 percent of the population has been converted from the traditional tribal beliefs to some form of Christianity. Adherence to dogma, either traditional or Christian, is flexible. Converts, especially those in rural areas, generally retain traditional beliefs simultaneously with their adopted Christian religious practices.

The traditional belief states that all men and animals possess the same principal life force, *imana*, which is manifested in a physical existence. In animals this invisible soul disappears when the creature dies, but, in humans it is transformed into *abazimu*, a spirit of the dead. It eventually eliminates the personal identity of the human to become an energy force in the spiritual world. Imana, the term also used to designate the creator god, is the most powerful force and source of energy, but is least concerned with worldly activities. Rituals and mediators allay impending disaster that might be caused by malevolent spirits.

Missionaries, especially the Missionaries of Africa (White Fathers), the Catholic religious order, have been active since the late 19th century. Certain similarities between tribal religion and Christianity account for much of their success. In addition to proselytizing, the Catholic church has been instrumental in establishing educational, medical, and social work facilities, contributing greatly to the development of an elite and leadership class. Before the revolution the schools instructed mostly Tutsi, but the number of Hutu students was slowly increasing (see Education, ch. 7). During the intercaste conflict the missions became places of refuge for Tutsi escapees. The church introduced and promoted principles of equality, inadvertently suggesting the abusiveness of the hierarchical system of the Tutsi monarchical system and thus contributing to its overthrow. Since independence the youth organizations begun under religious auspices have turned to social and political activities.

Islam, Hinduism, and Buddhism are practiced by members of the small Asian community. Approximately 1 percent of the non-Rwandan African population professes to be Moselm. Non-Christian religions have not actively sought converts, but their members are influential in urban centers as a result of their economic and mercantile activities.

High God and Spirits

Imana is the core of the traditional religion. He and a group of nondivinatory spirits are accorded specific functions in the invisible world. Although many spirits are of local origin, the belief in Imana as the external first cause of all good is universal throughout Rwanda. Imana's names indicate the roles he performs in relationship to man. Reverential titles include: Rurema, the creator; Rugaba, the giver; Rwagisha, the enricher; Iya-Mbere, the eternal; Rugira, always active; and Rugabo, the knowing.

The saying "Imana Y'i Rwanda," or "Rwanda is Imana's country," indicates the nation's strong dependency on the being and his role as the uninvolved protector of the country. His ties to the people are reemphasized by the proverb "If Imana is walking elsewhere during the day, he will come home at night to Rwanda." "We have done our best, it is up to him," indicates the fatalistic attitude and total resignation to his will which pervade the lives of most Rwandans. His name is used in naming children, as words of comfort, warnings against complacency, blessing, salutations, and during rites associated with marriage and death. Oaths take the form of "May Imana give me a stroke" or "May I be killed by Imana." In instances when a long-desired child is born, people say to the new mother, "Imana has removed your shame."

Individuals hold informal ceremonies imploring Imana's blessings. There is a tradition that before retiring a woman may leave a pitcher of water for Imana with the hope that he will make her fertile. At times the word "Imana" is used to flatter the spirit, somewhat contradictory to the belief that they cannot alter the will of Imana, regardless of the amount of sacrifice offered to him.

The departed ancestors form a group of malicious spirits called *abazimu*. They bring misfortune, sickness, crop failure, and cattle epidemic because they envy the living the cherished things they had to leave behind. Their power, actuated by the male spirits, or grandfathers, extends only over their own clan. The living members of a family must consult a diviner to discover the reason for the ancestor's anger. Respect is shown principally by joining a secret cult group. Hutu placate the hostile ancestral spirits more frequently than do Tutsi, who manifest an attitude of reverence without fear or subservience.

Rituals and Cults

Traditional rituals focus upon the spiritual quality of things and attempt to influence or manipulate the supernatural force inherent in all objects. A favorable result is obtained only when rituals are performed properly by the appropriate practitioner at an auspicious time. Ritual practices are directed toward calming the lesser spirits who might wish to cause harm to humans. Most rituals are performed during the main harvesttime, between July and October, when choice beer can be brewed, but events in the life cycle of the individual also prompt a desire for special blessings and ceremonies.

Ryangombe, a historical culture hero, is the most powerful spirit and leader of all ancestors (see Historical Setting, ch. 2). He is propitiated by the *babandwa*, a politicoreligious fraternity, who perform rituals, chants, and dances in his honor. They are not a permanent group and meet only once a year during July, at which time initiation takes place. There are two steps in membership: that of the initiate, or *kwatura*, and that of the chief, or *ziingo*. During their festival the members of the fraternity paint themselves and decorate the spirit huts. A member of the group appears as the personification of the spirit of Ryangombe, carrying his sacred spear. After a ritual is performed, all members purify themselves at the stream.

The most recently established cult in the northern and north-western areas of Rwanda is dedicated to a female ancestor, Nyabiingi. She protects and aids those who bring her gifts and offerings. During the 1950's the society existed as a loosely organized membership and had no initiation ceremonies.

A Hutu ritual involves the belief that the smooth, round stones found in brooks have in them the power of Imana and can bring blessings to the possessor. Several stones are collected and placed in a small hut, or *ndaro*, outside the *kraal*. They receive daily offerings of meat, milk products, broken pots, pumpkin shells, and beer. Eventually, they give birth to 20 or 30 additional stones. The technique of multiplication is taken for granted as supernatural conception demonstrating spiritual fertility.

Magicoreligious Practitioners

Several magicoreligious practitioners perform specific functions meeting the spiritual needs of the community. The priests act as mediators between spirits and men. Their position is hereditary, but occasionally a man may be seized by the spirit and imbued with the power of mediation. With the proper offering, the priest will go into a state of religious ecstasy, speak to the spirits, and utter prophesies and oracles.

Medical practitioners known as *abafumu* (singular, *umufumu*) possess powers to communicate with the dead and to ward off misfortunes and diseases caused by the supernatural powers of malevolent spirits. The insignia of office—a leopard skin, a headdress of cowtail, and a gourd rattle—and instruction in the various curing techniques are either passed from father to son or are earned by apprenticeship to a practicing *umufumu*. *Abafumu* interpret dreams, call together the spirits during secret seances, and predict the future. Some *abafumu* called *ababvubyi*, generally members of the Bashara clan, perform special ceremonies that cause rain. Lucrative benefits come from rainmaking, but it is a dangerous profession, since failure to cause rain allows the client to impose a punishment on the *ababvubyi*. Other practitioners include the *abahenyi*, known for their effective curses and incantations; the *umulozi*, or bewitchers; and the *abashitsi*, or catcher of thieves. The *bahuzi* discover poisoners and treat persons struck by lightning. As respected members of the society, the *abafumu* are paid a fee and may become wealthy and politically powerful.

Divination, Curing, and Witchcraft

Divining through ancestral spirits is among the *umufumu*'s arts. Chicken divining is most common, the fowl providing the medium through which the practitioner consults the oracle. The patterns of the entrails reveal to the diviner the fate of the client. At times the *umufumu* examines the jawbone of a sheep to determine the course of the future.

The diviner, usually a member of the Abakono clan, is also an expert in curing. External application of medication in the form of amulets is a favorite treatment. Modern medicines, such as pills, may be wrapped in leaves and strapped to the area of illness. Internal medication is used only if the patient's condition does not improve after external treatment. It is generally believed that it is the diviner's power, not the object itself, which will bring relief. Most rural Rwandans consult the diviner; only if he fails will they consent to treatment by modern means. Although this practice is changing somewhat, traditional techniques are still preferred because of the belief in the spiritual cause of illness.

In addition to his function as an amulet maker, the diviner has the ability to identify a person who is operating as a witch and to prevent him or her from harming others by casting spells. Witches, or *abarosi*, are held responsible in any disaster, such as an unaccountable death, devastation of the harvest, epidemic, or sterility. The witches use poisons and practice "contagious" magic, a technique of using a piece of the victim's body, hair, or fingernail parings in order to gain power of his soul. When discovered, the witch is subject to ordeals that establish guilt or innocence. Those found guilty are beaten or driven into the bush.

Charms and Taboos

Charms, or *amarozi*, made of sticks and the hair or horns of animals are used to ward off evil and to generate supernatural power for their possessor. Diviners transfer supernatural energy to the material object by means of magical formulas, and the more powerful the diviner, the more potent the charms. Most people, even those converted to Christianity, use amulets for luck in hunting, finding a wife, or curing sick cows. Special amulets are made for infants to insure their health by protecting them against intestinal worms, diarrhea, skin irritations, and snakebite.

It is widely believed that personal well-being depends on the observance of ritual prohibitions, or *imiziro*. Some taboos are universally observed, whereas others, such as self-imposed taboos against drinking milk or eating particular types of meat, apply only to members of specific clans. Most Rwandans will refuse to eat chicken and eggs. Major social taboos such as incest are rarely broken, but minor transgressions are more common. It is believed that if a woman whistles her husband will die. A woman must not speak while kneading sorghum dough, nor should she touch any metal. A pregnant woman should not look upon a

Westerner or hear a gunshot, for if she does her child will suffer. A strongly held taboo states that, if the umbilical cord is lost during the lifetime of an individual, great harm may occur. Another belief is that if milk is boiled a cattle herd will die.

Christianity

Many elements of Christianity were accepted with relative ease because of the similarity between certain traditional beliefs and Western religious dogma. Doctrines concerning the existence of a nonmaterial soul, a supreme being, and the life of the spirit after death were held by both systems. Catholic missionaries, especially the White Fathers were most successful in obtaining converts.

Catholic Missionary Activity

Proselytizing began in 1900 at Sáve in the south-central section of the country. The White Fathers made contact with and attempted to convert persons in the court of Mwami Yuhi V Musinga. Mission stations were set up almost immediately at Gisaka and Zaza, and the first converts were 17 Hutu and 9 Tutsi. In 1905 the bishop, assisted by the German Commissioner, obtained permission to set up a mission station in Kabgayi. Initially, the Tutsi were reluctant to accept Christianity, as they were not favorably disposed toward the doctrine of brotherhood that was being spread by the missionaries. By 1916, however, the Mwami and many of his court had willingly accepted the tenets of Catholicism and had been baptized.

The Belgian Administration encouraged and assisted the missionaries, for it felt that colonial goals could be more easily realized in a society embracing Christian social and moral principles. Missionaries provided the tools that might quicken economic development. Although the Belgians did not promote Catholicism as a state religion, there was close and continuing consultation between the political and ecclesiastical authorities as to goals and methods.

Before 1922 Rwanda had been a part of the ecclesiastical district of the Vicarate of Kivu with Burundi, the country adjacent to the south. By the time it became a separate entity, there were nearly 25,000 Catholics, and numerous seminaries and convents had already been established. By the mid-1920's the need for educational facilities was growing, since the Tutsi were requesting religious instruction. The missionaries, although dedicated to promoting equality and the brotherhood of mankind, were impressed by the superior social position of the Tutsi and, although still concerned with intergroup tensions and prejudices, welcomed Tutsi students into the schools.

Missionary activity came to a standstill in 1928, when famine plagued the country. Missionaries set up public health facilities and expanded their ministry in the direction of public welfare.

In 1931, as the result of another drive for converts, there was a great increase in both the number of baptized Catholics and facilities for ministering to the congregations. When famine again ravaged the country in 1943–44 with diseases that killed as many as 300,000 people, the missionaries, with the aid of the chiefs, ministered to the people, and religious instruction was again laid aside for emergency medical assistance. By 1949, when the disaster was over, plans for educational assistance. especially secondary schools, were begun. The Marist brothers had set up a training school at Byimana, and several congregations of sisters, now drawing many Rwandan girls to the convent, were instructing children in religious education and in general subjects. Church officials began to improve the techniques of instruction, upgrading the general education programs and establishing new parishes at the same time. Attempts to establish so-called Catholic Action organizations were begun, but most Rwandan Catholics were not eager to join. Those who became members generally came from the elite Tutsi stratum of society.

Throughout its ministry the Catholic church has attempted to ameliorate the problems of intergroup, Hutu-Tutsi tensions. Before the 1940's it recognized the disadvantages of the feudal system, but concerned itself exclusively with spiritual matters, education, and health. Some missionaries believed that, by using the superior position of the Tutsi who were converting to Christianity, the spread of the Catholic faith would eventually dissolve the inequalities of the existing social system. By the late 1950's, however, the problems created by rival political factions caused the church to condemn the situation of inequality.

The church supported the Hutu masses by sponsoring their petitions to the United Nations, but they offered active support and asylum at mission stations to the Tutsi fleeing the country. During the time of revolution the church attempted to reason with the leaders of the rebellion, many of whom had received much of their education at the Catholic seminaries. Catholic and Protestant missions were successful in preventing mass reprisals against the Tutsi, who were vulnerable because of invasion attempts by refugee Tutsi, and were also instrumental in helping to relocate refugees in other parts of Rwanda and in neighboring countries (see Historical Setting, ch. 2).

Contemporary Catholic Activity

Figures published by the Government indicate that in 1967 there were approximately 1,350,000 baptized Catholics and 400,000 catechumens, or persons under religious instruction. For administrative purposes the membership was divided into four dioceses (see table 6). The parishes that compose the dioceses are administered by over 330 priests, who are assisted by approximately 180 male and 485 female religious, many of whom are Rwandans. The Catholic church maintains numerous seminaries and elementary and secondary schools throughout the country (see Education, ch. 7). The Rwandan Constitution allows full freedom to the religious institutions and communities, saying that ". . . they shall regulate and administer their affairs autonomously, on the condition that they do not infringe upon the prerogative of the state nor mix in the political domain."

Catholic missionary publications report that the Church is assisting the nation in developing an African group of capable religious and secular leaders. It has been instrumental in programs dealing with increased employment, family problems, and community development. Student movements, which began in Catholic schools, have spread controversial ideas. In 1969 many seminary-educated Rwandans were in positions of leadership and power.

Protestant Missionary Activity

Protestant missionary activity began with the work of the Bethel Missionary Society in 1900. Under the guidance of Reverend Johanssen, a station was established near Nyanza. The German Lutheran Belfeld Mission was established in 1907. Between 1908 and 1910 Protestant mission organizations began to set up churches, schools, and dispensaries, concentrating their efforts on Rubengera, Remera, and Zaza. By 1921 their work had been expanded, and Protestant missionaries were traveling and teaching throughout the territory. The Free Swedish Mission Society began its work in 1936, building schools and hospitals.

By 1963 there were six missionary associations working among the 170,645 persons who constituted the Protestant population (see table 7). The major Protestant mission centers were at Gitare, Gisenyi, Shyira, Rubengera, Kibuye, Kirinda, Kibogora, Gihundwe, Butare, Nantanga, Runyombyi, Kigeme, Shyogwa, Rutogbe, Remera, Kigali, Kayenzi, Gatsibo, Gahini, and Nyamata.

Protestant denominations have never had the influence that Catholic groups have had, and during recent years their activities in the country have been decreasing. The Protestants have at-

Table 6. Roman Catholic Population of Rwanda, 1962

Diocese	Bishop	Parishes	Members	
			Baptized	Catechumens
Ruhengeri___Msgr. Phocas Nikwigize_____		Kinigi Murama Janja Nemba Runaba Nyagashinga Bymba	107,562	67,900
Nyundo_____Msgr. Aloys Bigirumwami___		Rambura Muramba Murandi Mushubati Nyanga Mubuga Birambo Nyamasheke Shangi Cyangugu Mwezi Mibirizi	154,820	53,072
Butare_____Msgr. John Baptist Gahamanyi		Kanzi Kibeho Tshianika Kaduha Nyanza Muyunzwe	258,322	69,568
Kabgayi____Msgr. Joseph Sibomana_____		Rulindo Rwankuba Kanyanza Kamonyi Biyimana Kigali Nyamata Zaza Lubengera Rwamagana Nyarbuye	232,486	84,640
TOTAL_____		36	753,190	275,180

Source: Adapted from *Pro Mundi Vita*, Ruanda: Strength and Weakness of the
Christian Centre of Africa, 1963, p. 30. No breakdown by diocese after 1962.

tempted to expand their influence by sponsoring movements such
as the Agricultural Aid Foundation and Back to the Bible Broadcasts, but because of internal administrative problems, lack of
interest on the part of the citizens, and the strong influence of
the Catholic church, Protestant conversion attempts have not
been significant.

Table 7. Rwanda Christians, 1963, Approximate

Denomination	Places of worship	Members	Ordained ministers	Schools
Anglicans	826	85,260	29	
Baptists	51	4,233	2	1
Free Methodist		4,356	8	5
Pentecostal	50	9,201	5	1
Presbyterian (Belgian)	214	8,756	2	1
Seventh Day Adventists	326	58,839		
TOTAL	1,467	170,645	46	8

Source: Adapted from H. W. Coxill and Kenneth Grubb (eds.), *World Christian Handbook*, p. 83. Published in 1968, but most figures accurate only to 1963.

Other Religions

Islam has never been a popular religion in the country, possibly because of traditional accounts of battles with Arab slave traders. Asians and a very small number of converted Africans, known locally as the Swahili, constitute the 1 percent of the population that belongs to the Moslem faith. Concentrated primarily in Butare, Nyanza, Gitarama, Kigali and Rwamagana, they operate a limited number of Koranic schools devoted exclusively to religious teaching. There are also a small number of Hindus, Buddhists, and Greek Orthodox; almost all of these are of non-African descent.

SOCIAL STRUCTURE

The traditional sociopolitical system was based upon three factors: the hierarchical Tutsi-Hutu caste division of inequality, sanctioned by divine order and operating through the patron-client system, or *ubuhake;* a strong family orientation as opposed to a communal or village organization; and the superiority of the male as expressed in the customs of patrilineal descent and paternal authority.

Under this now defunct system, the Mwami (king) held eminent domain over all land and livestock. These were controlled and managed by the royal princes, who allocated authority to relatives and personal favorites. These Tutsi cattle owners, functioning as chiefs and subchiefs, granted patronage, protection, and the use of cattle to their Hutu client-farmer. Each client had the right to work a plot of land allotted to him by the lord and to keep a portion of the produce, but the patron expected a share as usufruct payment. Although the farmer could share his land rights with his children and relatives, the Mwami, because of his symbolic ownership rights, could tax cultivated land, seize it as a penalty for crimes, and demand its return if feudal obligations were not fulfilled.

In the feudal *ubuhake* relationship, the Tutsi *shebuja*, lord, entrusted his *garagu*, or serf, with cattle, the symbol of the contract between the two parties. Ownership remained with the Tutsi and allowed the lord to expect services and produce from the serfs, who were given protection and privileges by their masters. Contracts were also formalized by an exchange of gifts which gave each party a sense of security in his contractual relationship with the other.

The stipulations imposed on the serfs were extensive. Generally, the Hutu retained the milk and calves born of the cattle entrusted to them, except for the increase of cows specified by the overlords. The serfs could not kill or dispose of the cattle, nor could they leave the *shebujas* territory. If the *garagu* neglected his duties, the *shebuja* had the option of asking for the return of the cattle. This occurred frequently and for the slightest transgressions. If, however, the *garagu* was diligent and ambitious in managing the cattle, he might eventually become a patron and contract cattle to others. The relationship usually passed from father to son for both the patron and client. Generally, possession of the inherited land and cattle united a man and his ancestors in such a way that he was eternally indebted to them for their goodness.

The Tutsi lords, as representatives of the Mwami, considered work with a hoe demeaning and made their living solely by owning and dealing in cattle. Through their contracts with the Hutu, the Tutsi perpetuated a system in which it was unnecessary for most of them to do any manual labor. At times, an impoverished Tutsi would work the land but, generally, his clan would make arrangements for him to borrow cattle and thereby maintain his superior status and prestige.

In order to control the Tutsi lords and Hutu peasantry, the Mwami maintained an elaborate court at Nyanza. Positions of honor included: *ntore,* or vassals and military aides directly responsible to the Mwami (this term was also used to designate the royal dancers); *abiru,* or guardians of customs and the *kalinga,* or the royal drum, which was the symbol of Tutsi authority; *abashoshi,* or young attendants who would eventually gain positions of authority and prestige; *bakoma,* or persons with supernatural powers, soothsayers, magicians, and historiographers; *abasisi,* or the cook who had the complete trust of the Mwami (poisoning was always considered a danger); *nitalinda,* or huntsmen and couriers; *nitimwana,* or artisans; and the female attendants and servants who constantly accompanied the Mwami.

Each of these positions was attained only through dedication and service to the Mwami.

Changes affecting the traditional, hiearchical, sociopolitical order began as early as the 1940's. By that time many of the Tutsi chiefs had been converted to Christianity and had been influenced by Western thought and customs. More importantly, Hutu students having contact with education were being exposed to and were discussing egalitarian ideas. Partly because of the teachings of Catholic missionaries, monogamy was replacing polygyny, which had allowed the lords, through assistance from several wives, to hold large estates. In addition, the formerly effective system by which lords parceled out land to subchiefs in trusteeships was breaking down.

The Belgian Administration, with its technical knowledge as well as authority, had its effect on the old order. In need of a clerical staff, colonial officials utilized local, mission-educated Rwandans, generally Tutsi, but with some Hutu representation. The prestige positions at the Mwami's court lost their appeal, and the Mwami was deserted by many of his followers, who now saw the colonial administration as an alternative to his authority. Education and Westernization in appearance became the new avenues to prestige and status.

As a result of the Hutu revolt in 1959, independence, and a gradual shift toward a monied economy, the relationship between the Tutsi overlords and agricultural serfs has changed. According to the Constitution, ". . . the Rwanda Republic ensures the equality of all its citizens without distinction of race, origin, sex or religion." The egalitarian base of the new governmental form is constitutionally reinforced: "The privileges of castes are abolished and may not be restored. No new privileges may be instituted." The right of suffrage to all nationals of both sexes is granted by the Constitution.

Resourceful Hutu, using their educational opportunities and administrative and technical skills, are seeking full economic and social equality. Their hopes for future improvement of social standing is increasing, whereas the position of the Tutsi in the republican society in 1969 was still undefined.

The feudal land tenure system was theoretically abolished by the Constitution: "Private property, individual or collective is inviolable. It may not be threatened except in cases of public need legally attested and subject to just and prior indemnity." New property codes, now under consideration, will attempt to legalize ownership claims by possession and habitation, since a system of land title has not yet been established. Only when the traditional land tenure system is totally eliminated will the standard of living for independent agriculturalists be improved (see Agriculture, ch. 9).

The small, elite group of young Hutu and Tutsi men who have acquired more than a few years of schooling are reluctant to enter social service professions, such as medical work, where they are badly needed. They prefer the prestige ascribed to Government and civil administration. Since the revolution, social change and the establishment of a new social system have been under the leadership of President Kayibanda and the hand-picked, often seminary-educated Hutu who have risen to middle- and upper-level Government positions (see Political and Governmental Systems, ch. 6).

SOCIAL VALUES

Although the 1960's have been a decade of ferment because of the changes caused by revolution, by the pervasive effects of Christian teachings over the past 70 years, and by the growing economic system and commercial enterprise, the traditional values have been slow to change. In spite of the national upheaval and turmoil, the people generally retain preindependence attitudes toward the relationship of man to his world. The overall fatalistic attitude toward the will of Imana, the emphasis placed upon the family, the solidarity of blood kin, and the acceptance of ancestral spirits in the family circle are still maintained. Even the reversal of the sociopolitical hierarchy has probably had little effect on the basic values held by rural Rwandans. There has been movement toward a community-oriented, nationalistic, egalitarian society in response to European and Christian value systems, but the great majority retain traditional values.

An important source for traditional beliefs is oral tradition, which subtly indicates the most important attitudes of the society. Proverbs, axioms, and sayings express feelings and instructions for proper behavior which reflect the philosophy of the society. In the absence of written history and limited formal education, oral tradition imparted by the family and peer group continues to be the most pervasive means of providing guidelines for the young, and insuring the smooth operation of society.

A survey of proverbs indicates a preoccupation with values such as personal destiny, fertility, dignity, reciprocity, eloquence, societal solidarity, and acceptance of one's role in the social structure.

Fatalism and man's resignation to his inability to determine the course of the future are indicated in many proverbs. These generally deal with an understanding of man's personal destiny.

Integrity, understanding oneself, and the exercise of personal judgment are believed to be developed within the individual. Although each man is subject to the arbitrary decisions of Imana, "The sculpture of hearts has not made them the same." Each man can determine his own course, since "Goodness of the heart can change destiny." Within limits, any particular man can affect the course of history and gain personal fulfillment. The only way to obtain happiness is to work with one's destiny, not to try to escape it, since "You can outdistance that which is running after you but not what is running inside you."

Man is frail, mortal, and insignificant because "Death is inevitable, to die is the ransom of life." Although Rwandans do not happily join the ancestors, for "To get old is to be robbed, old age is an enemy," they believe that the brief life that man has can be used to attain peace of mind if one develops the appropriate personality traits.

The most desired personality traits are illustrated by proverbs: perseverance and steadfastness, "Slowly, slowly is the safari"; contentment with what one has, "Lameness is better than the grave"; humility, "He who feels sufficient in his wisdom is not wise"; choice of companions, "You don't tie a bad goat near you"; search for knowledge and experience, "If a small bird cannot fly it will not know where the ripe grain is." Practicality in all situations is stressed, and quarrels should be avoided at all cost. Initiative, self-reliance, and cooperation with others are means toward success and dignity. Actions toward others must be reciprocal, however, in that favors received must be returned in like kind.

Rules for social interaction are also derived from proverbs. "The hammer will not grow higher than the one who makes it" (do not feel superior to one's father or teacher), "Laws are more than a case in court" (people with power have the advantage over those who are right), and "The hen does not crow if the rooster is there" (indicating the relationship between the wife and the head of the household).

A principal goal in life is parenthood, since "Nothing is more agreeable to the heart than to reproduce oneself in children." Children are highly valued, and childlessness is regarded as a misfortune as indicated by the proverb "The greatest sorrow is to have no children to mourn for you." The desire for offspring is reinforced by the belief in a relationship between the living and deceased blood kin. Solidarity of those who live together is essential because it is the relationship with the living which brings earthly satisfaction and the harmony with the ancestors which allows life and fertility to be transmitted down through the generations.

To speak is a social duty. "The fact of knowing, like fire, comes from your neighbor" shows the way in which knowledge spreads. Words are considered treasures. They are most prized when the speaker is concise, eloquent, has a rich vocabulary, and can speak in allusions. Direct statements that are blunt or to the point are considered boorish and can be badly misinterpreted, since one never speaks what is on his mind. Guile is considered an attribute because "The man who tells no lies cannot feed his children." Exaggerated stories are generally a part of an evening's entertainment, and at times men compete with each other at these bragging sessions.

The Ideal Man

The qualities of an ideal male are clearly defined: He exemplifies goodness, politeness, dignity, and courage. Knowing the proper behavior for all situations, he is sincere and sociable in personal relations, but is cunning in using his rhetorical skills for deception in negotiations. A man must have respect for human life and should love children, the elderly, and the crippled, but he need not extend this feeling to men in inferior social positions. Finally, hospitality to his guests is a sacred duty.

Personality traits that men must guard against include imprudence, idleness, avarice, stubborness, injustice, pride, arrogance, and ingratitude.

The Ideal Woman

The ideal female is fertile, hardworking, and modest and has been trained in artful silence and reticence. As a careful listener, she can generally repeat most conversations verbatim. It is proper for a wife to be shy and gentle, but a husband also admires a woman who is good in bargaining, managing his property, and negotiating for him in his absence. Through their cleverness, some women become formidable matriarchs.

Women are symbolically one with the earth and must act accordingly. As vessels of fertility, women may not, according to traditional beliefs, jump, step over brooks, or climb ladders. Within her, she has all the potential of life; she fulfills her societal role and receives esteem in proportion to the number of children she bears. If she performs her duties well, fecundity may be transmitted to the seeds she plants, bringing prosperity to all.

Women, especially mothers, receive a great deal of respect but very little authority in decisionmaking. Her position in the society is determined by the marriage her family contracts. Probably few women are interested in the voting rights accorded to them by the Constitution. The ideal woman functions almost entirely within the circle of home and family. Traditionally, Hutu women assisted their husbands in the fields, and Tutsi noblewomen wove mats, containers, and baskets. In 1969 a small number of women attended the homemaking classes at various mission and Government centers, but no women's clubs had been established.

The Importance of Cattle

Cattle are not primarily a source of food, but are regarded as living gold, constituting a symbol of prestige and the most highly prized form of wealth (see Agriculture, ch. 9). Cattle were, and to some extent still are, the basis of the patron-client relationship that dominated the social structure. An exchange of cattle usually confirmed important agreements, and they remained the preferred form of bridewealth, even after a monetary economy was introduced.

The traditional greeting "May you have herds" and the response "I wish you herds of females" are still used. It is a profound compliment to say that a woman's features resemble a cow. In 1968, although the patron-client relationship had been theoretically abolished, it was still common for Hutu who had attained economic power to demonstrate their position by walking their cattle down the main thoroughfares on Sunday mornings.

Myths, legends, and epics illustrate the manner in which men and their cows share a common life. When the herds are prosperous, fertile, and healthy the owners will have good lives; if the cattle are having a difficult time, men will inevitably share their sorrows.

The Importance of Beer

Beer is a necessity for all socially significant communal gatherings, such as marriages, funerals, contract negotiations, and divination rites. At times it is used as a medium of exchange or as a gift. It is made from bananas, sorghum, millet, or honey, and large quantities are brewed during the harvest season, from July to October, when most festivals occur.

All adults, especially males, are beer drinkers. On social occasions it is offered to guests as an expression of homage, for amusement, or as mere refreshment. To refuse beer is a serious insult. Drunkenness is not considered a vice but, rather, the mark of a prosperous man.

Reed straws are usually provided for drinking beer since a communal pot holds the liquid. The type of pot indicates the status of the drinkers, as there are different types of pots for persons of different social positions.

CHAPTER 6

POLITICAL AND GOVERNMENTAL SYSTEMS, POLITICAL DYNAMICS AND VALUES, FOREIGN RELATIONS

Rwanda's Constitution provides for a unitary republic with a strong central administration and separate but interdependent executive, legislative, and judicial branches of government. The preponderance of power, however, is delegated to the executive branch, and the Constitution directs and empowers the President of the Republic to ". . . coordinate the general activity of the three branches of power of the Republic." The Constitution also designates the President as the supreme head of the Armed Forces.

The President and the National Assembly share the right to introduce legislation, but most legislation is drafted and proposed by the President and his Council of Ministers, who together form the Government. The Supreme Court, the highest of the four judicial levels in the legal system, must pass on the constitutionality of legislation or presidential decrees before promulgation by the President. The Supreme Court justices are appointed by the President and may be dismissed by him with the majority agreement of the National Assembly.

In early 1969 there were 10 administrative divisions (prefectures) and 141 subdivisions (communes). The prefects, chief administrative officers of the prefectures, are appointed by, and responsible to, the President through the Council of Ministers. The communes, the lowest administrative level, have elected councils that are supervised by the prefectural governments.

The President, the 47 deputies of the National Assembly, and the members of the 141 communal councils are elected by direct universal suffrage. Voting is obligatory for all adult Rwandans. In 1969 all elected officials were members of the Party of the Hutu Emancipation Movement (Parti du mouvement de l'emancipation Hutu—PARMEHUTU), the governing and only political party. As the founder and president of PARMEHUTU and as President of the Republic, Grégoire Kayibanda was the preeminent political and official figure in early 1969. His political power and prestige are enhanced by the circumstance that the Hutu majority credits him with achieving the overthrow of the ancient Tutsi monarchy.

The major foreign policy issues relate to Rwanda's landlocked position; the status of the Tutsi refugees in all neighboring states; and the need for economic, technical, and military assistance. In the Organization of African Unity (OAU) and the United Nations (UN) Rwanda pursues an independent policy with a general pro-Western orientation, reflecting a constitutional bar against internal Communist activity or propaganda.

POLITICAL AND GOVERNMENT SYSTEMS

In early 1969 PARMEHUTU was the only political party and President Kayibanda as the party president controlled directly all of its many activities. Important decisions on domestic and foreign policy frequently have been announced by Kayibanda in his role as party chief and, on various occasions in 1967 and 1968, he admonished the public in general and Government officials in particular to look to PARMEHUTU for guidance on all matters of policy and practice, and asserted that all laws should be modeled on party theory.

Kayibanda exercises his control through the two key party organs: the Council of Representatives and the National Executive Bureau, both of which were established in 1967. The council, which has seven special commissions, is composed of the bureaus of the 10 party secretariats on the prefectural level. The National Executive Bureau consists of an administrator, selected by and from within the council; an executive secretary, appointed by the party president; a propaganda chief; a counselor; and three assistants.

Broad, general policy decisions are formulated at the annual party congress, which is attended by all party members from the central, prefectural, and communal levels. More specific decisions are made by Kayibanda through the Council of Representatives and are implemented within the party through the National Executive Bureau.

In early 1969 the 47 National Assembly deputies, the members of the 141 communal councils, and all senior officials of the executive branch were members of PARMEHUTU. There was a strong feeling of party loyalty, in addition to personal loyalty to Kayibanda, and he had thus been able to work closely, harmoniously, and effectively with and through the National Assembly.

In a speech on Democratic Day, January 28, 1969, Kayibanda announced that he had expelled from the party eight senior members, two of whom were former members of the Council of Minissters. Kayibanda's action was in response to a National Assembly Commission of Enquiry, which stated that the individuals had profited illegally in their transactions with the Government as a result of their senior positions in the party and the Government. In announcing the dismissals, Kayibanda cited as the more significant act of wrongdoing the circumstance that "dishonesty divides the party."

The Structure of Government

The Executive Branch

The Constitution, which was passed by the National Assembly and promulgated by the President on November 24, 1962, designates the President as the Head of State and the supreme head of the Army. Among the numerous prerogatives reserved to the President are those of declaring war, concluding an armistice, promulgating emergency measures and decrees, declaring a state of emergency, and suspending the National Assembly for a maximum period of 15 days.

A key component of presidential influence is the power to appoint and dismiss civil, military, and judicial officials. With the advice, but not necessarily the consent, of the National Assembly, the President appoints the members of the Supreme Court; with the agreement of a majority of the National Assembly, he may dismiss the Supreme Court justices. Without reference to the National Assembly, the President appoints the Council of Ministers; the Vice President; and all other civil, military, and judicial officials. As of early 1969 the post of Vice President had never been filled. The only significant restriction of his appointive power is a constitutional prohibition against the appointment of a presidential relative ". . . by blood or marriage to the second degree" as Vice President, President of the Supreme Court, or minister (see fig. 4).

The ministers are responsible only to the President, with whom they form the Government. The Government shares with the National Assembly the right to initiate legislation and in fact drafts most legislative measures. The President and his ministers regularly attend Assembly sessions, and the Assembly is required to keep the President informed of the Assembly agenda. The National Assembly in turn may make verbal inquiries of the President as to Government policy and activity to which the President must reply directly or through the appropriate minister.

If on a matter of "general policy" two-fifths of the Assembly were dissatisfied with the reply of the President or one of his ministers, the deputies could file a motion of censure. Three days after the motion had been filed, it would be put to a vote. If an

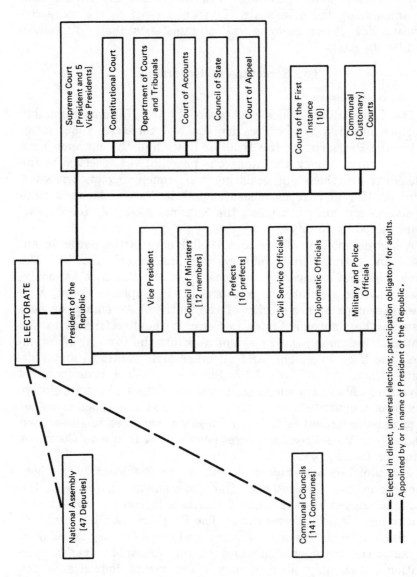

Figure 4. *The structure of government of Rwanda.*

- - - - Elected in direct, universal elections; participation obligatory for adults.
——— Appointed by or in name of President of the Republic.

Supreme Court
[President and 5 Vice Presidents]
- Constitutional Court
- Department of Courts and Tribunals
- Court of Accounts
- Council of State
- Court of Appeal

Courts of the First Instance [10]

Communal [Customary] Courts

ELECTORATE

President of the Republic
- Vice President
- Council of Ministers [12 members]
- Prefects [10 prefects]
- Civil Service Officials
- Diplomatic Officials
- Military and Police Officials

National Assembly [47 Deputies]

Communal Councils [141 Communes]

absolute majority of at least four-fifths of the deputies approved the censure motion, the President and his government would resign. The President of the National Assembly would then act as Head of State pending the outcome of a presidential election that would he held within 30 days.

The President and his ministers enjoy legal immunity that may be lifted only by a majority of three-fourths of the deputies voting in a secret ballot. A majority of four-fifths of the deputies can declare the President to be "unworthy" of the office, in which case the Supreme Court would be obligated to announce the forfeiture of office by the President.

The Constitution states that the President, who may appoint and dismiss the ministers at discretion, must consult the Council of Ministers on vital Government matters, including ". . . decisions affecting the general policy of the State . . ." and ". . . appointments and dismissals to all higher offices of the State within the administration, the judiciary, the army and the foreign service."

In early 1969 there were 12 members of the Council of Ministers heading the following ministries: Agriculture and Animal Husbandry; Commerce, Mines, and Industry; Family and Community Development; Finance; Information and Tourism; International Cooperation and the Plan; Justice and Interior; National Education; Police and National Guard; Posts, Telecommunications and Transport; Public Health; and Public Works and Energy. With the exception of the Ministry of Police and National Guard, which is staffed by police and military personnel, the ministers have small civil service staffs to assist them. Because of the scarcity of adequately trained Rwandans, most ministers in early 1969 continued to rely upon senior foreign advisers, most of whom were Belgian.

The Minister of Justice and Interior exercises direct supervisory control for the President over the prefects, the chiefs of the 10 major administrative divisions and, through the prefects, of the 141 communal councils. The prefects, who also hold important positions in the PARMEHUTU party structure, implement Government-PARMEHUTU decisions and directives and supervise the activities of the communal councils.

The mayor and the councillors are elected for 4 year terms, but may be dismissed by the prefect should his directions be ignored or disobeyed. The information available in early 1969 indicated that the primary activities of both the prefectural and communal administrations were those of tax collection, maintenance of law and order, execution of local public works projects, and implementation of special projects for the various ministries.

The Constitution states that the National Assembly ". . . shall control action . . ." of the President. The powers reserved to the Assembly for this purpose, however, either are diluted by sharing with the President or are of a severe nature, such as a vote of censure, to be used only as a last resort. In addition, President Kayibanda wields extensive influence as leader of the PARMEHUTU, of which all deputies to the Assembly are members, and several of his ministers were elected as deputies and have retained their votes in the Assembly.

The Assembly is administered by Secretariat composed of a President, a Vice President, and a Secretary General, who are elected by and from within the assembly membership. The Assembly holds two ordinary sessions yearly. Except by a majority vote of two-thirds of the deputies, neither session may exceed 3 months. The President of the Republic, the President of the Assembly, or an absolute majority of the deputies may convene an extraordinary session that may not exceed 15 days and may discuss only the topic or topics cited in the convening order.

The Assembly may be dissolved only if during 3 consecutive years it has passed two or more censure motions or if the National Congress should approve a dissolution by a majority vote. The National Congress is composed of the Government, the National Assembly, and the communal councilors. If the Assembly were dissolved, the Government would have to resign immediately. The Council of State, a department of the Supreme Court, would act as the caretaker government and would supervise the general elections that would be held not less than 20 nor more than 40 days after the Assembly dissolution.

The budget and all tax measures must be passed by the Assembly and may not be the subject of governmental proclamations or decrees. All legislation passed by the Assembly is forwarded both to the President and to the Constitutional Court, a department of the Supreme Court. The Constitutional Court advises the President on the constitutionality of the proposed legislation. If the Supreme Court rules that the proposed legislation is unconstitutional, the President returns the bill to the Assembly for a second reading. If the Supreme Court rules favorably, the President within 15 days of the passage of the legislation either signs it into law or returns it to the Assembly for reconsideration. The signed and approved legislation must be published in the *Official Journal of the Republic* within 15 days of signature. It enters into force 10 days after publication.

Deputies have parliamentary immunity and may be expelled from the Assembly only after a secret vote with an absolute majority of four-fiths of the members. Deputies may serve as ministers but may hold no other position for profit or gain.

The Judicial System

The Constitution and numerous legislative acts provide for an extensive judicial structure headed by the Supreme Court. There is also an extensive body of criminal and civil law based primarily on Belgian procedures and precedents. In early 1969, however, there were few Rwandan lawyers and, although the Government has expressed its intention to codify customary law, little progress has been made.

The Constitution provides for four ordinary jurisdictions: communal tribunals (customary courts); Courts of the First Instance; the Court of Appeal; and the Supreme Court. The Constitution also designates four special jurisdictions: councils of war; military courts; police courts; and tribunals of commerce. Other jurisdictions may be created by legislation.

The Supreme Court is headed by a President, and the five departments of the court are headed by Vice Presidents. The six justices when sitting together act as the Constitutional Court, ruling on the constitutionality of Assembly legislation and Presidential decrees before promulgation. The justices also sit together as the Supreme Court, acting as the appellate court from the communal customary courts on the infrequent appeals brought up on issues involving customary law. The Supreme Court also resolves "institutional conflicts between the different organs of the State" and has sole jurisdiction to try Government officials or deputies who have been indicted by the National Assembly.

The Supreme Court's Department of Courts and Tribunals supervises the work of courts of all lower jurisdictions. The Court of Accounts acts as an audit review office on Government expenditures in the name, and on behalf of the National Assembly, and, presumably, is analogous to the United States General Accounting Office.

Another department of the Supreme Court, the Court of Appeal, technically is a separate legal jurisdiction. It functions as the appellate court for cases heard in one of the 10 Courts of the First Instance. These courts, one of which is situated in each prefecture, try only those cases involving written law, of which there is a low workload.

The fifth department of the Supreme Court is the Council of State, which would function only if the Assembly were dissolved.

This council would be composed of the President of the Supreme Court and the five Vice Presidents.

In early 1969 almost all criminal and civil disputes continued to be heard by the customary courts. These courts are described in official publications as cantonal or communal courts and are designated as the "fourth" and lowest judicial level. The courts are generally ad hoc affairs in which, in conformity with customary law, criminal or civil disputes are resolved by the elders, who are influential members of the community. There are few known appeals from these decisions.

There are in addition a number of police courts. These courts handle only minor cases, most of which are the "disturbance of the peace" variety, or cases for related infractions of village or communal codes. The information available in early 1969 indicated that records are not maintained for cases tried in either the customary or police courts.

The Electoral System

The election procedure and qualifications for voters and candidates are controlled by legislation passed in July 1967. It provides for direct universal suffrage by native-born or naturalized Rwandans 18 years of age or older. Participation in elections and referendums is obligatory unless the individual has been temporarily or permanently prohibited from voting. Those temporarily prohibited include all military and police personnel. Persons who have been convicted of murder or assassination, treason, or desertion from the military are excluded from voting, as are "those who have been deprived of their procreative faculty."

All elective offices are for 4-year terms, but there are separate elections for central and local government positions. The communal councilors holding office in early 1969 had been elected in 1967, whereas President Kayibanda and the Assembly deputies had been elected in 1965.

With a few minor exceptions, those eligible to seek election to the communal councils must be Rwandan citizens who are eligible to vote, 21 years of age, neither polygamous nor involved in concubinage, and have resided in a commune for 6 months. The exceptions include certain categories of former convicts, persons who have declared bankruptcy, and individuals who are permanently disabled.

To be eligible to stand for election to the National Assembly, an individual must be eligible for election as a communal councilor and must have completed primary school. To be eligible as a candidate for the presidency, the individual must be a male communal councilor at least 35 but no more than 60 years of age, who is eligible for Assembly membership. In addition, members of the "Nyiginya dynasty of the Bahindiro tribe," the clan of the former Tutsi monarchs, are ineligible.

FOREIGN RELATIONS

In early 1969 foreign policy as formulated by President Kayibanda and as implemented by the Ministry of International Cooperation and the Plan, continued to be generally pro-Western and specifically anti-Communist. The primary issues, however, were the acquisition of foreign economic aid and assistance, and the status of Rwandan refugees in neighboring states. The minister, Thadée Bagaragaza, was the most influential and powerful member of the Council of Ministers.

The foreign relations section of the ministry was small and, because of a shortage both of funds and qualified personnel, Rwanda had only five small diplomatic missions abroad in early 1969.

Relations With African States

Rwanda's relations with its immediate neighbors of Uganda, Tanzania, Burundi, and Congo (Kinshasa) have revolved primarily around the issues of the Tutsi refugees in those states and Rwanda's need as a landlocked nation for easy access to seaports and ocean trade.

Burundi

In early 1969 relations between Rwanda and Burundi were less strained than at any time since both became independent in 1962. Although formal diplomatic relations had not been established, the open hostility and mutual fear and suspicion that characterized relations between 1962 and 1966 had by 1969 been replaced by correct, if limited, diplomatic intercourse.

The historic enmity between the Tutsi-ruled Kingdoms of Rwanda and Burundi was altered but not lessened by the successful Hutu revolt in Rwanda in 1959–60 and the establishment of a Hutu-dominated republican state in 1962 (see ch. 2, Historical Setting). Between 1959 and 1964, scores of thousands of Tutsi fled to Burundi. In late 1963 and 1964 some of these Tutsi launched small, poorly equipped invasions of Rwanda in unsuccessful attempts to restore Tutsi domination. The Rwandan Government asserted that the Burundi authorities not only had failed to prevent such activities, but had in fact instigated and assisted the Tutsi invaders. The Tutsi monarchical government in Burundi, on the other hand, feared that the Hutu revolt would spread from Rwanda to Burundi.

Relations between the two states improved markedly after the assumption of power in Burundi by a group of military officers under the leadership of Michel Micombero in November 1966. Rwanda was the first state to grant recognition to the Micombero government. Efforts by the Burundi Government to persuade the Tutsi refugees to settle permanently were more sucessful in 1966–68 than in early years. These efforts were helped in part by Rwandan legislation in early 1966 that prohibited any refugee returning to Rwanda from reclaiming lands occupied during the refugee's absence.

Congo (Kinshasa)

Although a large number of Tutsi fled to the Congo between 1959 and 1964, their presence in Congo (Kinshasa) was not a major problem between the two states following their independence from Belgium. In November, 1967, however, Congloese President Joseph Mobutu requested Rwanda to hand over for trial by the Congolese Government, the 119 white mercenaries who had fled from the Congo into Rwanda. When Rwanda refused the request, Mobutu on January 11, 1968 broke off diplomatic relations.

Throughout the dispute with Congo (Kinshasa) over the mercenaries, President Kayibanda insisted that his Government was acting in conformity with resolutions passed by the OAU. As a result of several months of negotiations that involved officials of the OAU, the International Red Cross, and several European governments, the mercenaries were evacuated on April 24, 1968. In September 1968 President Mobutu announced that his Government had decided "not to oppose" the resumption of normal relations with Rwanda, and diplomatic relations were resumed in early 1969.

East African Community

In 1968 there were an estimated 68,000 Tutsi refugees resident in Uganda, and between 5,000 and 10,000 in Tanzania. Since early 1964, however, the presence of the refugees had created no serious problems.

Rwanda's relations with the states of East Africa are directly related to its landlocked position and its need for access to seaports. After the establishment of the East African Community (EAC) in December 1967, President Kayibanda on several occasions expressed an interest in joining the EAC, probably in a limited way as an associate member, but as of early 1969 Rwanda had not made formal application for membership (see ch. 8, Foreign Economic Relations).

President Kayibanda maintains a close personal relationship with several of the leaders of neighboring states through his attendance at the annual meetings of the East and Central Africa Heads of State. The other Heads of State usually attending these meetings are those of Burundi, Central African Republic, Congo (Brazzaville), Congo (Kinshasa), Ethiopa, Kenya, Malawi, Somalia, Sudan, Tanzania, Uganda, and Zambia.

Organization of African Unity

Rwanda joined the OAU immediately after achieving independence and has been an active member of the ad hoc commission on refugees. Rwanda adheres to the general position of other members of the OAU in opposition to the Governments of South Africa and Rhodesia and to Portugal's control of Angola and Mozambique.

Because the Rwandan Government believed that the OAU Secretary General, Diallo Telli, had taken the side of Congo (Kinshasa) in the Congo-Rwanda dispute over the white mercenaries, President Kayibanda in his speech to the OAU Summit Conference in September 1968, was sharply critical of Telli and actively opposed his reelection. The Secretary General of Rwanda's Ministry of International Cooperation and the Plan, Fidele Nkundabagacenzi, was an unsuccessful candidate to replace Telli.

The United Nations and Relations with Non-African States

Because Rwanda maintains few foreign diplomatic missions, it views its participation in the activities in the United Nations (UN) as particularly important. In early 1969 the Rwandan Ambassador to the United States, Celestin Kabanda, also served as the Permanent Representative to the UN. His various speeches and statements before the General Assembly and UN agencies have outlined Rwanda's policy position on many major international events and questions.

Rwanda maintains close diplomatic relations with the Republic of China, and has been sharply critical of the Peoples' Republic of China for policies "designed to spread armed conflict throughout the world" and for supporting subversion in Africa "by military training or arming of rebels." Rwanda recognizes the Republic of Korea, and the Federal Republic of Germany is a source of economic and technical aid and assistance.

Rwanda has maintained a generally neutral position in the disputes between Israel and the Arab States and in the conflict in Vietnam. In UN deliberations on the Kashmir dispute between India and Pakistan, Rwanda has favored a referendum in Kashmir to resolve the issue, a position favorable to Pakistan.

Rwanda's generally pro-West position on many international issues has not precluded strong criticism of the role of Western nations with respect to African problems. Criticism of Communist China has been coupled with statements that "the attitude of Portugal is insulting to Africa and a challenge to the moral conscience of mankind." Rwandan spokesmen have complained that UN resolutions on Rhodesia have been thwarted by the members of NATO, who were described as "the accomplices of the inveterate colonialists."

In early 1969 Rwanda continued to maintain very close relations with Belgium, the former colonial power. Belgium continued to be the major source of aid and assistance in economic, technical, and military matters, and Belgian advisers and consultants held important positions and were active in Rwanda's development efforts (see Foreign Economic Relations, ch. 8; The Armed Forces, ch. 10).

CHAPTER 7

PUBLIC INFORMATION, EDUCATION, AND ARTISTIC AND INTELLECTUAL EXPRESSION

In 1969 face-to-face, word-of-mouth communication continued to be the most important method of transmission of information and opinion. The combined, largely identical audience of the Government-owned radio station and the three small periodicals was probably less than 500,000. The majority of the population was largely unaffected by any of the formal, modern information media.

Despite a significant expansion of the educational system since independence, the number of secondary and university graduates, particularly in vocational and technical fields, will be inadequate to meet the country's manpower needs in the foreseeable future. In the late 1960's the Government's efforts were directed to a stabilization of the primary school enrollment in order to improve the quality of the system, and to an expansion of the secondary school system in order to accommodate more primary school graduates. Although Government expenditures on eduaction in the late 1960's usually represented over one-fourth of the total budget, only an estimated 3 percent of the school-age children completed primary school.

Artistic expression remains traditional in form and content. Musical expression is of major importance in daily life, and the oral literature is rich in folk tales, myths, and proverbs. Rhetorical expression is particularly valued.

PUBLIC INFORMATION

Radio

In early 1969 the domestic radio station, the Government-owned Radio of the Rwandan Republic (Radio Diffusion République Ruandaise, popularly known as Radio Kigali) broadcast for less than 100 hours weekly over a 50-kilowatt shortwave transmitter on the 49.52 meter band, or 6058 kilocycles. The station was built and equipped by the Federal Republic of Germany in 1965 in exchange for the privilege of building and operating a large relay station for Deutsche Welle (Voice of Germany). The relay station broadcasts are in German and English and are directed at an all-Africa audience, not primarily at Rwanda (see Foreign Relations, ch. 6).

Information on the number of radio receivers in the country was not available in early 1969. In 1964 there were an estimated 20,000 receivers, reaching an adult audience of about 230,000. In 1969 the number of sets in use probably did not exceed 35,000, with an audience of perhaps 400,000 (see Industry, ch. 9).

Press

Because of the widespread practice of group reading, in early 1969 the audience for the three regularly published periodicals was probably about 400,000. The periodicals contain limited news and comments on world affairs and occasional news about events in other African countries.

The French-language monthly, *Rwanda Carrefour d'Afrique* (Crossroads of Africa), which was published in Kigali by the Ministry of Information and Tourism, contained news of Government programs and activities. A small Kinyarwanda-language weekly, *Kinyamateka*, which contained mostly religious news and comments, was published in Kabgayi.

Another Kinyarwanda periodical, *Imvaho*, was published twice monthly in Kigali. In 1965 the registered circulation was about 27,000, but in 1968 the circulation reportedly had increased to about 40,000. *Imvaho* contained more current news of events outside the country than the others, but the emphasis was on local affairs.

Other Media

In early 1969 there was a very limited circulation of foreign newspapers, periodicals, and other printed material exclusive of religious tracts imported by the various missionary organizations. In 1965 the seven local libraries reportedly had a combined holding of less than 2,000 books, which was an average of 1 book per 200 people, and the five bookstores were largely concerned with religious publications.

EDUCATION

Educational Development in the Preindependence Period

Before the arrival of Roman Catholic and Protestant missionaries in 1900, only an informal system of education functioned within the framework of the ethnic group, clan, and family. This education consisted basically of the transmission of the pattern of accepted social, spiritual, economic, and political behavior and knowledge of the practical functions of daily life. From the beginning of missionary activity, however, simple literacy as well as religious learning was regarded as an important part of the conversion process to Christianity. As each new Roman Catholic and Protestant mission post was founded, therefore, a primary school at the mission station and numerous outlying "bush" schools were established.

In 1925 the Belgian Administration decided to conduct all primary education through missionary institutions. A program of subsidization was instituted in 1930 for Belgian Roman Catholic mission schools that complied with standards of instruction specified by the Administration's Department of Education; non-Belgian mission schools did not receive subsidies until 1946. Aside from setting instructional standards for subsidized schools, the Administration's direct role in the educational process remained limited. Public schools, staffed by civil servant teachers and supported completely by the Government, were not created until the 1950's.

Throughout the Trusteeship period, from 1946 to 1962, primary education was emphasized to the almost complete exclusion of higher learning, and a majority of the students were Tutsi (see Historical Setting, ch. 2). Within the formal primary school system, there were separate educational institutions for Africans and non-Africans. Subsidized schools for Africans were divided into lower and upper primary schools. The curriculum in the lower primary schools was composed of 2 years of studies taught in Kinyarwanda and included hygiene, physical education, gardening, and manual training in addition to the rudiments of elementary school subjects. Most students completing the lower primary course entered a 3-year upper primary school in which the lower primary school courses were continued but with increased emphasis on manual or agricultural training. The teaching of French was compulsory in boys' schools but optional in girls' schools. After 1948 a small number of boys attended 4-year upper primary schools designed to prepare them for secondary or postprimary education. Special attention was given to the study of French, and less emphasis was placed on vocational training than in the regular upper primary schools.

The number of students enrolled in subsidized primary schools in the combined territory of Rwanda and Burundi in 1950 was about 103,000. The statistics did not show the distribution of pupils in the two levels of primary schools, but the majority were in lower primary schools. There were also 343,800 pupils in unofficial, mission-operated nonsubsidized schools known as chapel and reading schools (*écoles de simple lecture*). The students in these schools received only the most rudimentary instruction in addition to religious training, and the schools were not considered to be true primary school institutions.

Until the mid-1950's secondary education was offered at only one educational center in the Territory, the Groupe Scolaire in Astrida (now Butare), established in 1929 by the Roman Catholic order of the Brothers of Charity (Frères de la Charité). In addition to its secondary program, which was on a lower academic level than the equivalent programs in Belgium, the Groupe Scolaire provided teacher training and some technical and vocational education. Some expansion of technical and vocational education programs occurred in the immediate post-World War II period, but postprimary education of all types continued to be extremely limited. In 1956 only 4,336 African students in the Territory of Rwanda and Burundi, or less than 1 percent of those of postprimary age, were enrolled in general secondary, teacher training, or vocational-technical schools.

In the period immediately before independence, the number of postprimary facilities, particularly those for general secondary education and for teacher training, increased, and the level of instruction in the secondary schools was gradually upgraded. A large vocational school was established in Kigali: it offered courses in mechanics, masonry, carpentry, and tailoring, and several craft schools were set up. In 1956 a preuniversity institute was opened in Astrida as a link between the low level of secondary education and university education. There were no institutions of higher learning in the Territory, but the few students who completed secondary school and were properly qualified could study at the Lovanium University (Université Lovanian) or at the Official University (Université Officielle) in the Belgian Congo, both of which were established in the mid-1950's, or at an overseas university.

A study commission from the University of Liège (Belgium) which was sent out in 1957 to survey the Territory's educational conditions and needs noted that, despite relatively large expenditures on education, the number of schools was inadequate in comparison with the school-age population. It stated further that children who were in school received only limited benefits from their attendance. The main reasons cited for these conclusions were an inadequately trained teaching staff, a curriculum that was too heavily oriented toward Europe, and social and health problems.

The Educational System in the Postindependence Period

In 1969 the educational system consisted of subsidized schools administered by Roman Catholic or Protestant organizations, nonaided religious schools, and public schools. About four-fifths of all primary schools and most secondary-level schools were Government-approved, mission-operated schools. The Government underwrote teachers' salaries and certain other costs, such as the acquisition of approved teaching materials, in schools operated by religious groups, which conformed to Government regulations on curricula and teachers' qualifications. The educational system as a whole was under the jurisdiction of the Ministry of National Education, which exercised supervision through school inspectors. Under the Constitution primary education was compulsory for all children up to the age of 15, but few children remained in school until this age.

The Government's strong emphasis on the expansion of educational opportunities in the postindependence period was reflected in the large proportion of total expenditures allocated to the Ministry of National Education. The ministry's budget was increased from RF164 million in 1963 to RF356 million in 1967 (for the value of the Rwanda franc, see Glossary), of which approximately three-fourths was spent on teachers' salaries. As a percentage of total expenditures, however, its budget declined from 30 percent in 1963 to 22 percent in 1966 before increasing to about 27 percent in 1968 (see Public Finance, ch. 8). Most of the absolute increase in the ministry's budget was necessitated by rising costs per pupil rather than by expanded enrollments, particularly in the late 1960's.

Budget figures did not reflect total expenditures on education, however, since an important part of the cost of official schools and approved mission-operated schools was financed by non-Government sources. Primary education, fully paid for by the state, absorbed about 70 percent of the ministry's budget in the late 1960's. The Government underwrote only part of the cost of secondary education through its subsidization program. Pupils' living costs at secondary level schools, all of which were boarding schools, were paid for by the parents, and the salaries of the large number of technical assistance personnel who taught in secondary level institutions were paid for through foreign aid programs. The whole cost of the country's university was financed through foreign aid; the Government's only expenditure for higher education was on scholarships for some students studying abroad (see Foreign Economic Relations, ch. 8).

Primary Education

Since 1963–64, when a major reform of the educational system was undertaken, the 6 years of primary education have been

Table 8. Enrollment in Primary Schools in Rwanda, 1960–61 to 1967–68

Year	Boys	Girls	Total	Number of classes	Number of teachers
1960–61	133,986	63,670	197,656	-----	-----
1961–62	175,314	85,992	261,306	-----	-----
1962–63	202,396	113,456	315,852	8,385	4,695
1963–64	222,462	134,176	356,638	8,861	4,892
1964–65	213,627	138,779	352,406	8,511	5,287
1965–66	195,867	134,203	330,070	8,076	4,920
1966–67	199,478	146,176	345,654	7,893	5,274
1967–68	215,748	156,436	372,184	9,059	5,921

Source: Adapted from Rwanda, Ministère de la Coopération Internationale et du Plan, Direction de l'Office Général des Statistiques, *Bulletin de Statistique*, No. 15, Octobre 1967, p. 2; Rwanda, Secrétariat d'Etat au Plan National de Développement, Direction de l'Office Général des Statistiques, *Bulletin de Statistique*, No. 17, Avril 1968, pp. 7, 8.

divided into 2 cycles. The first cycle (*premier cycle*) of 4 years, known as the literacy cycle and taught in Kinyarwanda, is intended to give children a basic knowledge of such subjects as arithmetic, geography, history, civics, religion, and reading. Student successfully completing an examination at the end of the fourth year are admitted to the 2-year second cycle (*deuxième cycle*). This cycle is taught in French and is designed to prepare students for secondary or technical education.

Primary school enrollment increased rapidly in the years immediately before independence. To accommodate expanded enrollment, the Government introduced a system of double sessions for the first 3 years of primary school. Because of subsequent overcrowding in the second and third grades, the Government fixed the admission age for the first class at 6 years of age by the start of the school year. This measure was fully implemented in 1964–65, and the number of primary school students declined. In the late 1960's, however, enrollment was expanding again (see table 8).

About 60 percent of the primary school age population attended school in the late 1960's. An estimated 85 percent of all boys and 65 percent of all girls who reached school age each year enrolled in the first year of primary school, but few completed the elementary program. Only about 25 percent of all school-age children advanced as far as the fourth year of primary school, which education officials considered to be the minimum amount of schooling necessary for any retention of learning, and only an estimated 3 percent went as far as the sixth primary year. In addition to a high rate of attrition from class to class, there was also a large

Table 9. Enrollment by Primary School Classes in Rwanda, 1967-68

Class	Boys	Repeaters (in percent)	Girls	Repeaters (in percent)	Total
First_____	72,745	32.1	57,986	33.1	130,731
Second_____	44,371	22.4	34,209	21.8	78,580
Third_____	34,138	21.7	26,175	21.3	60,313
Fourth_____	28,181	21.5	20,300	19.8	48,481
Fifth_____	20,677	16.1	11,842	14.2	32,519
Sixth_____	15,636	16.1	5,924	21.1	21,560
TOTAL_____	215,748	25.2	156,436	25.0	372,184

Source: Adapted from Rwanda, Secrétariat d'Etat au Plan National de Développement, Direction de l'Office Général des Statistiques, *Bulletin de Statistique*, No. 17. Avril 1968, pp. 2-5.

number of repeaters, particularly in the early classes (see table 9).

One of the main reasons for the poor record of the primary school system was the high proportion of unqualified teachers. Approximately 63 percent of all primary school teachers in 1967–68 were considered to be insufficiently qualified because they had a maximum of 2 years of secondary education, and many of the teachers had not gone beyond primary school. Another reason was a shortage of teachers and facilities. In 1967–68 there were 62 students per teacher and 41 students per class on the national level; in some prefectures the ratios were considerably above the average.

Secondary Education

The secondary school system expanded more rapidly than the primary school system in the postindependence period, but facilities still remained very limited (see table 10). Students who completed the sixth year of primary school took an official examination covering French, arithmetic, and civics for admission to secondary school. The number of places available in the secondary schools determined the passing score each year, which was lower for girls than for boys. In 1964–65, for example, only 16 percent of the 11,550 students who took the examination were admitted to secondary level programs. Students not admitted could attend a seventh year of school (*7eme complémentaire*), where home economics and farming methods were taught.

Secondary level education was divided into three main branches: general secondary education, teacher training, and technical and vocational training. About 55 percent of all secondary level students were enrolled in general secondary schools; teacher training accounted for about 35 percent of enrollments; and technical and vocational, for about 10 percent. The most serious imbalance in

Table 10. Enrollment in Secondary Schools in Rwanda, 1960–61 to 1967–68

Year	General orientation course	Modern and classical humanities	Technical training	Vocational training*	Total
1960–61	-----	1,055	165	1,063	2,283
1961–62	-----	1,211	199	1,470	2,880
1962–63	-----	1,528	362	2,283	4,173
1963–64	-----	1,852	373	2,634	4,859
1964–65	3,932	1,846	329	1,693	7,800
1965–66	3,834	2,127	314	2,010	8,285
1966–67	3,932	2,102	366	1,950	8,350
1967–68	3,879	2,182	326	2,455	8,842

*Includes teacher training.

Source: Adapted from Rwanda, Ministère de la Coopération Internationale et du
Plan, Direction de l'Office Général des Statistiques, *Bulletin de Statistique*,
No. 15, Octobre 1967, p. 5; and Rwanda, Secrétariat d'Etat au Plan
National de Développement, Direction de l'Office Général des Statistiques,
Bulletin de Statistique, No. 17, Avril 1968, p. 10.

the secondary system was that nearly 30 percent of all boys
studied courses, based on Greek and Latin, in private religious
institutions known as junior seminaries.

All secondary level instruction was in French. The general secondary education and teacher training curricula were based on
the National Catholic Federation of Intermediate Education of
Belgium (Federation Nationale de l'Enseignement Moyen Catho-
lique of Belgium), including those in schools operated by Protestant missions. Some Africanization of the history and geography
curricula had taken place by the late 1960's, but adaptation of
other subjects to the needs of the country was proceeding slowly.
In 1967–68 there were 6,195 boys in 34 boys' schools and 10
seminaries and 2,647 girls in 20 girls' schools. Only 37 percent of
the 580 secondary school teachers were Rwandan; a similar number were Belgian; and the rest were mostly French or Canadian.

General secondary education, after the 1964 educational reform,
consisted of a 6- or 7-year program. The first cycle of 3 years
was regarded as a general orientation course (*tronc commun
d'orientation*) leading to general, technical, or teacher training
study programs. In 1965–66, 13 boys' schools and 12 girls' schools
offered this cycle. The second cycle of general training was a 3-
year course in modern or classical humanities (*sections moyennes
générales*) leading to university studies. Three schools for boys
and one for girls taught modern humanities. Classical humanities,
which could be studied without attending the general orientation
course, was given at six institutions, five of which were junior
seminaries.

Teacher training at the secondary level was provided at three
types of institutions. *Ecoles de moniteurs auxiliaires*, for boys,

and *écoles de monitrices auxiliaires,* for girls, offered a 2-year postprimary course to prepare aides for primary school teachers; however, because of the shortage of qualified primary teachers, graduates of the six schools in this category served as teachers. *Ecoles normales inférieures* graduated qualified primary school teachers after a 5-year course, which included the first 3 years of general secondary education and 2 years of pedagogical training; only seven boys' schools and four girls' schools offered this course. *Ecoles normales moyennes* provided a 7-year course, which included 5 years of general secondary education followed by 2 years of teaching studies. Graduates of the three boys' schools and one girls' school in this category were qualified to teach in the first cycle of general secondary education.

Several types of technical and vocational training were offered at the secondary level. Two-year programs to train aides in crafts and trades were provided at two boys' schools; one offered courses in carpentry, ceramics, and sculpture; and the other offered courses in carpentry and masonry. These programs, as well as a 2-year program to train girls as midwife aides or as social aides, were intended primarily for students who had completed 2 or 3 years of general secondary education, but students could enter the programs directly after primary school. The Official Trade School (Ecole de Métiers Officielle) of Kicukiro in Kigali offered 4-year postprimary courses in carpentry, cabinetmaking, mechanics, automechanics, electricity, and welding. In the late 1960's Belgium and the Netherlands were financing an expansion of the school's capacity from 330 to 730 students. Students who had completed the general orientation cycle (*tronc commun*) could take 4-year courses (*sections moyennes orientées*) at the Groupe Scolaire in Butare to train as medical, agricultural, and veterinary assistants or as business administrators. At the same level there were 4-year courses to train girls as social assistants or nurses.

Higher Education

The National University of Rwanda (Université Nationale du Rwanda) at Butare was established in 1963 by the Government and the Roman Catholic Dominican Order of Canada as an autonomous, public institution. In 1967–68, 161 students were enrolled in the University's four faculties of letters, economics and social sciences, medicine, and physical sciences. About two-thirds of the University's teaching staff of 45 professors were Belgian or Canadian. Admission to the University was based on successful completion of the 3-year *sections moyennes générales* or the 4-year *sections moyennes orientées.* Two-, 3-, or 5-year courses were available in the faculties of letters, science, and social science; and 3-, 4-, and 7-year courses, in the faculty of medicine.

A second institution of higher education, the National Pedagogical Institute (Institut Pédagogique National), at Butare, provided teacher training in the University's faculties of letters and science in conjunction with their regular courses. Students who succesfully completed the 3-year combined program were qualified to teach the general orientation cycle of secondary school, and those who finished the 5-year joint program were quaiified to teach in the second cycle of secondary school. In 1967–68, 72 students were enrolled in the Institute.

A total of 156 Rwandans were reportedly enrolled at institutions of higher education outside the country in 1967–68. In fact, there were hardly enough qualified secondary school graduates to fill the places at the University and to accept the scholarships offered by foreign countries. An additional 97 students were enrolled in secondary level schools outside the country in the same year. There were also two higher seminaries in the country, which had an enrollment of 55 students in the 1965–66.

ARTISTIC AND INTELLECTUAL EXPRESSION

Music

Musical expression is of vital significance in the daily lives of all Rwandans. The ritual and the traditional ceremonies associated with birth, marriage, death, harvest, hunting, and numerous other social events are frequently expressed in songs, dances, and instrumental music (see Religion, ch. 5).

The music of each ethnic group has a distinctive style. The Hutu have different categories of songs for social occasions, such as beer drinking, hunting, and harvesting; before the 1959 Hutu revolution they had numerous songs which, through puns and various types of subtle and often vulgar innuendoes, satirized and ridiculed the Tutsi and the Europeans.

The Tutsi songs traditionally centered on Tutsi conquests in war and on the beauty and wonderful attributes of their cattle. Unlike the Hutu songs, Tutsi songs show a pronounced Arabic influence, particularly in the use of intervals smaller than half tones and of a hummed introduction patterned on the Arabic *maqam*.

The Twa songs are more directly concerned with hunting, the preferred Twa occupation. During the period of the Tutsi monarchy, Twa singers often served as entertainers in the courts of the nobels, often singing ribald, offcolor songs.

Before the overthrow of the monarchy, the Mwami's court was the center for training young Tutsi nobles in various art forms, with emphasis on the composition and recitation of poems and songs dedicated to war and cattle. The court was musically dominated, however, by the Royal Drummers, a group which gained considerable renown both within and outside of Africa. Although drum playing is no longer Tutsi dominated, it continues to be of major artistic importance.

A full drum "orchestra" typically has seven or nine drums. The smallest drum, sometimes called the soprano drum, sets the rhythm for each tune and is backed up by some or all of the following drums: a tenor, a harmonist alto, two baritone, two bass, and two double bass. The director of the orchestra often, but not always, plays the soprano drum.

The other widely used musical instrument is the *lulunga*, an eight-string instrument somewhat similar to a harp. It is usually played alone, often as the background music for singing or dancing, but it is sometimes used to provide a melodic interlude and counterpoint to drums.

The traditional dances of the Tutsi were often related to their primary interests of cattle and war. Both the traditional and the present-day Hutu dances—since independence the more frequently seen public dances—are more often expressions of emotions, desires, and thanksgiving related to weddings, births, and events such as successful harvests and hunting (see Family, ch. 5). One popular stylized dance, often performed at weddings and after harvests, involves two groups of young women, each alternately singing as accompaniment to the dancing of the other.

Although most of the dancing is informal and done at kin group gatherings, there are various semiprofessional dancers, such as the Intore Dancers from Gitarama prefecture. Each Intore Dancer is dressed in colorful regalia that includes a leopardskin draped from the waist to the knees, two strands of beaded cloth, crossed over his chest in baldric fashion, a plumed necklace, a headband of feathers, and a small string of bells tied to each ankle. Each dancer holds either a small bow in one hand and an arrow in the other, or a long, light spear. The dance ensemble is composed of musicians, singers, and dancers. The dancers have a leader who is, in effect, the choreographer, but each dancer is free to improvise.

Literature

Oral

There is a rich tradition of oral literature in the form of myths, folk tales, poetry, and proverbs. Speech, particularly rhetorical expression, is considered a form of artistic expression and is highly regarded, and most male Rwandans express themselves well (see Social Values, ch. 5).

Many of the popular myths and folk tales impart a moral or a message and it is primarily through oral literature that traditions and values are transmitted from generation to generation. The extensive use and repetition of pungent proverbs both in interpret and explain the seemingly capricious ways of nature and the spirits (see Religion, ch. 5). The ability of the clever to outwit the brutal, and the value of working together for the common good are also popular themes in folk stories and proverbs.

Written

In early 1969 there was still little written literature. Abbé Alexe Kagame, a Tutsi Catholic priest who in early 1969 resided in Congo (Kinshasa) has written extensively on the oral poetry of the Tutsi and has written down numerous poems in Kinyarwanda and French.

The only known novel by a Rwandan was written in French by S. Naigiziki. The novel, *Escapade Ruandaise,* which concerns traditional village and family life and is of some anthropological significance, was published in Brussels in 1950.

Arts and Crafts

Most art is either utilitarian or is related to the decoration of utilitarian objects. The most prevalent form of artistic expression is in the decoration of hut or room dividers, mats, baskets, and knife scabbards. The ornamentation usually is a combination of geometrical and rectilinear designs, often into a triangular pattern. Black and white in contrast are the most widely used colors, but red or red and black contrasts are also used.

There is some wood carvings, mostly of drums, knife scabbards, and knife handles. Wooden bowls and jugs are often given simple linear decorations that also serve as a means of showing ownership.

Basket weaving is very extensive because of the utilitarian need, but the female specialists consider it a matter of pride to produce only high quality and decorative items. Working with the pithy fibers of the papyrus, bast, banana, and other fibrous materials and using only a rough awl, the artisan creates freely, using either a weaving or coiling technique. Coiling is more common, particularly for thick-walled baskets and bowls, as coils are more resistant to shock and pressure than woven containers. The coiling technique is preferred when making waterproof cups, lids for the gourd bottles used for beer, and rings used to keep vessels in an upright position and for carrying bundles on the head.

Baskets vary according to use, but the most common are convex flattened globes or bells. The base and lid of a convex basket are similar, but the lid of the bell-shaped basket is higher, which creates a symmetrical shape. Various sizes are used for the

104

storage of salt, pepper, beans, and many other foods. Small oblong baskets are used to hold beer pots when visitors are entertained (see Social Values, ch. 5).

Most of the fibers used for baskets dry into shades of yellow or tan. Many baskets are decorated with strips of black or mauve fibers, dyed with mud from the marshes and arranged in geometric patterns. Simple zig zag patterns are common. Sometimes triangles are added, tiered in a pattern composed of squares, rectangles, and strips in V shapes or spirals. These combinations of narrow strips subtly represent the natural latticework of banana leaves. Banana leaves are a common artistic theme because of the importance of the banana plant, which is the source of banana beer, considered a necessity in social relations (see Social Structure, ch. 5). Both the base and the lid of the basket have the same pattern. More sophisticated basket styles include trimmings of white and blue beads, with the white arranged in geometrical figures that form triangles and diamonds.

All the baskets, plain or embellished, are socially valuable and utilitarian. In general, the number of baskets a family has and the skill and artistry displayed in them indicate the social status of the household.

The other arts and crafts are not well developed. The Twa do some clay pottery making, but they generally do little ornamentation. Ironworking was formerly important, particularly in the manufacture of war lances, which also had a symbolic and spiritual value, but in early 1969 this was of marginal significance.

CHAPTER 8

ECONOMIC AND FINANCIAL SYSTEMS, DOMESTIC TRADE, FOREIGN ECONOMIC RELATIONS

In the late 1960's Rwanda remained a very poor agricultural country with a largely subsistence economy, despite increased economic activity in the postindependence period. Land scarcity and rapid population growth continually threatened the country's economic viability. These two problems made the attainment of a level of stability from which economic development could be launched an extremely long-term process. Short-term prospects were dependent primarily on the growth of output of foodstuffs and exports. Food-crop production failed to keep pace with the high population growth rate in most years after independence. In the late 1960's various projects to expand food supplies were under way, but it appeared doubtful that per capita availability of foodstuffs would increase in the immediate future. Export prospects were more favorable because of an anticipated expansion in earnings from the principal export crops, resulting from increases in both quality and quantity.

From 1959 to 1965 Rwanda suffered from political and social instability, which had serious economic repercussions. Although national income accounts data are incomplete and unreliable, available information indicated that national output declined between 1959 and 1964. The main cause of the decline was a substantial decrease in food-crop production, which accounts for approximately 60 percent of total gross domestic product (see Glossary), as well as in export-crop output, which is the single most important determinant of the level of national monetary income.

In the mid-1960's a general economic revival began. The secondary sector (manufacturing, processing, power, and construction) and the tertiary sector (transport, commerce, housing, Government, and other services) expanded considerably, as manufacturing and trading companies, which in preindependence period had served Rwanda from their headquarters in Burundi, established local firms. Agricultural production recovered, although the output of coffee, the major export crop, was still below its record 1959 level. Gross domestic product, including the imputed value of subsistence agriculture, consequently rose from an estimated RF6.5 billion in current prices in 1964 to an estimated RF12.9 billion in current prices in 1966 (for the value of the Rwandan franc, see Glossary). Gross domestic product at fixed 1959 prices, which eliminates the effect of changes in prices and reflects only changes in volume, rose from an estimated RF4.5 billion in 1964 to an estimated RF6.2 billion in 1966. Simultaneously, the monetary component of total gross domestic product was thought to have risen from 40 to 50 percent, primarily as a result of an increase in marketed foodstuffs. Per capita income, however, increased very little in the mid-1960's because of the high population growth rate. In 1966 it was estimated at RF4,000 in current prices.

Despite the recovery of most sectors of the economy in the mid-1960's, the monetary and financial situation continued to deteriorate. In April 1966 the currency was devalued and a rather austere and restrictive program of monetary and fiscal reform was initiated by the country's central bank under the guidance of the International Monetary Fund (IMF) and Belgian monetary and fiscal experts. As a result of these measures, slow but steady progress was made toward the achievement of economic equilibrium in the following 3 years. In 1969 the principal goal of governmental economic policy continued to be the maintenance of sound monetary and fiscal policies, primarily through a balanced budget and credit restrictions, as the essential condition for the attainment of economic stability.

Government officials recognized that future economic stability was also dependent on accelerating the rate of both public and private investment which, in turn, was contingent on the achievement of some public savings and an increase in foreign aid. Investment activities in the late 1960's were guided by a 5-year development plan, the Interim Emergency Plan (Plan Intérimaire d'Urgence), prepared by the Government with French technical assistance. The plan was originally intended to apply to the 1966–70 period, but it was not adopted by the National Assembly until mid-1967; therefore, the terminal year of the plan period had to be extended to 1972. The plan had the additional weakness of being expressed in predevaluation prices. Finally, because of the very rudimentary nature of the country's national income accounts, it was not possible to check the plan's targets for consistency with each other or to assess whether the investments forecast in the plan would lead to the projected growth rate.

The general objectives of the plan included: an increase in financial resources to ensure budgetary equilibrium and to expand the supply of funds available for public investment; an increase in foreign exchange resources through expanded production for export; an expansion in domestic capital accumulation; creation of an administrative and institutional framework conducive to economic growth; and an increase in the number and quality of trained personnel through appropriate educational policies. Specific goals of the plan were: an average annual increase of 5 percent in total gross domestic product and of 9.6 percent in monetary gross domestic product; a decline in nonmonetary gross domestic product from about 60 percent to 49 percent of total gross domestic product; creation of an additional 27,300 salaried positions; and an increase of at least 70 percent in the value of exports.

Gross monetary investment for the 5 years was originally estimated at RF4.8 billion (predevaluation prices), of which RF3.4 billion would be financed from public resources and RF1.4 billion would be privately financed. About four-fifths of total investment was to be derived from foreign sources. Nonmonetary investment, representing the imputed value of approximately 47 working days per active adult, was estimated at RF830 million. The basic strategy behind the plan, improvement of the country's infrastructure and diversification of agricultural export production, was indicated by the sectoral distribution of investment. About 57 percent of total resources were to be invested in the productive sector, primarily in agriculture. Allocations for economic infrastructure, mainly road construction, were projected at 15 percent of total investments. Social and administrative infrastructure was to receive 28 percent of total resources, mainly for secondary education and technical training.

In early 1969 little information was available on the plan's implementation. In view of the country's economic performance in the early and mid-1960's, however, the plan's aggregate targets appeared to be somewhat overambitious. In particular, it was questionable whether the public sector investment target could be achieved, since the level of national public savings was extremely low and considerable delays were encountered in the disbursement of foreign aid.

FOREIGN ECONOMIC RELATIONS

The country's foreign trade depends heavily on the exportation of a few semiprocessed agricultural products and mineral ores, and on importation for consumption and investment. The balance of merchandise trade consistently showed a deficit after 1964, when separate foreign trade statistical reporting for Rwanda and

Burundi was initiated. The deficit increased from U.S.$0.5 million in 1964 to U.S.$8.7 million in 1966 before declining to U.S.$6.3 million in 1967. The deficit would have been considerably greater, however, if all imports and exports were valued at the Rwandan border instead of at the point of entry into or exit out of the African continent, which is usually Mombasa, Kenya, since the value of exports would have been lower and the value of imports higher.

Composition of Trade

Exports

The level of export earnings is the single most important determinant of national income, amounting to approximately one-fifth of monetary gross domestic product at current prices in the mid-1960's. Not only do exports provide income directly to producers, but the investment of these earnings in the local economy or their expenditure on domestically produced goods and services also has a secondary effect on national income. Thus, the effects of an increase or decrease in export income are multiple, giving rise to a secondary expansion or contraction of various magnitudes in national income, the level of employment, Government revenue, domestic capital formation, imports, and the money supply.

Despite fluctuations in the world market prices and in the quantities of major exports, the value of exports showed, on the whole, a small but steady increase between 1964 and 1967, reflecting a general recovery of agricultural production, both of food and export crops, after severe economic dislocations immediately before and after independence (see Agriculture, ch. 9) (see table 11). Approximately 60 to 70 percent of the value of exports was derived from agricultural raw materials and foodstuffs; the remainder was contributed by mineral production. Although a major campaign to diversify the export base was initiated in the postindependence period, centering essentially on tea and pyrethrum (a flower used in the manufacture of insecticides), coffee and tin ore together consistently accounted for approximately 90 percent of export earnings. Coffee, the main source of foreign exchange earnings, accounted for 54 to 60 percent of the total value of exports in the 1964–67 period.

In the mid-1960's coffee production began to recover from a 65-percent decline in output between 1959 and 1963, but by 1967 the volume of exports had still not exceeded the 1959 level.

Biennial fluctuations in the quantity of coffee exports during the 1964–67 period were rather large, but the value of coffee exports was more stable because of countervailing world price movements. In addition, the prices offered for Rwandan coffee, a mild arabica that is similar to Colombian or Central American arabicas, were relatively high, mainly because it reaches the New York market in July and August when stocks are normally low and coffee is sold at a premium (see Domestic Trade).

Government planners projected exportable coffee production to expand steadily in the late 1960's and early 1970's (see Agriculture, ch. 9). Actual export possibilities, however, are limited by a quota established under the International Coffee Agreement (ICA). When the ICA was renewed for 5 years in 1968, Rwanda's basic quota was set at 150,000 bags or 9,000 metric tons as compared with 212,000 bags, or 12,720 tons, under the old agreement, because of the sharp decrease in coffee output in the 1959–63 period. An adjustment clause in the new ICA, as in the old one, provides for an increase in the country's export allotment when tonnage available for export exceeds the basic quota, up to a maximum of 260,000 bags, or 15,600 metric tons. Output was expected to exceed this maximum, even without much improvement in yield, because of new trees coming into production in the late 1960's. Surplus production would have to be sold to markets not covered by the agreement, but nonquota sales in the future were expected to become increasingly difficult.

The volume of tin ore exports, the second largest earner of foreign exchange, fluctuated in the 1964–67 period, but was generally stable; prices on the London Metal Exchange, however, rose 110 percent over the 4 years (see Industry, ch. 9). Exports of tin ore were expected to stabilize at slightly less than 2,000 metric tons per year in the late 1960's and early 1970's, mainly because of declining ore reserves, and world market prices were expected to weaken.

Exports of tea and pyrethrum grew slowly but fairly steadily in the 1960's as increased acreage planted in these two crops came into fuller production (see Agriculture, ch. 9). The volume of both commodities was projected to increase rapidly in the future; as a result, Government planners expected dependence on the earning power of coffee and tin ore to lessen slowly. Pyrethrum exports were projected to reach 2,500 metric tons in 1972. A pyrethrum-extraction plant, producing 25-percent pyrethrine extract, was expected to be in full operation by that date, which would reduce the total volume to be exported to about 150 metric tons, permitting air transport, and which would increase the total value (see Industry, ch 9). The volume of tea exports was projected to rise to 1,800 metric tons in 1972, and an expected improvement in quality, which is below that of Rwanda's East African competitors, should increase the total value of the crop.

111

Table 11. *Quantity and Value of Rwandan Exports, 1964–67*
(in metric tons and thousands of U.S. dollars)

	1964		1965		1966		1967	
	Quantity	Value	Quantity	Value	Quantity	Value	Quantity	Value
Coffee	8,272	6,286	10,260	7,352	8,803	6,567	11,163	7,744
Tin ore	2,051	4,072	2,037	5,060	1,805	3,739	2,144	4,165
Pyrethrum	408	254	419	276	412	241	525	295
Tea	308	204	332	220	341	258	321	236
Other	6,425	732	3,470	738	3,160	935	3,441	1,531
TOTAL	17,464	11,548	16,518	13,646	14,521	11,740	17,594	13,971

Source: Adapted from Rwanda, Ministère de la Coopération Internationale et du Plan, *Etude de Développement-Plan Intérimaire d'Urgence*, I, p. 210; "Le marché du Rwanda," *Marchés Tropicaux et Mediterranéens*, No. 1145, Octobre 21, 1967, p. 2755; Rwanda, Ministère de la Coopération Internationale et du Plan, Direction de l'Office Général des Statistiques, *Bulletin de Statistique*, No. 16, Janvier 1968, p. 51.

Imports

In 1964, when the country established its own central bank, the Government retained an import-licensing system and a multiple currency system that had been introduced in 1960 by the then-existing central bank for Rwanda and Burundi (See Banking and Currency). Under this combined system there was an official rate of exchange for financing governmental imports and essential private imports, and a free rate of exchange for financing nonpriority imports. In spite of these measures, imports rose sharply during 1965 as a result of deficit financing (see table 12). Prices for imported goods increased rapidly as scarcities developed with the increasing restrictiveness of import licensing. In April 1966, when the currency was devalued, imports were liberalized as part of a stabilization program, but the import licensing system was retained to implement the Government's policy of favoring imports of capital goods and necessary consumer goods. In 1966 and 1967 the value of imports declined slightly.

The composition of imports is directly related to the country's low level of development. Consumer goods imports during the 1964–67 period accounted for an averaged 39 percent of the total annual value of imports; textiles, the largest single imported item, represented about 20 percent of the total. Capital goods and transport equipment accounted for an averaged value of 27 percent; intermediate goods and fuels averaged 29 percent of the total; and miscellaneous goods averaged 3 percent. Although it was impossible to discern any major trends in the composition of imports during the 1960's, Government planners projected imports

Table 12. *Quantity and Value of Rwandan Imports, 1964–67*
(in metric tons and thousands of U.S. dollars)

Commodity group	1964 Quantity	1964 Value	1965 Quantity	1965 Value	1966 Quantity	1966 Value	1967 Quantity	1967 Value
Foodstuffs:								
Vegetables, grains, etc.	2,089	610	4,125	1,088	5,835	1,461	4,424	963
Fats and oils	1,252	382	1,023	444	798	387	675	272
Salt	4,261	248	4,953	276	5,870	291	6,223	331
Beverages	887	240	623	240	806	206	1,375	190
Meats	185	166	379	360	297	254	265	252
Sugar and sugar products	465	126	901	196	2,869	283	3,112	381
Tobacco	21	66	16	50	11	31	22	57
Subtotal	9,160	1,838	12,020	2,654	16,486	2,913	16,096	2,446
Clothing:								
Textiles	1,627	2,760	1,926	3,032	4,144	4,934	3,802	4,717
Shoes	114	226	168	306	50	145	173	313
Subtotal	1,741	2,986	2,094	3,338	4,194	5,079	3,975	5,030
Health and Hygiene:								
Pharmaceuticals	164	298	126	470	200	398	125	299
Soaps and detergents	118	62	235	160	99	15	56	31
Subtotal	282	360	361	630	299	413	181	330
Transport and Energy:								
Vehicles	622	1,026	1,624	2,696	1,253	2,050	1,436	2,169
Hydrocarbons	9,051	918	13,148	1,382	12,535	1,399	13,583	1,222
Subtotal	9,673	1,944	14,772	4,078	13,788	3,449	15,019	3,391

Table 12—Continued.

Commodity group	1964		1965		1966		1967	
	Quantity	Value	Quantity	Value	Quantity	Value	Quantity	Value
Machines and Tools:								
Mechanical equipment	406	604	798	1,462	1,462	1,915	662	1,252
Electrical equipment	257	384	691	1,586	426	737	308	601
Tools	505	284	1,618	974	1,552	684	1,063	594
Subtotal	1,168	1,272	3,107	4,022	3,440	3,336	2,033	2,447
Manufactured Products and Raw Materials:								
Chemicals	572	286	949	524	1,653	886	1,790	692
Iron, steel, copper, aluminum	1,438	846	2,877	1,274	4,170	1,601	3,887	1,882
Paper and paper products	428	308	706	348	558	294	795	403
Cement	6,656	358	12,062	714	10,712	539	13,318	639
Asbestos-cement products	831	178	1,615	448	1,142	293	1,230	250
Plastics and rubber	163	244	384	456	319	449	372	564
Wood and wood products	1,152	316	1,992	270	1,913	365	1,583	459
Minerals and mineral products	65	102	223	262	150	192	392	184
Subtotal	11,305	2,638	20,808	4,296	20,617	4,619	23,367	5,073
Miscellaneous	1,847	970	2,679	1,926	749	663	490	1,505
GRAND TOTAL	35,176	12,008	55,841	20,944	59,573	20,472	61,161	20,222

Source: Adapted from Rwanda, Ministry of International Cooperation and Planning, External Documentation, *Invest in Rwanda*, 1967, p. 42; "Le marché du Rwanda," *Marchés Tropicaux and Mediterranéens*, No. 1145, Octobre 21, 1967, p. 2756; Rwanda, Ministère de la Coopération Internationale et du Plan, Direction de l'Office Général des Statistiques, *Bulletin de Statistique*, No. 16, Janvier 1968, pp. 61–68.

of consumer goods to decrease to 28 percent of the total value of imports by the mid-1970's, imports of capital goods and transport equipment to increase to 40 percent, and imports of intermediate goods and fuels to remain fairly constant.

Direction of Trade

Despite a gradual diversification of trading partners since independence, Belgium remained the largest single supplier of imports, particularly of iron and steel and of mechanical and electrical equipment, and the second largest single market for exports, accounting for most of the tin ore sold (see table 13). Imports from Belgium's partners in the European Economic Community (EEC), especially of West German capital goods, expanded considerably after independence, and the share of total imports supplied by the EEC rose from 38 percent in 1964 to 46 percent in 1967; however, the partners continued to be minor export markets.

The emergence of the United States as the largest single market for exports was the major change in the pattern of trade after independence. About 90 percent of coffee exports were sold on the American market in the 1960's, in spite of the preferential treatment which coffee received in the EEC because of Rwanda's associated membership. The United States also purchased about one-half of pyrethrum exports. Imports from the United States increased faster than total imports between 1964 and 1967, primarily because of Food for Peace-Public Law 480 commodity assistance, but its share remained limited, amounting to less than 7 percent in 1967. As a result, the United States was the only major partner with which Rwanda had a favorable trade balance.

The country's main trade imbalance in the late 1960's was with Japan, the main supplier of cotton and synthetic textiles, but a minor export market. A large deficit persisted in trade with Uganda, the major source of cement, fuel, and tools. Exports to Uganda, consisting mainly of foodstuffs and some minerals, expanded their share in total trade slightly, but imports nearly doubled between 1964 and 1967, because of a reorientation of Rwanda's international trade flows through Uganda rather than through Burundi as in the early 1960's; this development was accompanied by a decline in trade with Burundi (see Domestic Trade).

Foreign Aid

Most public sector investment after independence was financed by foreign aid, since internal resources available for development expenditure were extremely limited. Almost all foreign aid received was in the form of grants, both to finance projects and, increasingly, to support technical assistance personnel. Even though its contribution to the cost of projects was relatively small, the Government encountered difficulties in financing the local expenditures incurred through the acceptance of foreign aid, such as housing for technical assistance personnel and vehicles and buildings for projects. Figures on the total amount of aid actually received by the country were not available in 1969. It appeared that annual disbursements of project aid declined after

Table 13. Direction of Trade of Rwanda, 1964–67
(in thousands of U.S. dollars)

	1964	1965	1966	1967
Destination of Exports:				
Belgium	4,080	5,142	3,930	4,367
West Germany	------	28	107	8
France	------	36	110	83
Netherlands	4	142	160	111
Italy	2	4	10	------
United Kingdom	206	186	200	114
United States*	------	216	{6,460}	2,056
Consigned Mombasa	6,394	7,302		5,922
Burundi	196	116	84	336
Uganda	28	86	146	621
Japan	------	------	------	216
Other	638	388	533	137
TOTAL	11,548	13,646	11,740	13,971
Source of Imports:				
Belgium	3,000	5,480	5,615	5,615
West Germany	860	2,340	1,987	1,867
France	320	500	446	1,175
Netherlands	280	740	454	334
Italy	100	280	228	225
United Kingdom	460	880	914	712
United States	240	940	1,315	1,390
Burundi	1,800	1,160	537	777
Uganda	1,400	3,540	2,846	2,725
Japan	780	920	2,192	2,481
Other	2,768	4,164	3,938	2,921
TOTAL	12,008	20,944	20,472	20,222

*Most of the goods consigned to Mombasa are subsequently exported to the United States.

Source: Adapted from Rwanda, Ministère de la Coopération Internationale et du Plan, *Etude de Développement-Plan Intérimaire d'Urgence*, I, p. 216; Rwanda, Ministère de la Coopération Internationale et du Plan, Direction de l'Office Général des Statistiques, *Bulletin de Statistique*, No. 8, Janvier 1966, p. 36; *ibid.*, *Bulletin de Statistique*, No. 16, Janvier 1968, pp. 92–93.

independence, whereas those for technical assistance increased. As a result of delays in project implementation, however, a large amount of foreign aid was in the pipeline in the late 1960's.

Belgium was the major source of external financing. In the immediate postindependence period, Belgium supplied budgetary support and financing for specific projects and technical assistance, but since 1965 Belgian aid has been channeled outside the budget (see Public Finance). Commitments to specific projects averaged about the equivalent of U.S.$1.4 million annually between 1963 and 1967, but disbursements lagged considerably behind authorizations. Commitments increased to about the equivalent of U.S.$2 million in 1968 and U.S.$3.1 million in 1969. Among the projects financed by Belgian aid were: enlargement of the Kigali airport; acquisition of telecommunications equipment; construction of housing for civil servants; distribution of improved seed; construction of a school for agricultural extension workers and a hospital complex; reclamation of marshland; provision of drinkable water in rural areas; and establishment of *paysannats* (planned agricultural settlements) (see Agriculture, ch 9).

In addition, Belgium supported the operation of an agricultural research organization, a tropical medicine organization, and a private Belgian agricultural extension organization. At the time of devaluation in 1966, Belgium provided the equivalent of a U.S.$600,000 grant and a U.S.$900,000 loan to finance general imports. It also provide the equivalent of U.S.$300,000 to establish a fund to cover the maintenance expenditures on foreign-financed infrastructure projects A large proportion of Belgian aid consisted of annual maintenance support for 200 to 250 technical assistance personnel. About half of them were teachers; the rest included Government officials, professors at the National University of Rwanda (Université Nationale du Rwanda) in Butare, and agricultural or military advisers. Belgium also provided a number of scholarships to Rwandan students for study in Belgium.

The second major source of foreign aid was the EEC through its European Development Fund (Fonds européen de développement—FED). Between 1958 and 1968 the equivalent of approximately U.S.$14 million was allocated by the FED to Rwanda for specific projects and studies, but disbursements lagged considerably behind authorizations. Most of the FED's activities were directed toward diversifying the agricultural base. About one-third of its commitments were for the establishment of four tea-growing *paysannats* and for studies on tea production, and one-fifth for the expansion of pyrethrum production. Another one-fifth of the authorizations were to finance the establishment of *paysannats* based on coffee in the Bugesera-Mayaga area (see Agriculture, ch. 9). Other projects which the FED agreed to finance included: construction of a teacher-training school, an agricultural training school, and an industrial park near Kigali; geological and power studies; and road surveys.

Economic and technical assistance also came from several other sources. In 1966 the United Nations authorized a grant equivalent to U.S.$1.3 million to construct a pilot pyrethrine extraction plant at Ruhengeri and a grant equivalent to U.S.$1.9 million to finance part of the cost of the National Pedagogical Institute (Institut Pédagogique National) at Butare (see Education, ch. 7). In 1967 it authorized a third grant equivalent to U.S.$543,000 to start a tannery in Kigali (see Industry, ch. 9). All of the United Nations projects required direct financial participation by the Government.

The United States, as part of the stabilization program initiated at the time of devaluation, authorized the equivalent of approximately U.S. $1.5 million in food under the P.L. 480 program; the counterpart funds from the local sale of these food supplies were used to finance the recurrent budget and development projects. In addition, it approved the equivalent of U.S.$1 million for the importation of American equipment and materials to conserve Rwanda's foreign exchange reserves. The United States also financed several small projects, including a water filtration plant at Kigali.

In 1966 the Republic of China signed a 5-year technical assistance agreement, equivalent to U.S.$1.5 million, to develop about 2,500 acres of rice, sugarcane, soybeans, and vegetables, and to build a sugar refinery (see Agriculture, ch. 9). Canada provided financial assistance for the operation of the National University of Rwanda (see Education, ch. 7). France provided technical assistance personnel in agriculture, national planning, industry, and education; it also financed marshland reclamation surveys and assumed responsibility for the operation of medical facilities in Ruhengeri Prefecture. The Federal Republic of Germany financed the construction of a radio station at Kigali, pavement of the road from Kigali to the nearby airport, and installation of a power line. In the late 1960's it extended a credit equivalent to U.S.$350,000 for the construction of a bridge over the Kagera River to improve road connections with Tanzania. Switzerland concentrated its aid on the development of a commercial cooperative to which it provided both staff and financial aid; it also sent out technical assistance personnel in several other areas (see Domestic Trade).

Private Foreign Investment

Much of the economy's private sector, particularly in industry, is dominated by foreign enterprises. The Government has recognized that private investment must play a major role in the country's economic development, since only a very limited amount of public savings is available for investment, and that the country will be dependent on foreign financial and technical resources for a considerable time. Therefore, it has taken steps to assure prospective investors of the security of invested capital and to provide the economic and political framework within which private firms can become established and expand.

The main instrument for encouraging private foreign investment is the Investment Code, enacted in 1964. Under its terms, a foreign business concern that is interested in investing in almost any activity outside of the commercial sector can enter into an agreement with the Government for favored status if the proposed investment is expected to contribute to the economic growth of the country. Various categories of favored status provide an approved enterprise with one or more of the following: exemption from duties and taxes on imported plant and equipment and raw materials used in the production process; exemption from or reduction of taxes on goods manufactured or processed by the firm; exemption from the tax on business profits for 5 years; and exemption from trade license fees, and mining and forest rents for 5 years. In early 1969 the effectiveness of these inducements in encouraging foreign investments in the country was unknown.

An investment guarantee concluded in 1967 with the United States Agency for International Development insures American investment in Rwanda against the noncommercial risks of expropriation, currency inconvertibility, and losses due to war, revolution, or insurrection. Extended risk guarantees are also available for new American investment in projects approved by the Rwandan Government. A similar agreement was signed with the Federal Republic of Germany in 1967.

Balance of Payments

The general picture of the country's economic and financial relations with all other countries is shown in its balance of payments statement. Data used in the compilation of Rwanda's balance of payments were subject to a large margin of error and often were incomplete. In particular, statistics on foreign payments were based on records of official foreign exchange; thus, imports financed without the use of official exchange, which were important in 1965, as well as part of the foreign aid flows were excluded. Therefore, balance of payments statements for Rwanda must be interpreted cautiously.

The current account, representing the flow of goods and services and transfer payments between Rwanda and the rest of the world, is divided into visible trade (goods), invisible trade (services), and transfers (unilateral transfers of wealth for which nothing is received in return). Between 1965 and 1967 the current account showed a significant annual deficit (see table 14). This deficit was primarily the results of the high level of imports and the high cost of freight and insurance payments, mostly for imports, on the invisible trade account. If public transfer payments (grants and technical assistance received by the Government from various foreign governments and international economic institutions) were included, the deficit on the current account would be somewhat reduced. The current account deficit was financed through foreign aid and through reductions in net foreign exchange reserves.

The capital account consists of changes in the assets and liabilities of Government and private enterprises and individuals and changes in the assets of the country's monetary institutions, the central bank and the commercial banks. There appeared to be a small net inflow of public and private long- and short-term capital in the 1965–67 period, but it was insufficient to offset the large deficits on the current account in 1965 and 1966, and the country's foreign exchange reserves were drawn down. Net foreign exchange reserves decreased by U.S.$2.6 million in 1965 and by U.S.$5.2 million in 1966. In the first half of 1967 they declined by a further U.S.$2.6 million, but in the second half of the year they increased by U.S.$4.4 million, and the first surplus since independence was achieved in the balance of payments. Throughout 1966, 1967, and 1968, net reserves were negative, but liabilities were generally smaller in 1968 than in the 2 previous years; at the end of 1968 net reserves were minus U.S.$121 million. Gross reserves declined during 1965, but increased in the next 3 years, following three IMF standby agreements (see Banking and Currency). At the end of 1968, gross reserves were U.S.$5.85 million, or roughly equivalent to 4 month's imports.

Economic Groupings

From 1922 until 1960, Rwanda, together with Burundi, was part of a customs and monetary union with the then Belgian Congo, within which the Congo was the dominant partner. Rwanda derived few, if any, economic benefits from the union

Table 14. Estimated Balance of Payments of Rwanda, 1965–67
(in millions of U.S. dollars)

	1965	1966	1967
Visible Trade:			
Exports f.o.b.	13.6	11.7	14.0
Imports f.o.b.[1]	−18.4	−17.3	−17.0
Balance of visible trade	−4.8	−5.6	−3.0
Invisible Trade (net):			
Freight, insurance	−2.5	−3.2	−3.4
Travel	−0.3	−0.3	−0.5
Government (not included elsewhere)	−0.3	0.3	0.1
Investment income	0.1	−0.1	0.1
Other Services	−0.1	0.1	−0.1
Balance of invisible trade	−3.1	−3.2	−3.8
Transfer Payments (net):			
Private	−0.9	0.2	1.4
Official[2]	n.a.	n.a.	n.a.
Balance of transfer payments	−0.9	0.2	1.4
TOTAL CURRENT ACCOUNT	−8.8	−8.6	−5.4
Nonmonetary Capital (net)	1.2	1.1	3.0
Monetary Capital (net)[3]	+2.6	+5.2	−1.8
Errors and Omissions	5.0	2.3	4.2

[1] Adjusted for estimated free market operations.
[2] Net official transfers (foreign aid) were not reported.
[3] A decline in reserves is signified by a positive sign.

Source: Adapted from Rwanda, Secrétariat d'Etat au Plan National de Développement, Direction de l'Office Général des Statistiques, *Bulletin de Statistique*, No. 17, Avril 1968, p. 54.

and remained the poorest and most isolated of the three Belgian territories—a supplier of foodstuffs to Burundi and the Congo and a market for their manufactured goods. When the Congo achieved independence in 1960, the union ceased to exist in practice, but Rwanda and Burundi maintained a monetary union, a common customs service, a common central bank, and a joint coffee-marketing board. On January 1, 1964, however, Rwanda terminated the union with Burundi over the specific issues of import-licensing policy and division of foreign currency, but the decision was considerably influenced by Government policymakers' general assessment that the union favored Burundi's interests and development to the detriment of Rwanda's. Since 1964 Rwanda has concentrated on developing economic links with East Africa, particularly with Uganda. In 1967 and 1968 President Grégoire Kayibanda, on several occasions, expressed an interest in some form of association with the East African Community, the institutional arrangement encompassing the common market and common services in which Kenya, Tanzania, and Uganda participate. As of early 1969, however, Rwanda had not applied for membership.

After the termination of the union with Burundi, Rwanda's only remaining formal economic link was associate membership in the EEC. Associate membership entitled Rwanda and the 17 other African associate members to two major benefits: technical and financial aid through the FED and duty-free entry for their exports into the EEC. Preferential treatment for its exports, however, had little effect on the direction of Rwanda's foreign trade. Only a small proportion of the country's exports of coffee, tea, and pyrethrum was sold to EEC countries, despite tariffs on nonassociated states' exports of these products to the EEC. Tin ore, which had duty-free entry from all countries, was the only major export for which the EEC was an important market.

DOMESTIC TRADE

The modernization of the economy, particularly the transformation of subsistence agricultural activity into market-oriented production and the concomitant drawing of increased numbers of persons into the monetary sector, depends largely on the efficient functioning of the distribution system. The small-scale farmer's opportunities for increasing his material well-being are primarily dependent upon the availability of a market for his produce. Incentive for increased production depends, in turn, on the ready availability, at reasonable prices, of those goods and services which he might desire.

The commercial sector, like the industrial sector, has expanded since independence and particularly since the breakup of the economic union with Burundi in 1964. This expansion was a result of the general economic revival, especially the recovery of agricultural production, and of the establishment of local offices by the major trading companies that previously operated in Rwanda from their Burundi headquarters. In 1966 the tertiary sector, excluding Government services, accounted for an estimated 8 percent of gross domestic product, including subsistence agriculture, at constant prices, as compared with approximately 6.5 percent in 1964. In the latter year 2,248 persons, or about 3 percent of the total public- and private-sector labor force, were estimated to be employed permanently or temporarily for cash wages or salaries in commerce and transportation (see Labor, ch. 9).

Dynamics and Channels of Trade

The structure and extent of domestic trade are influenced by the country's hilly-to-mountainous terrain and the dispersion of the population on isolated hillsides, the small number of urban centers, and the location of existing towns on the periphery of the country (see Living Patterns and Conditions, ch. 3). It is also affected by the existence of a small export sector grafted onto a still largely subsistence economy. As a result, the commercial sector, although expanding, is almost entirely concerned with the exchange of local products, the distribution of imported merchandise, and the collection of export produce. In the late 1960's the distribution system was still not fully effective as an integrating force on the entire economy.

Although the rural population is largely self-sufficient and the average agricultural family can produce nearly all its food requirements, exchanges of agricultural produce, livestock products, and handicrafts do take place within the rural economy. Aside from export crops, about 10 percent of food-crop production is marketed, mostly bananas (generally in the form of beer), legumes, potatoes, and cassava (see Agriculture, ch. 9). Most marketed food crops are supplied to Kigali and the few other towns, where the expansion in the number of urban residents, particularly Government personnel, had led to the growth of a cash market for local crops.

Rural exchanges generally take place at one of about 300 open-air local markets held periodically throughout the countryside, attracting persons within 2 hours' walking distance. The amounts traded at these traditional markets are usually small, limited to what the suppliers and customers can carry on their heads. At some of the larger rural markets, small-scale traders offer a limited range of local or imported consumer goods, such as cloth and housewares. Some of these traders also peddle their goods by bicycle to hillside dwellings.

Most retailing, however, is conducted in the urban commercial centers, normally the 10 prefecture capitals, and in secondary trade centers, which average one per commune. Small-scale retail trade is largely in the hands of Rwandans, but the larger retail trade is carried out by Asian and Arab establishments, many of which import consumer goods, particularly textiles and housewares, on their own account. General importing, especially of capital goods, is handled by a small number of European-owned export-import houses, often the branches of companies operating internationally or of companies established in Congo (Kinshasa) or in Burundi. Most of these firms maintain wholesale warehouses only in Kigali, but some have established outlets in a few other towns, from which small-scale Rwandan, Asian, and Arab retailers, religious missions, and company stores of large enterprises, such as the mining companies, are supplied. Small-scale retailers generally maintain limited stocks, and there are often local shortages of consumer goods pending fulfillment of orders from Kigali or wholesale branches in other towns.

Consumer goods prices vary regionally and seasonally, but are generally high. The causes of at least some of the price rises are heavy transport costs, poor credit facilities, and high import duties; in addition, most retailers have high markups because their sales volume is low. The Government has attempted to deal in three ways with the adverse effects of retail price distortions on consumption. First, a number of laws and Presidential decrees were passed in the mid-1960's to control and equalize prices througout the country, but the laws are unenforceable because of a lack of administrative personnel. Second, as part of the 1966 import-liberalization program, no tariffs are charged on imported lots worth less than RF20,000; the purpose of this measure is to provide an alternative trade channel for imported goods to be sold to the rural population, thereby limiting profit margins in existing channels (see Banking and Currency). Third, the Government has encouraged the expansion of cooperatives in the commercial field.

Work, Fidelity, Progress (Travail, Fidèlité, Progrès—TRAFI-PRO), a cooperative established in 1956 by the Roman Catholic church but staffed and financed since 1962 under the Swiss foreign aid program, is the main vehicle of government policy in the commercial sector. With a membership of 72,000 in early 1967, the cooperative operates in two main fields: the distribution of imported consumer goods through 28 branch stores and through sales from a fleet of trucks and the marketing of coffee. As a retail organization, TRAFIPRO's objective is to make available to both rural and urban residents a wide range of consumer goods at reasonable prices, uniform throughout the country, by operating on a moderate profit margin. Its activities have caused other merchants to lower their prices and have improved the purchasing power of the population.

The level of commercial activity within the country, particularly in the rural areas, depends directly on the volume and value of marketed cash crop production. In particular, domestic trade flourishes seasonally, with peaks coinciding with the main harvest and sale of the coffee crop, generally in April and May, and, to a lesser extent, with the smaller harvest in November. A small main harvest or a low world market price leads directly to a reduced level of domestic trade in all goods throughout the country, as well as to other immediate signs of an economic recession. A recession in commercial activity lasts until the next main harvest is brought to sale.

Husked and dried coffee beans are sold by the grower to licensed private agents, primarily Rwandans, or to TRAFIPRO purchasing agents at local markets throughout the coffee-growing regions; in 1967 TRAFIPRO bought approximately 20 percent of the crop. The minimum price to the farmer is fixed by the Office of Industrial Crops of Rwanda (Office des Cultures Industrielles du Rwanda—OCIR) on the basis of the Mombasa export price and the cost of various intermediate states, including a fair return to the purchasing agents and exporters. The minimum price was raised to RF35 per kilogram (equal to approximately 2.2 pounds) of green coffee at the time of devaluation, and in 1967 the Government guaranteed planters this minimum for at least 4 years (see Agriculture, ch. 9). The Government has continually urged farmers not to accept prices below the minimum, an indication that the official price is not always respected by the private buyers, particularly during the second harvest in November, when TRAFIPRO does not purchase coffee.

The purchasing agents sell the coffee crop to one of seven privately owned factories for processing (see Industry, ch. 9). The marketable coffee is then warehoused at OCIR's facilities in Kigali or in Ruhengeri, where it is graded. After classification, the coffee is sold to buyers overseas, mainly through local export houses at prices agreed to by OCIR, and is shipped to Mombasa under OCIR authorization.

The pyrethrum crop is purchased by two local cooperatives, which administer its processing, transportation, and marketing overseas. A German firm, under contract with the Government, markets overseas the tea grown on the paysannats, whereas European planters market their own production (see Agriculture, ch. 9). Most mineral production is marketed in Europe through the agency of a Belgian company, but some is sold on consignment to a British company in Uganda (see Industry, ch. 9).

Transportation

As a landlocked country, with neither internal rail facilities nor rail connections on its borders, Rwanda is dependent on road transport for the movement of its domestic and foreign trade (see Physical Environment, ch. 3). The road network is fairly dense and presents no major physical bottlenecks to internal or international traffic or to domestic communications. The main sections of the trunk network are normally well maintained, although the maintenance of other national and secondary roads is generally inadequate as a result of insufficient financing on the national level and a lack of technical guidance on the communal level.

Internal public road transport is undertaken by private carriers and by a Government-owned transport company, which provides biweekly service between Kigali and the prefecture capitals at the rate of RF1 per person per kilometer. In 1966 the company carried 59,000 passengers, an increase of nearly 40 percent over 1965. The number of private vehicles is increasing, but in 1967 there were only 2,353 passenger cars and 1,249 light and heavy trucks. There are also few bicycles, both because most people cannot afford them and because the hilly terrain makes them difficult to ride.

Until 1960, when the economic union with the Belgian Congo was terminated, most of the country's foreign trade was oriented toward the Atlantic Ocean. Since independence, however, practically all traffic has been redirected toward the Indian Ocean, using two main routes. The southern route encompasses 180 miles of transport by truck from Kigali to Bujumbura, Burundi; shipment across Lake Tanganyika to the Tanzanian port of Kigoma (125 miles); and about 1,000 miles by rail to Dar es Salaam, Tanzania. The northern route involves 360 miles of transport by truck from Kigali to Kampala, Uganda, via Kagitumba and about 800 miles of rail transport from Kampala to Mombasa, Kenya. Other northern exits to Kampala are Cyanika, via Kasese, Uganda, and Gatuna, via Kabale, Uganda (see frontispiece).

During the period of economic union with Burundi, the southern route was the more frequently used of the two, despite the necessity of two transshipments. After the breakup of the union in 1964, traffic was redirected toward the northern route. In the late 1960's about three-quarters of all imports and four-fifths of all exports took one of the northern exits. The southern route was economical only for trade originating in the southern prefectures of Cyangugu, Gikongoro, and Butare and for certain bulky shipments.

In order to improve external communications links and to reduce the heavy transport cost of international trade, two major road projects were under way in 1969. The first was the reconstruction of the Kigali-Byumba-Gatuna-Kabale route which, on completion, was expected to replace the Kigali-Kagitumba route as the main external road link and to reduce transport costs to and from Europe by about 15 percent. The second was the construction of a bridge over the Kagera River near the Tanzanian town of

Rusumo, linking Kigali with the western Tanzanian trunk road system via Kibungo. This link will considerably shorten the distance between Kigali and Dar es Salaam, avoid transshipments, and provide Rwanda with an alternative outlet to the ocean if the Burundi or Ugandan borders should ever be closed.

International trade traffic is handled by two transport companies. In 1963 the Government granted one of these companies, International Maritime Agency (Agence Maritime Internationale —AMI), a 10-year monopoly as sole agent for the movement of all Rwandan imports passing through Uganda. Such an arrangement has the advantages of lessening the complexity of transport operations and especially customs formalities between Rwanda and the maritime ports, of helping to prevent fraud, and of increasing reliability. The transport rates charged by AMI, however, are thought to be abnormally high; one study estimated that "reasonable" rates would be 15 to 20 percent below those charged by AMI in 1964. In addition, such an arrangement places practically all of the transport operations in Ugandan hands, thereby curtailing the activities and expansion of the domestic commercial and transport sectors and aggravating Rwanda's balance of payments position.

The principal airline facilities are an international-class airport near Kigali, capable of handling 4-engine jet aircraft, and the Kamembe airfield, outside Cyangugu, which is open to DC-4's. Airstrips at Butare, Ruhengeri, Gisenyi, and Gabiro are accessible to DC-3 aircraft, whereas those at Nemba, Nyabisindu, Kagitumba, Gako, and Bugarama can handle light aircraft. International carriers regularly serving Kigali are Sabena, Air Congo, and East African Airways. Internal service is provided by two Kigali-based charter companies. During 1967 the airports at Kigali, Kamembe, Butare, Ruhengeri, and Gisenyi handled a total of 17,040 passenger arrivals, 17,425 passenger departures, and 344 metric tons of freight.

Water transport is of negligible importance, despite the country's numerous lakes and rivers. A Congo (Kinshasa) shipping line and two private operators provide weekly service to towns on Lake Kivu. The amount of traffic is small, and the rates are high, but lake transport between Gisenyi and Cyangugu is still less expensive than road transport.

Tourism

With a wide range of scenic attractions, a varied and pleasant climate, and a diversity of wildlife, Rwanda has the potential to develop tourism into a major industry and an important source of foreign exchange earnings. The main points of attraction for tourists are Kagera National Park (Parc National de la Kagera) and Mutara Big Game Hunting Reserve (Zone de Chasse du Mutara), which is located on the western border of the park, where licensed hunting is permitted. The park and reserve, which cover one-tenth of the country, contain approximately 500,000 head of wildlife, including buffalo, zebras, elands, lions, antelopes, and hippopotami. Another tourist attraction is the National Park of the Volcanoes (Parc National des Volcans), which encompasses the Virunga range of five volcanoes on the Rwandan side of the Congo's Albert National Park (Parc National Albert) and which is the refuge of the nearly extinct mountain gorilla. Lake Kivu, with its sandy beaches and clear waters, is also a tourist center.

There are, however, major drawbacks to attracting increased numbers of tourists to Rwanda, such as the relatively high airfares from North America and Europe to this remote, little-known country; the better-publicized tourist attractions of the country's East African neighbors; and the rudimentary internal transportation system. Expansion of the tourist industry is also hindered by inadequate accommodations. In 1966 the Government signed an agreement with a Swiss-German firm to form an organization to build hotels in the capital and in tourist centers. A 200-room hotel in Kigali was to be built first, but it was not known in early 1969 whether construction had been undertaken.

BANKING AND CURRENCY
Monetary Institutions

During the period of economic union between the then Belgian Congo, Burundi, and Rwanda from 1922 until 1960, monetary issue and circulation were the responsibility of the Central Bank of the Belgian Congo and Ruanda-Urundi (Banque Centrale du Congo Belge et du Ruanda-Urundi). In mid-1960, when the Congo became independent, a separate central bank, the Issuing Bank of Rwanda and Burundi (Banque d'Emission du Rwanda et du Burundi—BERB), and a new currency unit were created for Rwanda and Burundi. The monetary union was ratified reluctantly by the two countries, particularly Rwanda, after independence. Rwanda's dissatisfaction with the operating policies of the BERB, which were believed by the Rwandans to favor Burundi, increased. When the two countries were unable to settle their differences over the BERB's allocation of foreign currency for imports in late 1963, Rwanda announced that the union was terminated.

After the liquidation of the BERB and of the joint currency system, the National Bank of Rwanda (Banque Nationale du Rwanda—BNR) was established in April 1964 and began operations in the following month. According to the establishing legislation, the principal functions of the BNR are to issue legal tender currency, to manage foreign exchange reserves, and to regulate and control credit. The BNR acts as banker to the Government and to the commercial banks. It also has responsibility for maintaining monetary stability and for pursuing credit and exchange policies conducive to the country's economic growth. The BNR has an authorized capital of RF30 million, which is entirely subscribed and fully paid up by the Government. It has headquarters in Kigali and agencies in Butare and Gisenyi.

Two private banks offered full commercial banking services. The Commercial Bank of Rwanda (Banque Commerciale du Rwanda—BCR), established in 1963, was financed primarily by a consortium of European and American banks, with the Government as the other principal stockholder. It maintained branches in Gisenyi and Butare in addition to its main office in Kigali. In early 1967 a second bank, the Bank of Kigali (Banque de Kigali), was organized by a consortium of Belgian banks. The principal activity of the two commercial banks was financing the movement of exports, particularly coffee, and, to a lesser extent, imports, and serving the foreign community. Encouragement of savings among Africans and the financing of African-owned enterprises were generally regarded as being outside their sphere of activity.

Money and Credit

After the establishment of the BNR in 1964, Rwandan currency notes were issued to replace the BERB currency then in circulation. The official value of the Rwandan franc, like that of the Rwanda-Burundi franc which it replaced, was set at parity with the Belgian franc, or 50 Rwandan francs per United States dollar. The BNR found it necessary to retain a multiple exchange rate for the franc and a system of import licensing, introduced originally by the BERB in 1960, because of a decline in capital inflows and a major reduction in coffee exports during the previous 4 years. Under this system, foreign currency was made available by the central bank at the official rate of exchange to finance Government imports and private imports classified by the bank as essential. Importers of nonessential goods had to obtain foreign currency at the free market rate of exchange. All export earnings had to be surrendered at the official rate of exchange.

Despite the retention of trade and exchange restrictions, the monetary and financial situation deteriorated further in 1964 and 1965. A persistent deficit in the overall budget, financed mostly by advances from BNR, let to a rapid decline in foreign exchange reserves (see Public Finance). Prices, particularly for imported goods, rose sharply as scarcities developed with the increasing restrictiveness of the import-licensing system. Concomitantly, the importance of the free exchange market grew, and by the end of 1965 the unofficial rate of exchange was more than double the official rate of 50 Rwandan francs per United States dollar.

In April 1966 the Government entered into a stabilization program with the IMF, designed to encourage exports and to establish a more realistic domestic price level for imported goods, thereby improving the balance of payments situation. The currency was devalued from 50 to 100 Rwandan francs per United States dollar, and a unitary exchange rate system was introduced. The par value of the Rwandan franc was set at 0.00888671 gram of fine gold (RF3,500 per troy ounce of fine gold). As part of the stabilization program, quantitative restrictions on imports and restrictions on invisible transactions were liberalized, and the minimum price to farmers for coffee was raised in order to increase the incentive for production. Stringent credit restrictions were introduced for the public and private sectors. Export tax rates and most import duties, particularly on luxuries, were revised upward (see Public Finance). In support of the stabilization program, the Government entered into a standby arrangement with the IMF for U.S. $5 million to ease temporary pressures on foreign exchange reserves. External assistance was also received in the form of balance of payments support from Belgium and commodity aid from the United States.

In spite of a sharp increase in Government revenue in 1966, the budgetary deficit persisted at a high level, and the limit on public sector credit was exceeded. Coffee exports declined from the 1965 level; and a large deficit was incurred in the balance of payments. The complete IMF standby was drawn on to finance the deficit. The Government entered into a second standby arrangement for U.S. $2 million in April 1967. Increased export earnings from coffee and tin ore resulted in a balance of payments surplus in 1967; the budgetary deficit was reduced, and price stability was maintained. In March 1968 the IMF accorded Rwanda a third standby arrangement for U.S. $3 million in view of the steady, although very slow, progress the Government had made toward economic stability. By January 1969 the Government had repurchased U.S. $3 million of the initial standby, and its total drawing stood at U.S. $7 million.

Money Supply

The money supply consists of currency in circulation and private demand deposits. Currency in circulation rose steadily from

RF568 million in December 1964 to RF1,032 million in December 1967 before declining slightly to RF987 million in December 1968, with seasonal peaks occurring generally during the second quarter of the year and seasonal lows during the first quarter (see table 15). Private demand deposits fluctuated with the seasonal expansion or contraction of financing for the movement of export crops, particularly coffee, but increased only from RF335 million in December 1964 to RF524 million in December 1968. The gradual expansion in the money supply between 1964 and 1968 was accompanied by a continuing monetization of the economy.

Credit

Commercial bank credit to the public and private sectors expanded from RF301 million in December 1964 to RF1,336 million in December 1968. Seasonal fluctuations in the level of loans as well as in the money supply took place in conjunction with crop financing, but fluctuations in bank credit were more marked than those in commercial bank deposits. Loans to the private sector reached their peak during June, July, and August as the banks extended credit for the movement of the coffee crop; the level of private credit then declined monthly as outstanding loads were paid off until the normal seasonal upswing began in May of the following year.

One of the most important aspects of the stabilization program begun at the time of devaluation was the imposition of credit ceilings on the two commercial banks and on BNR. The BNR advances to the Government were limited to the equivalent of one-half of the budgetary receipts of the previous year, but the ceilings were exceeded in 1966, 1967, and 1968. Restrictions on private sector credit applied primarily to imports. The BNR authorized credit for imports only when they arrived in the country, thereby forcing importers to finance their goods from sources outside Rwanda. This measure reduced domestic demand for credit and improved the country's foreign exchange reserve position. Adequate financing for exports was assured by allowing the credit ceiling to move cyclically, based on forecasts of the coffee harvest. Such a provision was necessary because coffee exporters had little liquidity, and practically all crop financing had to be obtained from the banks.

During 1968 loan ceilings were raised in response to criticism that the credit restrictions were slowing down the economy excessively. Such a move was expected to result in a drop in the average commercial bank interest rate from 9 percent in 1967 to 8 percent, as in 1965 and 1966; the prime rate, accorded only for the financing of exports, was expected to return to 3 percent. The

Table 15. Monetary Survey of Rwanda
(in millions of Rwandan francs)

	December [1] 1964	June [1] 1965	December [1] 1965	June [2] 1966	December [2] 1966	June [2] 1967	December [2] 1967	June [2] 1968
Net foreign assets	264	70	132	−282	−253	−513	−78	−268
Domestic credit	301	536	634	1,101	939	1,513	1,109	1,508
Government	(241)	(360)	(552)	(687)	(777)	(931)	(936)	(1,055)
Private sector	(60)	(176)	(82)	(414)	(162)	(582)	(173)	(453)
Money supply	903	1,008	1,168	1,360	1,215	1,512	1,473	1,751
Currency outside banks	(568)	(754)	(845)	(1,025)	(899)	(1,142)	(1,032)	(1,200)
Private demand deposits	(335)	(254)	(323)	(335)	(316)	(370)	(441)	(551)
Quasi-money (savings deposits)	10	26	22	18	30	22	34	37
Other items (net)	−348	−429	−426	−560	−560	−535	−475	−547

[1] Rwandan franc equals approximately U.S.$0.02.
[2] 1 Rwandan franc equals approximately U.S.$0.01.

Source: Adapted from International Monetary Fund, *International Financial Statistics*, XXII, No. 3, 1969, pp. 264–65.

BNR was also forced to create a second category of credit completely outside the credit ceiling limits to finance new investments judged to be of value to the country. These credits were granted only for industrial and commercial projects; and were denied to nonproductive construction, such as housing.

The major deficiency of the credit system in the postindependence period was the inability of small-scale farmers and entrepreneurs to obtain loans through existing commercial channels. Judged by the standards on which commercial bank loan policy was based, these persons did not possess the requisite collateral or other assets to qualify as sound credit risks and, thus, were ineligible for loans. The only source of credit available to them, therefore, were local moneylenders who generally charged usurious rates of interest. To a certain extent, however, the inability of farmers to obtain production credit was offset by the provision of free seedlings, insecticides, and handtools by semipublic agricultural organizations (see Agriculture, ch. 9).

Savings, Investment, and Capital Formation

The level of public national savings was extremely low. The capacity of the Government to generate a budgetary surplus was limited by a continuing rise in recurrent expenditures and maintenance costs on foreign-financed projects (see Public Finance). In the mid-1960's Government investment was only about RF100 million per year, financed through central bank advances and foreign budgetary aid. Savings and investment by other public entities, generally limited to the power company and the coffee-marketing organization, were also minor. Most public sector investment, therefore, was financed through foreign aid.

The main private sectors of the economy—subsistence agriculture, commercial agriculture, commerce, and industry—functioned independently of one another in savings and investment. The small amount of savings generated within any one sector was invested in that sector, and there was no flow of funds from one sector to another. The main component of private monetary investment was housing construction and realty, particularly in the period before devaluation but also in the late 1960's as investors sought one of the few outlets providing rapid amortization and high returns on their invested capital.

There were few channels for the transmission of savings from one type of private economic activity to another or for the mobilization of domestic capital resources for public investment projects. The Rwandan Savings Bank (Caisse d'Epargne du Rwanda —CER) had very limited resources. In December 1967 private desposits totaled RF80 million, and private loans outstanding stood at RF61 million, most of them for housing construction and vehicle purchase. CER lending to the Government was also on a small scale; in December 1967 claims on the Government were RF125 million, consisting almost entirely of holdings of Treasury bills (see Public Finance). Postal accounts, or *comptes courants postaux*, were the only other channel through which small savings could be accumulated. In December 1967 total deposits stood at RF28.6 million, but approximately two-thirds of this amount was in public accounts.

In view of the absence of institutions to channel surplus funds within the economy into investment and the low level of domestic savings, the Government decided in 1967 to create a national development bank, but by early 1969 the bank had not begun operations. The projected functions of the bank included advising the Government on public sector development projects; assisting in the preparation of the development budget; examining investment proposals submitted under the Investment Code; and participating in development projects through the extension of loans or equity holdings. The bank's capital was set at RF50 million, of which RF27.5 million could be held only by public institutions; the remainder could be subscribed to by individuals or foreign or international organizations. The bank was expected to concentrate its resources and attention to the needs and development of the agricultural sector when it began operations.

Although no statistics were available on gross investment, it appeared that capital formation was proceeding slowly in the late 1960's and was restricted largely to the Asian community. Investment activity was thought to be still slightly below the 1959 level, when gross investment was estimated at 8 to 10 percent of gross domestic product. A large proportion of capital formation was not subject to statistical measurement, however, since it involved nonmonetary investment in the form of housing construction and land improvement in the rural sector.

PUBLIC FINANCE

Fiscal Administration

Responsibility for the recurrent budget, or *budget ordinaire*, rests with the Ministry of Finance. With the assistance of the other ministries, the Ministry prepares estimates of revenue and expenditure for each calendar year and, on behalf of the Government, presents them to the National Assembly for approval. Annual estimates of expenditure under the development budget, or *budget extraordinaire*, are prepared by the Ministry of International Cooperation and the Plan. The development budget has no receipts of its own. Most public investment is carried out with foreign air, and the various ministries initiate development projetcs relatively independently of the Ministry of International Cooperation and the Plan.

The Government levies both direct and indirect taxes. Direct taxes include an individual income tax, a tax on business profits, a capitation tax, and a tax on livestock. Indirect taxes are import duties, export taxes, and excise taxes. The livestock and capitation taxes are collected by the 141 communes, which retain a fixed proportion of the proceeds to finance communal responsibilities (in particular, road maintenance and the salaries of agricultural extension personnel) and forward the remainder to the Government. All other taxes levied by the Government are collected by Government tax agents.

Government Finance

Despite a rapid growth in Government receipts in the post-independence period, total expenditures consistently exceeded revenue by a wide margin; the tax system, the main source of revenue, was inadequate to finance the expansion in recurrent expenditure arising initially from the creation of a national administration and later from increased spending on education and defense. The recurrent budget deficit fluctuated between RF124 million and RF218 million from 1963 to 1967 and, together with the deficit in the development budget, represented from 16 percent (1967) to 65 percent (1963) of recurrent budget receipts (see table 16). In addition, deficits in accounts held at the Treasury increased the total Treasury deficit in most years, particularly in 1965. The overall deficit was financed through central bank advances to the Treasury, which had the effect of greatly reducing foreign exchange reserves, and, to a lesser extent, through the purchase of Treasury bills by the two local commercial banks and the savings bank.

Recurrent Expenditure

Recurrent expenditure increased by slightly more than 150 percent in current prices between 1963 and 1967, from RF547.5 million to RF1,382.6 million, although actual expenditures were below budgeted expenditures in every year after independence except 1965 (see table 17).

The growth of total expenditures in constant prices (real terms) was considerably less than in current prices because the salaries of Government personnel were raised by 30 percent after de-

Table 16. Consolidated Budget of Rwanda, 1963–68
(in millions of Rwandan francs)

	1963 [1]	1964 [1]	1965 [1]	1966 [2]	1967 [2] (provisional)	1968 [2] (budgeted)
Expenditures:						
Recurrent budget (Budget ordinaire)	547.5	659.6	887.2	1,321.8	1,375.3	1,382.6
Development budget (Budget extraordinaire)	1.9	56.5	79.6	102.3	79.7	100.0
Budget pour ordre[3] (net)						
Comptes hors budget[3] (net)	32.6	-----	110.5	9.6	54.4	-----
TOTAL EXPENDITURES	582.0	716.1	1,027.3	1,433.7	1,509.4	1,482.6
Receipts:						
Recurrent budget (Budget ordinaire)	333.6	493.4	619.3	1,170.7	1,251.2	1,378.3
Development budget (Budget extraordinaire)	-----	-----	-----	2.0	4.2	-----
Budget pour ordre[3] (net)						
Comptes hors budget[3] (net)	-----	55.7	-----	-----	-----	31.0
TOTAL RECEIPTS	333.6	549.1	619.3	1,172.7	1,255.4	1,409.3
Deficit (−) or *Surplus* (+)	−248.4	−167.0	−408.0	−261.0	−254.0	−73.3
Financing						
Treasury bills[4]	-----	108.0	97.8	-----	141.0	-----
Central bank borrowing	193.7	77.8	250.1	274.5	115.9	73.3
Foreign aid	27.9	41.6	60.1	−13.5	−2.9	-----
Cash balances[4]	26.8	−60.4	-----	-----	-----	-----
TOTAL FINANCING	248.4	167.0	408.0	261.0	254.0	73.3

[1] Rwandan franc equals approximately U.S.$0.02.
[1] Rwandan franc equals approximately U.S.$0.01.
[3] The *budget pour ordre* and the *comptes hors budget* include Treasury operations made outside the recurrent and development budgets.
[4] An increase in cash balances is indicated by a negative sign.

Source: Adapted from Rwanda, Ministère de la Coopération Internationale et du Plan, Direction de l'Office Général des Statistiques, *Bulletin de Statistique*, No. 16, Janvier 1968, pp. 108, 111.

Table 17. *Recurrent Budget (Budget Ordinaire) Expenditure by Ministry, Rwanda, 1963-68*
(in millions of Rwandan francs)

Ministry[1]	1963[2] (actual)	1964[2] (actual)	1965[2] (actual)	1966[2] (actual)	1967[2] (provisional)	1968[2] (budgeted)
National Education	164.1	166.4	194.8	287.7	356.4	376.3
Police and National Guard	111.9	166.2	220.5	462.8	378.7	322.0
Public Works and Energy	45.4	56.2	44.0	71.6	95.4	108.7
Posts, Telecommunications and Transport	17.5	28.2	30.8	43.7	47.4	76.0
Agriculture and Animal Husbandry	29.7	40.1	38.4	51.5	50.0	64.7
Commerce, Mines, and Industry	2.2	3.5	5.3	6.4	9.6	7.4
Finance	32.5	40.2	55.7	73.5	69.6	60.4
International Cooperation and the Plan[4]	20.2	42.0	107.8	90.2	103.3	89.0
Information and Tourism	2.9	4.3	7.3	10.2	10.4	11.7
Justice and Interior	56.9	41.4	49.5	99.3	101.8	95.0
Public Health	51.6 }	56.4 }	64.2 }	80.8	102.3	110.8
Family and Community Development				14.0	17.2	12.0
Sovereignty[5]	12.6	14.7	18.9	30.1	33.2	48.6
TOTAL	547.5	659.6	837.2	1,321.8	1,375.3	1,382.6

[1] The President established the listed division of ministerial responsibilities in 1965; expenditures for 1963 and 1964 were reallocated to conform with this breakdown.
[2] 1 Rwandan franc equals approximately U.S.$0.02.
[3] 1 Rwandan franc equals approximately U.S.$0.01.
[4] Includes foreign affairs.
[5] Includes expenditures for the Presidency, National Assembly, and Supreme Court. In the 1968 budget it also includes appropriations for the Secretary of State for Civil Service and the Secretary of State for Plan Statistics.

Source: Adapted from Rwanda, Ministère de la Coopération Internationale et du Plan, *Etude de Développement-Plan Intérimaire d'Urgence*, I, p. 240; Rwanda, Ministère de la Coopération Internationale et du Plan, Direction de l'Office Général des Statistiques, *Bulletin de Statistique*, No. 10, Juillet 1966, p. 14; "Un budget équilibre pour 1968," *Rwanda Carrefour d'Afrique*, No. 75, Fevrier 1968, p. 11.

valuation and the cost of imported materials rose. Despite increased Government spending, the level of recurrent expenditure remained modest, amounting only to about 10 percent of total gross domestic product in current prices in the mid-1960's.

The Ministries of National Education and of Police and National Guard accounted for approximately one-half of total expenditures in the postindependence period. The increase in spending on education, not all of which is financed by the Government, was initially the result of expanded enrollments, but in the late 1960's it was primarily because of increased costs per pupil (see Education, ch. 7). Defense expenditures increased from 20 percent of total expenditures in 1963 to 35 percent in 1966 as the Government attempted to create and equip an Army in a very short time (see The Armed Forces, ch. 10). In 1967 military spending was limited to 80 percent of the original defense allocation, and in 1968 the defense budget was reduced further to 23 percent of total projected expenditures in an effort to contain the level of total expenditures.

Expenditures on economic services and on social services other than education increased in absolute terms after independence, but their proportion of total expenditures either remained fairly constant or decreased. The major factor limiting expansion of these services was the increased cost of education and defense, but the difficulty of finding qualified personnel, particularly for agricultural extension work and road maintenance, also kept the provision of economic and social services at an inadequate level.

Development Expenditure

In the postindependence period the Government financed only a small proportion of development expenditures from its own resources. Hardly any of the funds budgeted for development purposes in 1963 were spent in that year, and the balance was made available for expenditure in the following 3 years. Similarly, the balance of the 1964 budget was kept open for the next 2 years. Because of the carryover from the two previous budgets, there was no development budget in 1965. In 1966, RF102.3 million in development expenditure was undertaken by the Government, including some funds carried over from the 1963 and 1964 budgets. In 1967, RF79.7 million, composed of RF48.6 million carried over from the 1966 budget and RF31.1 million from that year's budget, was invested in development projects. Of the combined 1966 and 1967 development expenditures, approximately 28 percent was invested in buildings, a similar proportion in roads, 23 percent in telecommunications, and the remainder in such projects as agricultural diversification and airport construction. Approximately RF100 million in development expenditures were budgeted for 1968, but the procedure of automatically carrying over unexpended funds from the budgets of previous years was to be discontinued.

Recurrent Revenue

Government recurrent receipts in current prices nearly tripled between 1963 and 1967, from RF333.6 million to RF1,251.2, despite an annual shortfall between projected and actual receipts (see table 18). Approximately one-third of the expansion occurred in 1966, primarily as a result of an increase in indirect taxation, particularly export taxes, at the time of devaluation. Concomitantly, the relative importance of direct and indirect taxation within fiscal revenue was reversed, as indirect tax revenue rose from less than 40 percent of total receipts in the early 1960's to approximately 70 percent in the late 1960's. The changes in taxation also increased the incidence of taxation of export-crop producers in the rural sector who, before devaluation, had been estimated to pay about 4 percent of their incomes in taxes, as compared with about 14 percent for salaried urban dwellers.

Fiscal receipts were expected to increase faster than expenditures in the late 1960's and early 1970's. Government planners realized, however, that the tax base would have to be widened in order to absorb the budgetary deficit and thereby permit a further growth in recurrent expenditures and to achieve some public savings. An increase in taxation would not be unduly burdensome for the country, since recurrent revenue was only about 9 percent of total gross domestic product in the mid-1960's.
Indirect Taxes. Import duties played the dominant role in the tax system in the postindependence period. Two tariff charges were imposed on a nondiscriminatory basis to the goods of all foreign countries. One was a customs duty averaging 10 to 15 percent ad valorem, and the other was a revenue duty averaging 15 to 20 percent ad valorem. Many rates were raised by about 10 percent at the time of devaluation, but there were some reductions. Although revenue was the determining factor in the composition of the tariff schedule, some rates were adjusted to foster industrial and agricultural development. In particular, the structure of import duties was designed to tax consumer goods, particularly luxuries, rather heavily and to tax lightly, or to admit duty-free, most raw materials, intermediate and capital goods, and basic necessities. In 1966 and 1967 import duties represented about 17.7 percent of the value of imports.

Excise or consumption taxes were levied on alcoholic beverages and tobacco products in addition to the import duties on these

Table 18. *Recurrent Budget (Budget Ordinaire) Revenue, Rwanda, 1963–68*
(in millions of Rwandan francs)

	1963 [1] (actual)	1964 (actual)	1965 [1] (actual)	1966 [2] (actual)	1967 [2] (provisional)	1968 [2] (budgeted)
Direct Taxation:						
Taxes on property	26.5	61.5	58.2	56.3	61.3	65.5
Livestock taxes	----	52.5	48.7	41.3	39.4	41.0
Taxes on income and profits	107.7	219.7	196.1	267.7	317.1	337.9
Income taxes	12.4	21.5	28.2	66.4	84.6	100.3
Business profits taxes	27.0	26.5	39.0	75.3	101.3	102.0
Capitation tax	63.8	159.8	125.8	120.2	120.7	125.0
Total Direct Taxation	134.2	281.2	254.3	324.0	378.4	403.4
Indirect Taxation:						
Export taxes	----	----	29.0	197.0	188.6	200.0
Import taxes	----	----	146.7	323.0	350.4	400.0
Excise taxes	----	----	86.5	195.0	191.3	200.0
Miscellaneous indirect taxes	----	----	20.8	21.2	25.0	30.0
Total Indirect Taxation	162.1	156.0	283.0	736.2	755.3	880.0
Nonfiscal Income	37.3	56.2	82.0	110.5	117.5	145.0
GRAND TOTAL	333.6	493.4	619.3	1,170.7	1,251.2	1,878.4

[1] 1 Rwandan franc equals approximately U.S.$0.02.
[2] 1 Rwandan franc equals approximately U.S.$0.01.

Source: Adapted from Rwanda, Ministère de la Coopération Internationale et du Plan, Direction de l'Office Général des Statistiques, *Bulletin de Statistique*, No. 16, Janvier 1968, pp. 109–110.

goods. They were also imposed on domestically manufactured beer, mineral waters, and lemonade.

The tax base was significantly widened in 1966, when export taxes were first used as a major source of revenue. These taxes are generally criticized as being inequitable and a deterrent to the growing of cash crops for export, since they are in the nature of an income tax on the producers of primary products, as well as having highly unstable yields. The Government, however, regarded export taxes as an ideal way of collecting taxes from a large number of small producers, of stabilizing rural incomes, and of siphoning off windfall profits when world market prices were high.

At the time of devaluation, the rate for coffee was raised from 8 to 20 percent and that for tin ore from 3 to 20 percent. A 20-percent tax was placed on pyrethrum flowers, which previously had been exempt, and on tea, which had been taxed at 6 percent. In April 1967, however, export tax rates were modified further. The rates for coffee and tin ore were reduced to 10 percent, with an additional progressive duty applicable when the prices realized on the world market for these two commodities exceeded specified levels. The tax on tea was reduced from 20 percent to RF10 per kilogram, and that on pyrethrum flowers to RF12 per kilogram. As a result of these changes, receipts from export taxes as a proportion of the value of exports dropped from 18 percent in 1966 to 13.5 percent in 1967.

Direct Taxes. Direct taxes were divided into property or personal taxes and taxes on income and profits. Livestock taxes were the most important tax on property. Cattle were taxed at RF200 a head, whereas sheep and goats were taxed at a lower rate. The yield of the livestock tax was considerably below the amount that should have been available on the basis of official livestock statistics. Since collection of capitation taxes, the other tax for which communal authorities were responsible, was reasonably efficient, it appeared that the number of livestock was probably overestimated in official statistics (see Agriculture, ch. 9).

The major taxes on income and profits were the capitation tax, an individual income tax, and a tax on business profits. The capitation tax of RF400 was payable by all adult males. From 1966 on, 35 percent of the yield of this tax and the tax on cattle, as opposed to 30 percent previously, was retained by the communes to finance their own responsibilities; this factor was the main reason for the decline in Government receipts from these two sources in the mid-1960's. Individual income tax rates were progressive, rising from 4 percent on the first RF25,000 of taxable income, to 6 percent on the next RF75,000, and to 10 percent on RF100,000 to RF200,000; few individuals earned taxable incomes above this amount. The rate of corporate taxation was 25 percent on the first RF500,000 of net profits, 30 percent on the next RF500,000, and 45 percent on net profits above that amount; the mining companies were the largest single source of revenue from corporate taxes.

CHAPTER 9
AGRICULTURE, INDUSTRY AND LABOR FORCE, AND LABOR RELATIONS

The economy is almost exclusively dependent on agriculture, primarily the subsistence production of food crops. Approximately 90 percent of the population derives its livelihood directly from agriculture, and additional persons find wage employment in activities closely linked to it. Agriculture is the largest single source of foreign exchange earnings, accounting for approximately 60 percent of total export proceeds (see Foreign Economic Relations, ch. 8). Subsistence and commercial agriculture contribute from two-thirds to three-quarters of gross domestic product (see Glossary) at constant prices. Additional gross domestic product is indirectly derived from the agricultural sector, since most industrial activity involves the processing of agricultural products, and increasing cash-crop production is expanding the rural market for domestically manufactured goods.

The country's diverse climate, soil, and topography provide the potential for productive and varied agriculture. Fulfillment of this potential is thwarted, however, by the concomitant problems of extremely high population density on existing arable land, increasing soil erosion, and depletion of soil fertility. An excessive cattle population, of little economic value, has also hindered agricultural development. In addition, traditional methods of cultivation are generally characterized by low productivity, and the fragmented nature of farmholdings and the country's hilly terrain have prevented the introduction of widespread mechanization.

The small-scale family holding is the basic unit of production. In general, farmers produce mainly foods for domestic consumption; when cash crops are grown, their cultivation is secondary to that of food crops. The major food crops are bananas, used primarily for brewing beer; sweet potatoes; cassava; sorghum; and legumes. The country is usually self-sufficient in agricultural produce, but food output has generally failed to keep pace with the high population growth rate. Moreover, the economy is extremely vulnerable to temporary declines in production and even to famine because of bad weather.

Commercial production for export is based primarily on coffee, which was introduced as a small-scale producers' cash crop in the 1920's and 1930's. The Government, however, has initiated a diversification program to expand the production of tea and pyrethrum (a flower used in the production of insecticides) in order to reduce the economy's almost complete dependence on the world market earning power of coffee. This program also includes development of the livestock industry and the integration of livestock into a system of mixed farming in place of the present system of practicing animal and crop husbandry side by side.

The industrial base is extremely limited, and most manufacturing and processing activity occurs at the artisan or workshop level. The weakness of the industrial sector is the result primarily of the concentration of industrial enterprises in the Democratic Republic of the Congo (Congo-Kinshasa) and Burundi before independence. Industrial activity was stimulated by independence, but expansion of the sector is hindered by the small size of the domestic market for industrial goods, the absence of a class of African entrepreneurs, the lack of skilled labor, the low productivity of labor, and the limited domestic availability of capital. Industrial development has also suffered from hesitation on the part of local and foreign investors because of political and social disturbances in the immediate preindependence and postindependence periods.

In 1964 an estimated 74,290 persons, or 5.7 percent of those considered to be in the working-age group, were employed permanently or temporarily for cash wages or salaries. Approximately two-thirds of the paid labor force was employed in private industry, primarily in agriculture, mining, and construction, and one-third in public service. Only a very small proportion of the work force is skilled, since many persons undertake employment only on a temporary basis and therefore are rarely employed long enough to acquire an advancement in skills. In early 1969 there was no organized labor movement, but the country was a member of the International Labour Organisation.

AGRICULTURE

Land Use and Development

Land Use

The country's hilly-to-mountainous terrain and numerous lakes and marshes considerably reduce the amount of land available for agricultural use. On the basis of land surveys conducted in the mid-1960's by the Ministry of Agriculture, it was estimated that only 70.4 percent of the total land area of 10,168 square miles was

144

suitable for agricultural exploitation. Approximately 28.5 percent of the land area was unexploitable because of its relief or hydrology, and another 1.1 percent was reserved for industrial-residential activity. Of the 7,157 square miles of land available for agricultural use, the Ministry of Agriculture estimated that 43.6 percent was suitable for cultivation, 44.1 percent for pasture, and 12.3 percent for forest or afforestation (see table 19). In the late 1960's more than 85 percent of the estimated 3,121 square miles of arable land, located principally on hillsides in the central plateau region, was under cultivation; the only tracts of unexploited arable land were in the east, where climatic factors make cultivation uncertain.

The primary factor affecting the productive use of arable and grazing land is its susceptibility to soil erosion and depletion of fertility. Most of the land under cultivation is located on slopes of 10 to 25 percent, whereas in certain areas, particularly in the north, slopes of 40 to 50 percent are farmed. About 70 percent of the arable land area has a slope of more than 5 percent, and about 60 percent of the grazing land area has a slope of more than 10 percent, the degrees of incline at which the risks of soil erosion become aggravated for cultivable and grazing land.

During the Trusteeship period the Belgian Administration undertook an extensive soil conservation program, based primarily on digging anti-erosion ditches and planting hedges. By 1960 approximately 1,400 square miles of arable land, or 45 percent of all cultivable land, and 250 square miles of pasture land, or 8 percent of all grazing land, were protected against erosion. After independence, however, this type of erosion control work was largely discontinued; in the mid-1960's it was estimated that 45 percent of all cultivable land and 40 percent of all grazing land needed to be protected against erosion. Certain soil conservation practices introduced during the preindependence period, such as leaving buffer strips of fallow between cultivated plots, intercropping, mulching, and planting crops in rows across the slope of the terrain, have continued to be implemented to varying degrees.

In the most densely populated and intensely cultivated areas of the country, major problems of soil exhaustion and depletion of fertility have arisen as a result of the lack of arable land. Traditionally, under shifting cultivation, the population farmed an area until the soil lost its fertility and then migrated to new areas. More recently, under a pattern of settled agriculture, farmers alternated cropping periods with resting periods, during which the natural vegetation cover is regenerated. Increased pressure on the land, however, has necessitated a drastic shortening of the fallow

Table 19. Projected Land Utilization in Rwanda in 1966

Prefecture	Total area (in square miles)	Estimated population (1966)	Average population density (per square mile)	Area of agricultural land* (in square miles)	Cultivable land (in square miles)	Forest land (in square miles)	Grazing land (in square miles)	Average population density of cultivable land (per square mile)
Butare	707	454,022	642	613	273	57	288	663
Byumba	1,925	385,856	175	1,211	378	68	765	889
Cyangugu	859	258,496	301	741	352	261	128	734
Gikongoro	846	294,470	348	628	304	83	241	969
Gisenyi	925	344,534	373	387	270	16	10	1,276
Gitarama	865	431,883	499	741	333	68	340	1,297
Kibungo	1,596	224,203	141	1,065	530	136	399	423
Kibuye	510	207,242	406	304	132	18	154	1,570
Kigali	1,255	309,943	247	962	331	35	596	936
Ruhengeri	680	461,057	678	505	218	140	147	2,115
TOTAL	10,168	3,321,706	327	7,157	3,121	882	3,154	1,064

*Agricultural land comprises cultivable land, grazing land, and land under forests (excluding primary forests) or land scheduled to be reforested (excluding primary forests).

Source: Adapted from Rwanda, Ministère de la Coopération Internationale et du Plan, Direction de l'Office Général des Statistiques, *Bulletin de Statistique*, No. 12, Janvier 1967, p. 2.

period or even continuous use of the land. In the late 1960's it was estimated that only 30 percent of the land area was fallow and that in certain overpopulated areas it was considerably less than this figure. Insufficient fallowing, in conjunction with inadequate crop rotation and the use of traditional cultivation techniques, has resulted in soil exhaustion and progressively lower output per unit of arable land cultivated in the most overpopulated regions. The use of fertilizers to prevent or counteract soil impoverishment has been negligible, and little use has been made of manure, despite the important role of cattle in the agricultural system of all farmers.

In the late 1960's it was estimated on the basis of existing population growth and methods of cultivation that all arable land would be in use in approximately 10 years. Population pressure in many regions has already led to a reduction in the cultivable area, the cultivation of pastureland and higher mountain elevations, and the drainage and cultivation of marshes, particularly small- and medium-sized ones at higher altitudes, during the dry season. These methods of counteracting pressure on the land, however, further aggravate the dangers of erosion which, in turn, reduce the amount of arable land and especially its productive capacity.

The primary response of the Belgian Administration, as well as the postindependence Government, to the problems of increasing population pressure on the arable land area has been to establish *paysannats* (planned agricultural settlements) in underpopulated or underutilized regions; the settlements are based on detailed studies of the areas' men-livestock-land potential and on plans which make intensive agricultural and pastoral exploitation possible. By early 1966 a total of 16,060 families had been settled on 24 *paysannats*. Approximately 78 percent of these families were on coffee-growing *paysannats*; 16 percent were on pyrethrum *paysannats*; 5 percent were on cotton *paysannats*; and 1 percent were on tea *paysannats*. Most *paysannats* are located in the Bugesera-Mayaga region, an underpopulated area of approximately 1,200 square miles east of the Akanyaru River and south of the Nyabarongo River; this region has generally fertile soils, but it is susceptible to tsetse fly infestation. The remaining *paysannats* are concentrated on the southwestern and north-central borders of the country. By the early 1970's the Government hopes to have approximately 55,000 families resettled on *paysannats*, mainly through the further development of the Bugesera-Mayaga region. Practically all of the financing for the establishment and functioning of *paysannats*, estimated at RF34,400 (1 Rwandan franc equals U.S.$0.01) a family on the basis of 1,000 families per *paysannat*, has been provided by the European Economic Community (EEC) and the Belgian Government.

Agricultural Regions

There are three broad agricultural regions that coincide, for the most part, with the climatic regions (see Physical Environment, ch. 3). Most of the land area under cultivation is located in the central plateau region, extending on both sides of the Congo-Nile watershed between 4,920 and 6,230 feet, where the climate, rainfall pattern, and soil structure provide the basis for productive and varied agriculture. Throughout this region, which receives an annual rainfall of 39 to 52 inches, the precipitation pattern is characterized by two distinctly marked peaks, each of which is followed by a dry spell of comparatively short duration. Most of the land surface is covered with relatively rich soil, often of volcanic origin, with a high humus content. Perennial crops flourish in this region, and it is normally possible to grow two crops a year of annual plants. The agricultural system is based on bananas, beans, sorghum, and sweet potatoes as the main food crops and on coffee as the primary cash crop. The country's livestock population is centered in this region.

In the mountains forming the Congo-Nile watershed above 6,230 feet, the amount of rainfall is high and well distributed, ranging from 50 to 72 inches in some parts of the Virunga Mountains. Much of the land surface, particularly in the north, is covered with volcanic soils, which correspond to the most fertile areas of the country. Tea and pyrethrum prosper in this region, and it is the principal area for the cultivation of peas, wheat, barley, finger millet, and potatoes.

In the eastern half of the country, situated between 3,280 and 4,920 feet, precipitation is irregularly distributed and rarely exceeds 39 inches annually. The dry seasons are more severe and prolonged than elsewhere in the country, and local droughts and food shortages are a constant possibility. The soils are less fertile and less retentive of moisture than in the central plateau region; the vegetation cover is wooded or grassy savanna. This generally semiarid, underpopulated region is better adapted to stockraising than to agriculture, but the distribution of livestock over much of the area is restricted by the presence of tsetse fly, which transmits trypanosomiasis (sleeping sickness in humans and nagana in animals).

Organization and Operation

The basic unit of production is the small-scale family holding. In the mid-1960's it was estimated that, depending on the area of the country, each family needed 5 to 12 acres of arable land to ensure an adequate standard of living and to prevent further soil erosion and depletion of soil fertility under prevailing agricultural techniques. The actual average-sized farmholding per family, however, was roughly estimated at 3.26 acres of arable land and 3.29 acres of grazing land for the country as a whole. On a prefecture basis, the average amount of cultivable land per family ranged from 1.6 acres in Kibuye and 1.8 acres in Ruhengeri to 3.5 acres in Kigali to 7.1 acres in Kibungo. The average amount of grazing land per household varied from 1.2 acres in Gisenyi and Ruhengeri to 3 acres in Gikongoro to 7.4 acres in Byumba. In the most densely populated regions, the area of land actually cultivated closely approximates the average amount of disposable arable land per family; in relatively underpopulated zones, however, the area are farmed is less than the amount of disposable land.

Farmholdings are rarely composed of contiguous plots of land, since dispersal of fragments is deliberately sought by the farmer as a risk-minimizing technique against complete crop failure resulting from climatic factors or soil conditions. Despite adaptations necessitated by local conditions, each farmholding is generally composed of: a *rugo*, or homestead, delimited by a small enclosure, where the family lives and the cattle spend the night; a banana grove, usually located near the homestead; a small parcel of land near the homestead where slow-maturing, often famine-reserve, food crops are grown; one or more parcels on a hillside, intensively cultivated and benefiting generally from fallowing, where the staple food crops, such as beans, peas, or sorghum, are cultivated; a piece of land in some low-lying zone to ensure food needs during the dry season; and a parcel of land, specially selected and often isolated from the others, for the family's coffee trees. Uncultivated land and fallow land are used as pastures.

The hilly terrain and the fragmentation of holdings make mechanization virtually impossible and the use of ox-drawn plows in the preparation of fields for cultivation difficult. The acreage under cultivation, therefore, is determined not only by differing patterns of land use, climatic conditions, and population pressure, but also by the amount of land which the family unit, the most prevalent form of labor, can cultivate with handtools. The hoe is the usual agricultural implement in the preparation and cultivation of cropped land; the pruning knife is the only other tool in widespread use.

The random distribution of farmholdings over the hillsides of most of the country has inhibited not only the introduction of improved production techniques, such as mechanization, but also regular contact among farmers within a localized area and between agricultural extension workers and farmers. Through the establishment of *paysannats*, the traditional difficulty of communications within the agricultural sector has been overcome by arranging individual holdings—each averaging 6 acres of arable land—along an access road in a systematic manner, with the homesteads located along the road and the main cash-crop field adjacent to the road. Such a layout facilitates transportation; mechanization of certain agricultural activities, such as insecticide spraying and harvesting; introduction of new agricultural methods; and provision of basic economic and social services.

In the late 1960's the land tenure system was ill defined following the removal of the feudal client-patron land rights system in the immediate preindependence and postindependence periods. It appeared that agricultural land was generally occupied on the basis of customary rules of tenure, whereby groups of elders or the head of an extended family group within a particular area conceded cultivation and grazing rights to the members of the local society. Under this system the farmer had, in effect, de facto ownership of his land on the basis of occupancy as long as he farmed or grazed the land. On *paysannats*, however, the customary land tenure system was to be replaced by individual land titles.

Production

Food Crops

Food crops for direct consumption on the farm are several times more important in terms of volume of output, expenditure of energy, and acreage cultivated than crops produced for the market. In the mid-1960's it was estimated that 96 to 97 percent of the land under cultivation was devoted to food crops. The value of output for subsistence was computed to be roughly equivalent to 10 times that of cash-crop production, and subsistence production accounted for about 99 percent of total agricultural output.

Despite individual differences, certain production techniques are characteristic of subsistence farmers. In general, the basic goal of the subsistence producer is to ensure his family's survival through provision of at least a minimum food supply. Given the frequent danger to crops from bad weather, the primary objective of the farmer, therefore, is to minimize the risk of failure rather than to achieve the maximum level of production and income. The self-sufficiency of each household through diversity, rather than concentration on the range of crops best suited to the prevailing soil and climatic conditions, is stressed. Intercropping is generally more characteristic than cropping in pure stands. The need for an increased food supply is normally achieved by expanding the area under cultivation rather than by attempting to increase the low productivity of the acreage already cultivated.

Finally, planting of food crops is generally done at the time of the year that experience has shown to be "safest," rather than at the correct time to produce the maximum yield. Similar considerations result in a repetitive pattern of cropping from year to year.

Figures on food-crop production are subject to a large degree of error, since approximately 90 percent of all output is consumed directly by the producers. Available statistics indicate that food production, although varying by as much as 30 percent from one year to the next, has failed to keep pace with the population growth rate (see table 20). Government statisticians estimate, for example, that the averaged 1962–65 total food production was only 3.5 percent higher than the 1958–59 averaged total output; excluding banana production, averaged total volume actually decreased by 30 percent between 1958–59 and 1962–65. The overall stagnation in food-crop tonnage is primarily the consequence of low yields, since the area under cultivation expanded after 1960; average yields range from 8 percent (finger millet) to 150 percent (cassava) below possible yields.

Bananas, a perennial crop, are the traditional staple of the central plateau region below 6,230 feet in altitude; they are consumed primarily in the form of "beer" (the diluted pulp is partially fermented) by the household. This high-yielding crop accounts for more than one-half of total food-crop tonnage in most years and occupies an estimated 18 to 20 percent of the cultivated land area. Bananas constitute a food reserve at the end of the dry season, since the trees bear year-round, and are a guarantee against famine if other crops fail. Bananas are the most frequently marketed food crop, since the beer does not keep well.

Legumes make an important contribution to food supplies throughout the country, providing the main source of protein for most people; they also fit well into the agricultural system, since their nitrogen-fixing properties help to restore soil fertility. At higher altitudes the staple legume is beans; at lower altitudes it is peas.

Sweet potatoes are grown in all regions. They are of particular importance in densely populated areas, since they require little acreage and are high yielding. Sweet potatoes are usually eaten fresh, but they can be stored for several months if they are sliced and sun-dried. Cassava is grown in low or average altitude zones, where it is valuable as a reserve against famine because it can be stored in the ground for up to 2 or 3 years; like sweet potatoes, cassava is not very demanding in its soil requirements. Potatoes are grown only in high altitude zones.

Maize is cultivated throughout the country, sorghum is grown in all but the low-lying zones, and finger millet is grown only in

Table 20. Estimated Food Crop Production of Rwanda, 1959, 1962–1967
(in metric tons)

	1959	1962	1963	1964	1965	1966	1967
Sorghum	130,500	167,800	127,000	147,200	130,700	143,900	145,200
Finger millet	5,700	3,100	2,100	1,200	2,100	1,800	1,200
Wheat	1,500	1,400	1,700	300	500	100	300
Rice	---	---	---	---	---	---	200
Maize	39,500	68,700	71,800	21,300	44,000	48,900	53,200
Potatoes	83,600	73,500	66,200	30,400	43,300	57,200	107,300
Sweet potatoes	487,200	656,700	421,300	238,800	203,200	257,100	360,000
Cassava	170,300	134,300	147,500	174,200	177,700	198,200	230,000
Beans	96,700	92,300	96,300	69,900	87,500	130,700	131,800
Peas	39,000	40,300	38,900	27,900	39,100	59,700	51,600
Peanuts	2,500	1,300	2,200	4,900	19,800	4,500	15,800
Bananas	849,600	1,471,800	879,200	1,033,300	1,202,300	1,452,000	1,560,000
TOTAL	1,906,100	2,711,200	1,854,200	1,749,400	1,950,200	2,354,100	2,656,600
Index*	100.0	142.2	97.3	91.8	102.3	128.5	139.4

*1959 =100.

Source: Adapted from Rwanda, Ministère de la Coopération Internationale et du Plan, Direction de l'Office Général des Statistiques, *Bulletin de Statistique*, No. 16, Janvier 1968, pp. 31–32.

high-altitude areas. These cereal crops are very tolerant in their soil requirements, are drought-resistant because of their low water requirements, but are low yielding. All three cereals are pounded to form flour for baking and porridge; sorghum is also used to make a fermented beverage.

Government planners are increasingly concerned about the failure of food-crop production to increase at a faster rate than the growth in population and about the concomitant decline in the nutritional level of the average household's food consumption. This concern is reinforced by the economy's continuing vulnerability to temporary declines in production and to famine resulting from climatic factors, since there are no stocks of food and the distribution system is inadequate. The planners project that production must grow by at least 3 percent a year to keep pace with the population growth rate; it is hoped, however, that production will grow by 5 percent annually to facilitate the monetization of the economy through the increased sale of surplus output. Given the scarcity of arable land, it is recognized that an expansion in food production will have to be achieved through increased yields, the introduction of improved farming techniques, and the development of new food crops.

Expectations of an increase in yields are based on the success of a program of selected seed multiplication and diffusion financed by the Belgian Government. The introduction of new food crops has focused on the development of peanuts, rice, soybeans, and sugarcane. Peanuts are grown to some extent throughout the country, but the dry climate and light soils of the east are particularly suited to their cultivation. Under the organization of a Belgian-financed private group, International Association for Overseas Rural Development (Association Internationale de Développement Rural Outre-Mer—AIDR), peanut-growing *paysannats* have been established in Kibungo Prefecture, and yields of about 1,070 pounds per acre have been obtained through a program of selected seed distribution.

Rice cultivation was introduced in the mid-1960's, with the technical assistance of the Republic of China, on approximately 700 acres of valley marshland in the prefectures of Kigali, Butare, Kibuye, and Cyangugu. With the use of selected seeds, rice farmers obtained average yields of nearly 1 metric ton per acre during the second year of cultivation. The Chinese have also assisted in the introduction of soybeans as a second crop, since the climate does not permit a double rice crop. Although the crop grows well and has the special characteristic of regenerating the soil, its introduction has met wih resistance since Rwandans find the beans difficult to cook. Sugarcane cultivation has also been developed with Chinese technical assistance on about 185 acres in the Nyabarongo River valley outside Kigali. The sugarcane is rotated with rice or vegetables and yields about 400 metric tons of sugarcane per acre, or 24 metric tons of processed sugar.

Cash Crops

Commercial agriculture contributes an estimated 5 to 7 percent of gross domestic product, including subsistence agriculture, at constant prices. Its products account for approximately 60 percent of export earnings (see Foreign Economic Relations, ch. 8). Cashcrop production provides the basis of the monetary economy and is the main source of income for the majority of the population. The spread of commercial agriculture is the primary factor in the increasing monetization of the economy.

The major cash crop is coffee, which contributes approximately one-half of total export earnings and about 90 percent of agricultural export earnings; it is also the primary determinant of the level of national income and commercial activity. The economy's almost complete dependence on the world market earning power of coffee, however, represents its major structural weakness. In an effort to reduce the dependence on coffee and thereby strengthen the economic base of the country, the Government is engaged in a diversification program to increase the role of tea and pyrethrum as cash crops so that, together, they equal in value the output of coffee.

Coffee. About one-half of the country, between an altitude of 4,100 and 6,230 feet, is suited to coffee cultivation. The best growing zones, however, lie between 4,920 and 5,900 feet, comprising the fertile, well-watered soils bordering Lake Kivu and an area in the center of the country north of Kigali (see fig. 5). Arabica coffee, which can command a premium on the world market if properly cultivated and processed, is grown on small plots by more than one-half of all households, or approximately 300,000 farmers. In the mid-1960's the average number of trees cultivated per farmer for the country as a whole was 105; on a prefecture basis the number ranged from 83 in Kibungo to 135 in Kigali. Some large-scale farmers, however, had as many as 1,000 to 2,000 trees under cultivation.

Coffee production expanded fairly steadily until 1959, although there was usually a slight decline in output in alternate years. Between 1959 and 1963, however, production decreased dramatically, as many trees were not harvested and as standards of cultivation fell, mainly as a result of the political events of 1960–61 (see Historical Setting, ch. 2). Concomitantly, the average output of parchment coffee (preroasted coffee) per acre declined from 1,177

154

pounds in 1959 to 319 pounds in 1963, and the average yield per tree decreased from 29.1 ounces to 7.4 ounces (see table 21). Output resumed an upward trend in 1964 as a result of an improvement in standards of cultivation and a continual expansion in the number of trees in production. By 1967 the average output of parchment coffee per acre, although still below the 1959 level, had increased to 660 pounds, and the average yield per tree had risen to 17.6 ounces.

The generally low productivity of the country's coffee trees is primarily the result of poor cultivation techniques, particularly the insufficient use of fertilizers, since the number of producing trees increased from 22.3 million in 1959 to 31.5 million in 1967. Experiments undertaken by the Institute of Agronomical Sciences of Rwanda Institut des Sciences Agronomiques du Rwanda— ISAR), an agricultural research organization, indicated that yields could be raised by 15 to 20 percent through the use of mineral fertilizers. On the basis of these studies it was also estimated that yields of marketable coffee would stabilize without the use of fertilizers at approximately 12 ounces per tree per year, or about 12,700 metric tons in 1969 and 15,000 metric tons in 1971, instead of the Government projected level of 15 ounces and 16,000 metric tons in 1969 and 22 ounces and 20,000 metric tons in 1971.

Achievement of the Government's 1971 coffee production target is dependent not only on the introduction of fertilizers, but also on the success of a coffee rehabilitation project designed to increase productivity through proper tree pruning, insecticide spraying, and biyearly mulching and manuring. Introduction of improved production techniques will be the responsibility of an expanded cadre of coffee extension workers; these agents, who numbered about two per commune in 1967, are employed by the Office of Industrial Crops of Rwanda (Office des Cultures Industrielles du Rwanda—OCIR), a Government-owned organization in charge of assisting farmers in improving their production, of fixing and maintaining a minimum buying price to the producer, and of classifying the coffee crop for export (see Domestic Trade, Foreign Economic Relations, ch. 8).

Production increases were also expected to result from the planting of a projected 8.3 million high-yielding trees between 1966 and 1968. These improved varieties, developed by one of ISAR's seed selection research stations, were distributed to farmers under the supervision and at the expense of OCIR. Based on a minimum maturation period of 3 years, about 11 million new coffee trees, many of which were planted on *paysannats* in the Bugesera-Mayaga region, were expected to start producing between 1967 and 1971. Continuation of OCIR's program of supply-

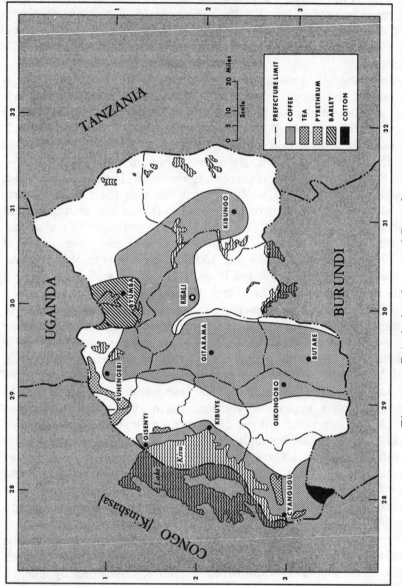

Figure 5. Principal cash crops of Rwanda, 1968.

Table 21. Estimated Cash Crop Production of Rwanda, 1959, 1962–1967
(in metric tons)

	1959	1962	1963	1964	1965	1966	1967
Coffee:							
Parchment	18,350	12,700	6,270	10,800	13,600	11,860	14,570
Marketable	13,700	9,500	4,700	8,100	10,200	8,600	10,900
Pyrethrum (dried flowers)	688	430	337	340	420	417	520
Tea (dried leaves)	100	210	300	320	332	361	430
Barley	1,425	275	300	939	1,163	750	2,197
Seed cotton	344	298	248	409	403	313	352

Source: Adapted from Rwanda, Ministère de la Coopération Internationale et du Plan, Direction de l'Office Général des Statistiques, *Bulletin de Statistique*, No. 15, Octobre 1967, pp. 34–35; *ibid*, *Bulletin de Statistique*, No. 16, Janvier 1968, p. 33; "Productions agricoles du Rwanda," *Rwanda Carrefour d'Afrique*, No. 43, Avril 1965, pp. 17–19.

ing insecticides and fertilizers to farmers in conjunction with ISAR, distributing free of charge the tools necessary for proper tree maintenance, and financing depulping plants should also affect production (see Industry).

Producers are assured a guaranteed minimum selling price for their coffee by the Government through the use of a stabilization fund, which is financed by levying a tax on every 2.2 pounds of coffee purchased from the grower (see Domestic Trade, ch. 8). Such a fund enables OCIR to subsidize prices to growers at a level higher than the world market price when that price begins to fall, thereby stabilizing growers' incomes. Between 1963 and 1965 it was necessary for OCIR to draw on the fund to subsidize producer's prices, but intervention in the market was not necessary during the following 2 years. It is impossible to determine the exact relationship between the level of the minimum price to growers and the quantity and quality of coffee production, although there are some indications that the increase in output after 1963 was partially in response to increases in the minimum price in 1964 and 1966.

Tea. Tea is an ideal crop for Rwanda, located more than 1,000 miles from the nearest seaport, since it has a higher shipping unit value than other cash crops grown or suitable for cultivation. In addition, world market prospects for tea are more favorable than for most other primary products. Approximately 42,000 acres of land, with an estimated productive capacity of 19,000 metric tons of tea, are potentially suitable for cultivation; about one-half of this land is comprised of swamps and marshes, which are the best and most productive areas for tea cultivation. ISAR obtains an average production of about 740 to 880 pounds of dried green tea per acre on hillsides and 1,056 to 1,232 pounds in swamps and marshes 6 to 7 years after planting, which is double the average world yield. The factory yield of dried black tea from green tea is about 20 percent.

Until 1963 tea production was largely carried out by private companies and European planters. The long-term nature of the crop, the large investment required to establish production, the specialized techniques of cultivation, and the need to process the crop shortly after picking made tea more suitable for estate production than for small-holder cultivation. Expansion of tea production and participation of small-scale farmers in the industry, however, were the primary focus of the agricultural diversification program initiated by the Government after independence. With the financial and technical assistance of the European Economic Community (EEC), which had underwritten the cost of 11 projects or studies on tea production by mid-1968, tea cultivation was introduced as a small-holders' cash crop on *paysannats* during the 1960's.

By the late 1960's nine tea plantations, clustered in the prefectures of Cyangugu, Gisenyi, and Byumba, were either in production or under cultivation. Two were run by private planters and two by European combines, with a total of about 1,500 acres under cultivation and in production. Three *paysannat* plantations financed by the EEC had about 2,300 acres under cultivation and in or nearing production out of a projected total of 4,000 acres. A fourth EEC-financed *paysannat* plantation, involving an estimated eventual goal of 2,500 acres, was in the process of being established in the late 1960's.

The eighth plantation was composed of a group of small-scale farmers, growing on private plots under the framework of a *paysannat*, with about 500 acres under cultivation and in production. The last was a Government-owned and operated plantation (*régie*), scheduled to become a *paysannat*, with about 250 acres under cultivation and in production. Taking into account only the yield of plantations actually operating or about to go into production in 1967, the Government estimated that output would reach 1,800 metric tons in 1971 or 1972 and would exceed 3,000 metric tons around 1975, since the yield of the EEC-financed plantations would not have an impact on production until after 1969.

Pyrethrum. Pyrethrum is a small daisy-like flower whose extract, pyrethrine, is used in the manufacture of insecticides. The area suitable to its production in Rwanda is limited to about 24,700 acres of well-watered volcanic soils above an altitude of 9,800 feet in Ruhengeri and Gisenyi Prefectures, where it is impossible to grow other cash crops. The pyrethrine content of the dried flowers cultivated on these fertile soils is considerably higher than the world average.

Until 1963 pyrethrum was primarily an estate crop grown by 19 private European farmers and two semipublic organizations (*régies*). In line with its emphasis on agricultural diversification, however, the Government introduced pyrethrum as a small holders' cash crop in the mid-1960's to 2,540 families on *paysannats* in Ruhengeri and Gisenyi Prefectures. By 1967 approximately 3,000 acres of pyrethrum were under cultivation, divided almost equally between the two *régies* and four *paysannats*, on the one hand, and the European plantations, on the other.

Production of pyrethrum, introduced before World War II, increased annually until 1955, when approximately 1,200 metric tons of dried flowers were produced. Output subsequently declined to 337 metric tons in 1963, after the closing of the processing factory at Goma, Congo (Kinshasa), where the 1.5 to 1.6 percent pyrethrine content of the dried flowers was extracted and stabilized in a 25-percent solution for export. Exporting the crop in the form of dried flowers considerably reduced producers' prices because of the high transport costs and, consequently, production declined. Sales were also reduced because foreign importers preferred the extract to the dried flowers.

Production began to increase after 1964 with the entry into production of the pyrethrum-growing *paysannats* and an agreement with Kenya, the world's largest pyrethrum producer, to process the Rwandan crop. Output was expected to continue to expand in the late 1960's and early 1970's as a results of a 1966 agreement with the EEC to finance the development of an additional 8,650 acres of pyrethrum on existing or new *paysannats* in Ruhengeri and Gisenyi Prefectures, involving about 5,000 families. By the early 1970's total production was projected to reach 2,500 to 3,000 metric tons of dried flowers on the approximately 11,650 acres under cultivation. Extension of production was expected to be facilitated further by the construction of a local extraction factory with an annual capacity of 3,000 metric tons of dried flowers under a 1968 agreement with the United Nations (see Industry).

Other Crops. A small amount of cotton is grown on a *paysannat* in the extreme southwest of the country in the Ruzizi Valley. Production has remained fairly constant at 300 to 400 metric tons of seed cotton because of continuing low productivity. A major extension of the acreage under cultivation is not possible for topographical reasons, and the maximum output of the area is projected at only 500 to 600 metric tons. Through the introduction of better cultivation techniques and regular spraying with DDT, however, Government agronomists hope to raise output to its maximum. Additional increases in national production were also expected from the introduction of cotton cultivation on a *paysannat* established in the mid-1960's in the Bugesera-Mayaga region.

Barley is grown by about 4,600 farmers in areas above an altitude of 5,900 feet in Byumba Prefecture. Production has varied considerably; it fell drastically in the early 1960's as a result of political disturbances in that region, but expanded to over 2,000 metric tons in 1967, the Government-anticipated production level for the late 1960's and early 1970's. Marketing, however, has become a problem, since the previous major customer, a brewery in Congo (Kinshasa), no longer imports from Rwanda.

Animal Husbandry

Most farmers supplement their cultivation activities with some form of livestock raising. Livestock, however, are rarely integrated into the farming system; rather, animal and crop husbandry are practiced side by side in a system of parallel husbandry, with little use made of cattle manure in the agricultural cycle. In most areas cattle are grazed on pastureland or uncultivated arable land during the day and are returned to the *rugo* at night. In the more densely populated and intensely cultivated zones, where there is little or no fallow or pastureland, cattle are grazed along the edges of cultivated fields. Goats and sheep are usually tethered at a stake within the *rugo* so that they will not destroy the crops, although occasionally they are taken to pasture in small herds.

In 1967 the number of livestock was roughly estimated at 682,-000 cattle, including 306,000 cows and 138,000 heifers; about 677,-000 goats, sheep, and pigs; and about 537,000 chickens (see table 22). The size of the cattle herd decreased by approximately 15 percent between 1958 and 1963 as a result of political unrest; in the mid-1960's the number of cattle was rising, but there were indications that the cattle population had been overestimated in official statistics. The number of goats, sheep, and pigs, however, continued to decline in the postindependence period from its late 1950's level, although the actual magnitude of the fall did not appear to be as great as the statistics indicated.

The cattle are generally characterized by extremely low rates of growth and low yields of milk, partly as a result of the prevalence of livestock diseases. The major epidemic diseases, such as rinderpest (cattle plague), anthrax, and contagious bovine pleuropneumonia, have been largely eradicated by mass vaccination programs. Parasitic diseases, endemic throughout most of the country, have not been eliminated and cause widespread death among calves, general debility in the rest of the herd, an increase in the cattle population's susceptibility to other diseases, and a decrease in the value of much of the meat and hides produced.

Approximately one-half of the cattle population is infected with cysticercosis, a tapeworm disease which deprives the affected animals of all commercial value. This disease is derived from the great human and animal population density, the proximity in which people and their animals live, and the lack of hygiene among farmers. There is no known cure for cysticercosis or other parasitic diseases, but the rate of infestation can be reduced by disrupting the evolutionary cycle of the parasites through proper human and animal hygiene. East Coast Fever, a disease carried by ticks, causes the death of an estimated 25 to 30 percent of all calves and presents a constant threat to all cattle that have not had their ticks removed through dipping or spraying. Nagana, the trypanosome-caused cattle disease related to sleeping sickness and carried

Table 22. Estimated Number of Livestock in Rwanda in 1967

Prefecture	Goats	Sheep	Pigs	Poultry	Cattle	Number of acres of pastureland per head of cattle
Butare	30,000	14,300	15,300	53,600	90,495	2.0
Byumba	130,700	29,300	5,700	187,400	128,524	3.8
Cyangugu	32,100	2,700	2,900	-----	23,648	3.5
Gikongoro	23,200	7,500	6,700	14,600	48,846	3.2
Gisenyi	32,300	12,000	1,100	27,000	42,413	1.5
Gitarama	33,400	7,800	3,100	36,700	124,200	1.8
Kibungo	80,500	10,400	400	88,000	75,219	3.4
Kibuye	35,400	6,400	1,800	52,400	41,127	2.4
Kigali	46,600	11,700	1,000	37,600	72,477	5.3
Ruhengeri	55,600	35,900	1,500	39,900	35,162	2.7
TOTAL 1967	499,800	138,000	39,500	537,200	682,111	3.0
1966	374,700	138,800	29,500	304,300	614,722	
1965	409,800	160,900	25,800	338,700	576,915	
1964	458,600	202,700	35,900	498,700	556,978	
1963	663,900	215,100	47,100	-----	500,299	
1959	983,000	296,000	50,000	-----	564,000	

Source: Adapted from Rwanda, Ministère de la Coopération Internationale et du Plan, Direction de l'Office Général des Statistiques, Bulletin de Statistique, No. 16, Janvier 1968, p. 35; ibid., Bulletin de Statistique, No. 14, Juillet 1967, p. 62.

by the tsetse fly, is widespread in the eastern region of the country. Tsetse eradication through bush clearing and spraying, however, is a long-term, costly, and difficult process.

Animal husbandry methods and range management practices also hinder the development of a productive livestock industry. The cattle population could be supported on the existing area of pastureland if it were used judiciously. Traditional range management practices, however, militate against the optimum use of the grazing capacity of available land. In particular, the practices of uncontrolled brush burning and of heavy grazing before the vegetation cover has completely regenerated have led to deterioration of the grasslands and increased soil depletion and erosion. Under actual range practices, therefore, it is estimated that each head of cattle requires an average minimum of about 4 acres of pasture to assure proper nourishment and to prevent overgrazing. Since there are few areas of the country where such a cattle-pasture ratio is possible, undernourishment and overstocking are extremely widespread.

Slaughtering, both to counteract overstocking problems and to increase the meat supply, has been hampered by the tradition of viewing livestock more as a symbol of wealth and prestige than as a commercial asset. Formerly, cattle played an important social and political role unrelated to their economic significance, but the prestige value attached to cattle appears to have declined to some extent since the abolition of *ubuhake* (a feudal patron-client relationship based on the use of cattle) and the redistribution of the cattle (see Historical Setting, ch. 2). The annual offtake is thought to have increased as a result of these changes, but it is impossible to determine even roughly the number of cattle butchered yearly, because most animals are slaughtered in the local markets or on the homesteads rather than in the officially registered slaughterhouses.

Government planners recognize that, unless improved methods of animal husbandry and range management are introduced, the country's livestock population will remain an unproductive and uneconomic asset and that the concomitant problems of overstocking and overgrazing will be exacerbated. Government attempts to improve the quality of natural pastures through such measures as planting forage crops, irrigation, and rotational grazing, however, have made little headway. The Government has been equally unsuccessful in substantially reducing the large number of unproductive and inferior cattle kept in the herd. Difficulty in achieving progress in the introduction of new practices has reinforced the widespread view that better utilization of the country's livestock potential depends basically on teaching farmers that it is the quality of cattle and not their numbers that is important.

Forestry and Fishing

Of the country's formerly extensive forest reserves in the mountains of the Congo-Nile watershed, less than 580 square miles of natural forest remain. There are about 215 square miles of wooded savanna in the eastern central plateau region; approximately 100 square miles of these woodlands consist of exotic trees, primarily eucalyptus, but only two-fifths of the area is exploitable. In the mid-1960's it was estimated that existing forests could produce about 3.3 million cubic feet of wood annually; this was approximately 25 times more than total wood consumption, which is considerably lower than in other African countries.

For many years the Government's policy has been to create sufficient forest cover to maintain climatic conditions suitable for agriculture, to conserve water supplies, to maintain soil stability in areas of potential erosion, and to provide wood for fuel and for agricultural and industrial purposes. A major afforestation program was undertaken by the Belgian Administration to enrich existing forests, to plant trees usable as firewood, and to restore the vegetation mantle in overgrazed or badly eroded areas. In the postindependence period this program has continued on a smaller scale at the local level through the planting of communal forests of fast-growing eucalyptus, black wattle, and cypress; afforestation is also an integral part of the establishment of *paysannats*.

Despite the fact that lakes cover an area of about 480 square miles, fishing remains a minor activity, partly because the lakes do not naturally offer considerable resources. Fishing is significant as a supplement to subsistence farming for many people living near the shores of Lakes Kivu, Muhazi, Mugesera, Reweru, Cyohoha, Ruhondo, Sake, Gaharwa, and Rumira. In 1967 the volume of production from these nine lakes was projected at 450 metric tons; an estimated 530 professional fishermen and 1,000 occasional fishermen worked the lakes, using approximately 1,000 small canoes and 2,000 nets. Lake Kivu was the most intensely exploited, but yielded only 15 percent of the total estimated catch. Tilapia, first stocked during the Trusteeship Period to raise the low natural productivity of the country's lakes, accounts for most fish production; tilapia multiplies better in the marshy lakes of the east than in Lake Kivu, accounting for the lake's low yields.

INDUSTRY

Factors Affecting Industrial Potential

The main constraint on industrial expansion is the limited size of the domestic market, which is affected, in turn, by the extremely low purchasing power of the country's relatively small population. The low monetary per capita income of the population has restricted the market for most goods and has permitted the establishment of only a few enterprises above the level of artisan workshops. Most of these larger scale firms manufacture goods within the potential purchasing power of the population. Excess capacity and a scale of operations conducive to high costs, however, are generally characteristic of the import-substitution industries already established; this is a result primarily of the limited size of the domestic market.

Expansion of industrial activity has also been affected by the limited supply of skilled labor, both technical and managerial, and by low labor productivity (see Labor). These factors, in conjunction with the limited domestic availability of capital, mean that a large number of unskilled laborers must be used to perform a given task. This raises the cost per unit of output which, in turn, increases the prices of fledgling industries and affects their competitiveness with imports.

In contrast to the constraints on industrial development presented by the limited domestic market and the supply and productivity of labor, the country's diverse climate and terrain offer considerable scope for developing a food industry based on a wide variety of products. In the late 1960's there still existed considerable scope for expanding the degree to which coffee, tea, and pyrethrum are processed. The major source of expanded industrial production of agricultural products, however, lay in the creation of new plants for canning or dehydrating fruits and vegetables; meat, dairy, and leather products; banana-based products, such as wine, vinegar, and woven fiber bags; and oilseed milling.

Textile production, based on imported materials, also provides a promising source for industrial expansion. The domestic market is strong in terms of import-substitution possibilities and of the increased demand for clothing and textiles by people entering the market economy. The relatively labor-intensive structure of textile production strengthens its role as a potential focus of industrial development. Footwear, beverages, and tobacco products are other basic consumer goods industries for which domestic demand can be expected to expand with the spread of cash

165

incomes. Extensive methane gas reserves represent a considerable source of long-range industrial possibilities through the production of nitrogen fertilizers, explosives, plastics, synthetic fibers, and other products of organic chemistry.

Increasing Government control over the country's political and social problems should stimulate industrial activity in the future by creating an atmosphere in which private investors would not lack confidence in the security of their investments as many did during the period from 1959 to 1965. The Government has also sought to encourage private and mixed foreign investment in manufacturing, processing, mining, power, construction, transportation, and tourism by granting approved enterprises favored status benefits (see Foreign Economic Relations, ch. 8). These benefits include duty-free importation of necessary machinery and materials and tax exemptions on the products produced and on profits.

Manufacturing

Structure and Organization

Processing of agricultural products, designed to increase their value in both the export market and the local market, is the major type of industrial production. A few consumer goods and some building materials are also produced, but the economy remains dependent on imports to fulfill its requirements of raw materials, intermediate and capital goods, and most consumer goods. In the late 1960's the majority of processing and manufacturing firms were operating below capacity.

Most of the firms engaged in food processing and manufacturing are small, and the industrial sector employs only a fraction of the wage labor force. The 1964 labor survey enumerated 2,282 persons, or 3 percent of the private and public sector labor force, as being employed by 71 manufacturing and processing firms (see Labor). Approximately 40 percent of these wage earners were employed in Kigali Prefecture; 20 percent, in Gisenyi Prefecture; and 15 percent, in Ruhengeri Prefecture. Of the firms enumerated, only 13 employed more than 50 persons, and 19 employed less than five persons.

The location of industrial establishments is determined primarily by accessibility to raw materials and markets. Processing plants and construction material firms are scattered throughout the country near the source of their raw materials. Most manufacturing firms are located in Kigali; however, a number of small-scale consumer goods establishments, engaged in activities such as baking, tailoring, and woodworking, are located in the other towns.

In early 1969 little information was available regarding ownership of industrial enterprises. It appeared that most manufacturing firms were European or Asian owned; several of these were branches of companies established in Burundi. Processing firms were either privately owned or owned by cooperatives. Many of the workshops in the country were organized and run as cooperatives under the auspices of some of the larger Roman Catholic missions. The few Africans in business generally operated one-man service firms, such as repairs or tailoring, that required relatively little initial capital.

Manufacturing and Processing Activity

Starting from a negligible base before independence, industrial activity began to expand after 1962 and particularly after the breakup of the economic union with Burundi in 1964 (see Foreign Economic Relations, ch. 8). Although national income figures identify only the contribution of the secondary sector as a whole to gross domestic product, it is estimated that manufacturing and processing increased from about 3 percent of gross domestic product, including subsistence agriculture, at constant prices in 1964 to about 8 percent in 1966. Part of this increase, however, was thought to be the result of an underestimation in 1964. The small contribution of manufacturing and processing to national income reflects the country's extremely limited industrial base and the low value-added component of processing, the main industrial activity.

Processing of Agricultural Products. Coffee beans are husked at about 360 communal centers scattered throughout the coffee-growing region. The beans are then processed at one of seven privately owned factories which have a total combined capacity of 22,440 pounds per hour, or 14,200 metric tons of marketable coffee per year, based on 100 working days; there is also one roasting plant (see Domestic Trade, ch. 8).

Green tea is converted into black tea at three factories. A factory at Mulindi with a capacity of 1,200 metric tons of black tea processes the output of the four plantations in Byumba Prefecture. Two factories, each with a capacity of 200 metric tons of dried tea, process the output of two European combine plantations in Cyangugu Prefecture; a fourth factory was scheduled to begin production in 1968 on one of the EEC-financed plantations in Cyangugu Prefecture.

Dried pyrethrum flowers are pressed for export at a plant outside Ruhengeri with an annual capacity of 3,000 metric tons of dried flowers. In 1968, however, the United Nations agreed to finance the construction of a pilot extraction factory at Ruhengeri which will yield 200 metric tons of pyrethrine extract from 3,000 metric tons of dried flowers.

Processing factories also exist for several food crops. A relatively large, modern mill at Ruhengeri, with a capacity of 880 pounds of flour an hour, processes most of the country's wheat production. A number of small-scale wheat-milling concerns are also established in the north, and a small quantity of sorghum, maize, and cassava is milled at the artisan level throughout the country. Flour from the larger grain mills is used by five modern bakeries and numerous small bakeries to make various kinds of bread.

In 1968 a pilot peanut-oil extraction plant began production at Kibungo as part of a Belgian project to test the feasibility of developing a peanut-oil industry; the plant's manually operated machines have an annual capacity of about 100 metric tons of oil. A sugar refinery, financed by the Republic of China, was under construction in 1968; it will process 100 metric tons of sugarcane a day.

The livestock-processing industry handles a very small fraction of the meat and dairy products consumed in the country. Several small slaughterhouses are scattered around the country, but no figures on their output have been available since 1959 when the Government's Veterinary Service ceased to control them. A dairy at Nyabisindu, the only one in operation, has a capacity of 1,850 gallons of milk a day, but produces only about 270 gallons daily; it also makes acceptable-quality butter.

Beverages and Tobacco. A large, modern brewery at Gisenyi annually produces about 3.8 million gallons of Pilsen-type beer for the local market. A small firm in the northwest with an annual capacity of about 48,000 gallons makes banana beer commercially, and household brewing of bananas or one of the cereal crops is extremely widespread. The Gisenyi brewery also makes carbonated beverages, as does a small firm in Kigali. A small quantity of cigars is manufactured from locally grown tobacco by a firm in Ruhengeri Prefecture.

Textiles, Clothing, and Footwear. The wearing apparel industry is dominated by a factory in Kigali which engages in three types of textile production: it repairs and reconditions about 500 tons of imported used clothing annually; it manufactures shirts, shorts, and pants from imported bleached and printed cloth; and it produces knit undershirts. A number of small tailors scattered around the country make clothing from imported cloth.

A blanket-weaving factory with an annual capacity of about 600,000 cotton blankets had been scheduled to begin manufacturing in mid-1967, but had not begun production by late 1968.

Two types of plastic shoes and rubber thongs are produced by a shoe factory in Kigali with an annual capacity of about 450,000 pairs. In mid-1968 an agreement was signed with the United States for the construction of a tannery in Kigali with an annual production of about 25,000 square feet of cowhide and 50,000 square feet of sheepskin. It was hoped that the tannery would provide the basis for leather shoemaking.

Wood, Paper, and Printing. Most lumber must be imported from neighboring countries, since there are only two small sawmills in the country. The imported lumber is used for building construction and by carpentry and woodworking workshops. A growing number of artisan workshops, as well as several larger firms, make furniture and other products such as windowframes, doors, and crates. A small firm in Cyangugu also makes pasteboard suitcases, but the plant has excess capacity. The Government printer in Kigali and the Roman Catholic Archdiosese printing press at Kabgayi produce newspapers, Government publications, pamphlets, business stationery, and related items.

Chemicals and Rubber. Only three industries produce chemical products. Three small soap factories, two at Kigali and one at Gisenyi, have a combined annual capacity of about 1,000 metric tons of household soap. A factory in Kigali manufactures about a ton of paints and varnish from imported materials per working day, although its capacity is double this production. A small pharmaceutical laboratory in Butare makes smallpox, rabies, and other vaccines.

Metal Products. The metal products industry consists primarily of the manufacture of relatively simple metal products from imported materials. One factory assembles steel furniture, such as beds, tables, and chairs, and steel construction materials. Three workshops produce metal frames and other forged items, and a small Kigali firm sharpens and polishes imported unfinished hoes, and another manufactures nails. A small factory in Cyangugu makes soldered aluminum boats and household utensils from imported materials; however, its capacity of 1.5 million pieces pieces annually exceeds local demand for pots, plates, and bowls.

A cooperative established in 1965, assembled 600 radios a month for domestic sale at half the price of imported ones. Its production was expected to increase to 1,000 radios per month when it moved into a new plant in Kigali in late 1968; it also planned to expand into phonographs, amplifiers, and interphones, as well as a wider range of radios. There are also a number of vehicle-repair and spare-parts garages and several forges, where used hoes and other agricultural implements are repaired.

Nonmetallic Mineral Products. Building materials are manufactured primarily on the workshop level. Imported cement is generally transformed into the necessary forms by the users, but two firms make cement blocks and pipes. Small brickworks and tileworks are scattered throughout the country. Lime is furnished by two firms in the northwest and by several small workshops near Cyangugu. A semi-industrial enterprise produces masonry materials.

Handicrafts. Handcrafted articles and items produced by individual artisans occupy an important place within the economy as the main source of objects essential to everyday living (see Artistic and Intellectual Expression, ch. 7). The largest volume of handcrafted goods is produced within the subsistence economy by the family or by persons who, in addition to their own agricultural activity, specialize in the production of such items. The main items produced are earthenware pottery, woven baskets and mats, forged iron, and some wooden articles. Large quantities of raffia baskets, banana-fiber rugs, ceramics, and wooden statuary are produced by trained craftsmen grouped in workshops operated by some of the larger Roman Catholic missions.

Mining

Mineral exploitation, although an important source of foreign exchange earnings, employment, and materials for the construction industry, does not play a major role in the economy. The mining sector contributed approximately 30 to 40 percent of the total value of exports between 1964 and 1967, but it accounted for only an estimated 2 percent of gross domestic product, including subsistence agriculture, at constant prices (see Foreign Economic Relations, ch. 8). In 1964 about 10 percent of the total private and public sector labor force was employed in mining, but the number of wage earners in mining was thought to have declined in the subsequent period (see Labor).

Minerals produced for export include tin (cassiterite), tungsten (wolfram), beryl, and columbium-tantalum. The local market absorbs most of the production of clay, sand, gravel, building stone, and lime. Most mining operations are carried out on a relatively small scale, mainly in open pits with simple techniques and by unskilled laborers. The four major mining companies also permit individual miners, grouped into cooperatives, to work deposits not suited to rational exploitation on the companies' concessions and to pan fine ore not recovered by the mechanical washers. These small-scale miners are required to sell their production to the mining companies. An estimated one-half of their output is smuggled to Uganda, however, because the prices offered by the companies are considered too low. Nevertheless, small-scale miners' production accounted for about one-fifth of the total known volume of mineral production in 1967.

Tin is second to coffee in foreign exchange earnings and accounts for most of the value derived from mineral exports. The main concessions are located on a west-east axis in the center of the country at Gatumba, Rutongo, Musha, and Rwinkwavu (see Physical Environment, ch. 3). Although the level of production is sensitive to fluctuations in the world market price, prices in the 1960's were at a profitable level, and production remained stable at 1,800 to 2,000 metric tons a year (see table 23). The rate of tin exploitation was expected to decrease in the 1970's as a result of weakening world prices and limited reserves, estimated in the mid-1960's at 65,000 metric tons.

Production of tungsten is even more affected by world market price fluctuations than that of tin. Prices were extremely unstable in the postindependence period, and output was generally low. Beryl and columbium-tantalum are both primarily recovered from tin ore, and their rate of exploitation is therefore dependent on the level of tin produced as well as on their profitability. Lithium production stopped in 1965 as a result of the exhaustion of known reserves. Gold production also stopped in 1965, according to official statistics, but it was thought that some gold was still being mined in the late 1960's and smuggled out of the country.

Power

With no known deposits of oil or coal, the country depends on hydroelectric power, imported oil, and firewood for its energy requirements. Firewood and oil supply practically all power, but the country's hydroelectric capacity is the most important source of energy. Large deposits of methane gas, dissolved in the depths of Lake Kivu, represent a power source of considerable long-term potential (see Physical Environment, ch. 3).

The bulk of electric power is generated and transmitted by Forces de l'Est, a Congolese public utility company, from its hydroelectric plant at Ntaruka, located between Lake Luhondo and Bulera, northeast of Ruhengeri. The station has an installed capacity of 7,500 kilowatts, out of a maximum of 11,250 kilowatts, and can provide 20 million kilowatt-hours of power annually. Its 70-kilovolt line feeds Kigali and the mining centers of Rutongo, Musha, and Rwinkwavu. Forces de l'Est also operates the Mururu hydroelectric plant on the Ruzizi River between Congo (Kinshasa) and Rwanda, south of Cyangugu. The plant's installed capacity of 12,600 kilowatts can be increased to a maximum of

Table 23. Mineral Production of Rwanda, 1959, 1962-67

(in metric tons)

	1959	1962	1963	1964	1965	1966	1967
Tin ore (cassiterite)_____	1,578	1,839	1,896	1,897	1,972	1,848	1,956
Tungsten ore (wolfram)____	143	238	12	154	232	325	538
Beryl_____	170	357	256	286	89	138	110
Lithium ore (amblygonite)__	2,690	326	368	5	23	_____	_____
Columbium-Tantalum_____	64	39	30	29	23	29	32
Gold (in pounds)_____	213	2	2	4	2	_____	_____

Source: Adapted from Rwanda, Ministère de la Coopération Internationale et du
Plan, Direction de l'Office Général des Statistiques, *Bulletin de Statistique*,
No. 13, Avril 1967, p. 79; *ibid.*, *Bulletin de Statistique*, No. 16, Janvier 1968,
p. 42.

28,200 kilowatts, and it can produce 70 million kilowatt-hours
annually. The station supplies only Cyangugu, a nearby airport
and a tea plantation in Rwanda, as well as Bukavu (Congo-Kinshasa) and Bujumbura, Burundi.

The National Water and Electricity Distributing Company
(Régie de Distribution d'Eau et d'Electricité du Pays—REGI-
DESO), a Government-owned enterprise, generates the remaining
electricity output. It operates a 1,100-kilowatt hydroelectric plant
at Gisenyi with a capacity of 5 million kilowatt-hours that serves
Gisenyi and Goma (Congo-Kinshasa). REGIDESO also maintains diesel-generating thermal stations at Butare, 555 kilowatts;
Nyabisindu, 70 kilowatts; Kibuye, 50 kilowatts; Gitarama, 90 kilowatts; Gisenyi, 550 kilowatts; and Byumba, 90 kilowatts.

In the mid-1960's the hydroelectric plants and the thermal
plants had excess capacity as a result of the very low demand for
electricity. In 1965, for instance, the Ntaruka and Mururu plants
had maximum demands of only three-sevenths of their combined
installed capacity, and the Butare and Nyabisindu plants were
operating at 10 percent of capacity. Between 1962 and 1966,
however, electricity consumption nearly doubled to 19.7 million
kilowatt-hours, despite a general stagnation in demand by the
mines, the largest consumers. On the basis of a study financed
by the European Economic Community, electricity consumption
was projected to increase by 14 percent annually between 1966
and 1972 and thereafter by about 6 percent a year. To provide
an adequate future power supply, the Government was considering, in the late 1960's, the feasibility of installing the third gen-
erating set at Ntaruka, which would bring its capacity up to the
maximum level, and of constructing a 7,500-kilowatt hydroelectric
plant on the Mukungwa River at the exit of Lake Luhondo. No
decision on these projects, however, had been reached by late
1968.

The methane gas deposits of Lake Kivu have been exploited to a very limited extent. An experimental collecting and purifying station operated by REGIDESO on the shores of Lake Kivu produces more than 1 million cubic meters of usable gas annually. The Bralirwa brewery in Gisenyi, the only industrial user of the gas, purchases about two-thirds of the plant's production for steam generation; the remainder is partly burned and partly stored. Government planners wish to exploit the deposits on a large scale for industrial fuels and for fertilizers and other synthetic chemical products. A larger scale operation, however, is limited by the extensive capital investment required, the difficulty of exporting the product except to neighboring countries, and the absence of a widespread regional market for fertilizers and other chemical products.

Construction

The construction industry comprised 134 private contracting firms in 1964, employing a total of 11,569 persons including the Government's public works department, or about 16 percent of the private and public wage sector labor force. The number of employees in each enterprise varies with the volume of work in progress, but the industry is characterized generally by small units; in 1964, 80 percent of private firms had fewer than 20 employees. Most of the large contracting firms are owned by non-Africans. Many major projects are undertaken by overseas contractors, using local labor.

Between 1962 and 1965 there were 472 reported completions of private buildings in the country, about equally divided between residential and nonresidential. Total floorspace was slightly more than 1 million square feet, three-quarters of this was in nonresidential construction. In the late 1960's the construction industry was experiencing a rapid expansion in business. During 1967, for example, 141 new construction permits were issued, involving a total floorspace of about 590,000 square feet; approximately two-thirds of the permits and four-fifths of the floorspace was for nonresidential construction. More than 60 percent of the permits were issued for Kigali, covering over 70 percent of the total projected floorspace; the second major center of construction was Butare Prefecture.

LABOR
Characteristics of the Labor Force
Composition

The only reliable labor statistics are based on a census conducted by the Government in 1964. In that year it was estimated that 74,290 persons were employed permanently or temporarily for salaries or cash wages. Of this total, 51,400 persons were employed in private or semipublic sector agriculture, mining, manufacturing and processing, construction, and services: 15,348 persons were central Government civil servants, teachers, or members of the Armed Forces; 6,000 persons were estimated to be employed as domestic servants; and 1,542 persons were added to compensate for a projected underestimation of 3 percent of the private and semipublic sector labor force (see table 24). Wage and salary earners represented 5.7 percent of the estimated potential work force of persons between the ages of 18 and 60 and about 11 percent of the adult male population. On a prefecture basis, the proportion of adult men in private and semipublic sector employment was: Kigali, 28 percent; Ruhengeri, 8.3 percent; Cyangugu, 8 percent; Gisenyi, 6.9 percent; Butare, 6.6 percent, Kibungu, 5 percent; Byumba, 4.3 percent; Gitarama, 3.9 percent; Kibuye, 2.8 percent; and Gikongoro, 2 percent.

The Government was the single largest employer in the country. Of 74,290 enumerated employees in private industry and public service, approximately 26,700 persons, in addition to an unknown number of persons in the public works department, were employed in the public sector. Within private industry the primary sector, agriculture and mining, accounted for about 45 percent of enumerated wage and salary earners.

Of the 1,536 enumerated private and semipublic sector establishments in 1964, only nine firms (four in agriculture, two in mining, one in construction, and two in services) employed more than 500 persons. Thirty-one firms employed 200 to 499 workers, 55 employed 100 to 199 workers, 297 employed 20 to 99 workers, 376 employed 5 to 19 workers, and 768 employed fewer than five workers. Approximately 58 percent of the establishments employing five or fewer people were commercial firms; a large proportion of construction and transport-warehousing firms were also in this category.

Little information was available in early 1969 regarding the ethnic composition of the labor force. In the past, although there was no legal discrimination in employment, there tended to be an ethnic division of functions; Europeans and Asians filled the highly skilled and well-paid posts because of the shortage of qualified and experienced Africans. By the late 1960's, however, two major changes had occurred. First, even though the country remainded dependent on a small number of foreign workers, Africans held the highest public service positions and many of the managerial and supervisory posts in private industry. Second, Hutu occupied practically all of the public service and private

Table 24. Projected Private and Semipublic Sector Employment in Rwanda in 1964[1]

	Agriculture Forestry	Mining	Manufacturing Processing	Construction	Water Electricity Sanitation[2]	Banking Commerce	Transport Warehousing	Services	Total Number of Employees
Butare	851	----	220	----	636	267	122	3,523	5,619
Byumba	1,459	530	42	----	45	33	36	1,009	3,154
Cyangugu	2,823	122	155	37	158	61	108	728	4,192
Gikongoro	----	316	5	65	66	3	29	764	1,248
Gisenyi	776	1,060	437	70	169	33	----	1,626	4,171
Gitarama	----	404	185	111	102	271	53	2,536	3,662
Kibungo	----	1,050	----	----	120	44	16	1,469	2,699
Kibuye	20	678	----	46	121	93	16	745	1,719
Kigali	2,745	2,713	901	8,496	442	956	102	2,427	18,782
Ruhengeri	1,261	534	337	2,744	186	89	38	965	6,154
TOTAL	9,935	7,407	2,282	11,569	2,045	1,850	520	15,792[3]	51,400

[1] Permanent workers, day laborers, seasonal and occasional workers, excluding central Government civil servants, teachers, and members of the Armed Forces.

[2] Employees of REGIDESO and the Ntaruka hydroelectric plant and workers in hospitals, dispensaries, and hygiene services.

[3] Of which 9,546 persons were employed in prefectural and communal administration, 1,803 persons in public organizations, tribunals, and embassies, 157 persons in private services such as hotels and restaurants, and 4,286 persons in religious missions.

Source: Adapted from Rwanda, Ministère de la Coopération Internationale et du Plan, Direction de l'Office Général des Statistiques, *Bulletin de Statistique*, No. 9, Avril 1966, p. 15.

industry skilled positions staffed by Africans, in contrast to the preindependence period when Tutsi filled the few posts staffed by Africans.

Unemployment

Statistics on unemployment are lacking, since there are no legal requirements for the registration of unemployed persons. It is known, however, that unemployment was a growing problem in the 1960's despite the increased demand for skilled and semi-skilled labor. Although there were few totally unemployed persons, since most Rwandans always retained a connection with the family farmholding, there was a large surplus of unskilled workers as well as a large number of persons in the agricultural sector, estimated at about one-quarter of the nonwage agricultural labor force, who were underemployed.

The main cause of growing unemployment was a decrease in the number of jobs available, which was aggravated by the high population growth rate and the absence of unused arable land. Wage and salary employment reached its highest level in 1954, but decreased in subsequent years, primarily as a result of a reduction in mining employment following increased mechanization. The departure of several large-scale European pyrethrum planters, who encountered difficulties in selling their production in the late 1950's and early 1960's, contributed to the decrease in employment opportunities, as did the closure of a number of small-scale enterprises that lost their main market in Congo (Kinshasa) when civil war erupted in that country in the early 1960's. The problem of unemployment was also affected in the immediate postindependence period by an apparent decrease in the previously sizable number of seasonal or permanent migrants to southern Uganda, mainly as a result of the presence of hostile Tutsi refugees along the border. There was also an apparent decrease in the formerly smaller number of migrants working in the mines in Katanga after political disturbances broke out in Congo (Kinshasa).

The failure of employment opportunities to expand at a faster rate than the population is a major concern to Government planners. The planners hoped that between 1964 and 1970 private and public sector wage employment would increase by 31 percent, in comparison with a projected population growth of 17 percent, through the creation of 23,700 new jobs, 15,000 of which would be in agriculture, mining, and construction. Additional persons were expected to find employment at the artisan level and in small-scale commercial establishments resulting from the growth in monetary income. Government planners also hoped that the concomitant problems of growing unemployment and increasing pressure on the land would be mitigated through the reestablishment of former levels of migration to Uganda and Congo (Kinshasa) and through the development of additional *paysannats*.

Migrant Labor and Stability

Of the 51,400 private and semipublic sector wage and salary earners enumerated in 1964, approximately 21 percent were classified as nonpermanent or as daily, seasonal, or occasional workers. The actual number of persons undertaking temporary employment within the country, however, was probably considerably higher than enumerated because census data were apparently incomplete. There were, for example, approximately 1,270 small-scale miners working on mining concessions in 1964 who were not enumerated, and the number of migrant workers in agriculture was probably underestimated. The agricultural sector had the highest proportion of temporary workers—45 percent. A large percentage of temporary workers, about 30 percent, were also employed in services, primarily by the religious missions. On a skills basis, approximately 25 percent of those classified as unskilled and about 13 percent of those listed as semiskilled were temporary.

There are various degrees of internal migration. Most workers leave their family farmholdings on a temporary basis to earn money for strictly defined and limited purposes and maintain strong economic and social ties with their rural families; when enough money is acquired, they return to their farms. Others stay indefinitely in the urban centers, but eventually return to the country. A small number of workers are semipermanent urban residents who return to the country in their old age; an even smaller number become permanently urbanized and sever all ties with the countryside.

A special type of migration is the permanent or seasonal emigration of Rwandan workers to Congo (Kinshasa) to work in the mines or to Uganda and, to a much lesser extent, to Tanzania and Congo (Kinshasa) to work in agriculture. Between 1959 and 1964 an estimated 9,500 men per year signed 3-year contracts with Union Minière du Haut Katanga to work in Congolese mines. A considerably larger but unknown number of persons migrate on an annual basis to southern Uganda to work on coffee and cotton plantations, often for the same employer year after year. Many of these workers eventually became permanent landholders in Uganda because of the increasing lack of arable land in Rwanda.

The rates of absenteeism and turnover within the labor force are extremely variable, depending on the branch of employment and the qualifications of the worker. Within the mining industry, the level of absenteeism is roughly estimated at 1.8 to 4 percent; in general, miners who are employed near their farms or who are married have a higher rate of absence than those whose farms are distant or who are single. The rate of absenteeism in the agricultural sector is considerable higher than in other sectors— an estimated 30 to 40 percent; absenteeism is affected by the same factors as in mining, but the proximity of a worker's own farm appears to exert more of an influence.

A certain amount of the high turnover rate in private industry, particularly among unskilled workers, is involuntary on the part of the employee, since many workers are employed on temporary contracts or are subject to seasonal fluctuations associated with agricultural planting and harvesting. The coffee harvesting season, in particular, provides expanded employment opportunities not only in agriculture, processing, and transport, but also in consumer goods industries and in commerce which benefit from increased demand at this time. Nevertheless, there is a high percentage of voluntary turnover; people leave their jobs to find others or leave wage employment completely to return to the countryside. The fluidity of the labor force, which rarely remains employed long enough to begin to acquire a significant level of advancement in skills or responsibility, combined with a generally inadequate level of education and nutrition, has resulted in low labor productivity.

Skills and Training

In 1964 about 63 percent of the private and semipublic sector labor force was classified as unskilled and 28 percent as semiskilled; only 9 percent of the enumerated workers were considered to be skilled. The highest proportion of unskilled labor, 80 percent or more, was employed in construction, mining, and public utilities; sanitary services, banking and commerce, and services had the greatest percentage of skilled workers—25, 22, and 18 percent, respectively.

No data were available regarding the ethnic division of skills, but it appeared that most skilled or supervisory positions in private industry were held by Europeans or Asians and that many key posts in the civil service were staffed by foreigners. Skilled Rwanda labor is not readily available, since most workers who have learned a technical speciality or who have had training in adminstration or accountancy are already employed in public service or private industry. The Government is making a major effort to expand the pool of skilled labor by concentrating its resources on education, particularly on increasing the number of places in secondary schools which encompass technical and vocational training, as well as general secondary education and teacher training (see Education, ch. 7). For categories of skills not requiring a secondary or higher education, most training is received on the job or in short-term training programs sponsored by the employer. Many of the larger Roman Catholic missions provide training in various crafts.

Wages and Working Conditions

Standards for wages and working conditions, as well as for labor organization and relations, are set forth in the Labor Code, enacted by the Government in 1967. The provisions of the code apply to all employers and employees, except civil servants and agricultural workers. The code provides for the establishment of a Labor Administrative Service, within a Ministry of Labor, to be responsible for the administration of laws regarding conditions of work, protection of workers, and social security. The Labor Administrative Service itself was to be composed of a General Directorate of Labor, which would prepare labor legislation and regulations, and of a labor inspectorate in each prefecture, which would ensure that labor laws and regulations were complied with. The code also provided for the establishment of a Labor Advisory Board, composed of an equal number of employers and employees, under the chairmanship of a Minister of Labor. Among other functions of the board, it was to be responsible for advising the Minister on minimum wage rates. In early 1969, however, it did not appear that the administrative machinery for implementing the Labor Code had been established, and there was no Ministry of Labor.

Wages and Benefits

Minimum-wage legislation was first introduced in 1949 by the Belgian Administration. The minimum renumeration was composed of three parts: a minimum daily salary for persons doing ordinary work, based on the estimated cost of living of a single worker, which was increased or decreased by 10 percent for persons doing heavy or light work, respectively; a food ration, which varied for the three types of work; and a housing allowance when free housing was not provided by the employer. In 1954 provision was made for the payment of a minimum daily total wage, encompassing a minimum salary and food and housing allowances. Employers, however, generally continued to pay workers a variable salary, to which was added a food ration and a housing allowance. In 1961 the minimum daily total wage was generally stabilized within each prefecture for various kinds of work, and it rose only slightly during the remainder of the 1960's. In practice, salaries for unskilled workers are higher in urban centers than in rural areas, and skilled workers are paid three to four times more than unskilled employees. Unskilled agricultural workers are paid between RF20 and RF30 a day, depending on the prefecture. Mining foremen receive RF116 a day; electricians, RF91; and auto mechanics, RF71. Government ministers earn RF390,000 a year, and primary school teachers receive about RF25,000 a year.

Fringe benefits enjoyed by public service employees and by persons in private industry working under contract include housing, pension rights, employment injury benefits, and leave provisions. The most important benefit is that of housing, either free or subsidized, which ensures rents well below the market rates. Medical or health services are provided by some employers for workers and their families. Workers are entitled to paid leave at the end of 1 year's service at the rate of 1 working day for every 2 months of uninterrupted service, with an increase of 1 working day for every 5 years of service.

Pension and employment injury benefits are covered by social security legislation enacted in 1962 and administered by the Social Fund, an autonomous body under Government supervision. The pension plan is financed by the employer and the employee, each of whom contributes 3 percent of the monthly salary. The workmen's compensation plan is financed by an employer contribution of 2 percent of the employee's monthly salary. The pensionable age is 55 years, and retirement from occupational activity is required for eligibility; the annual amount of pension equals one-tenth of total employer-employee contributions, including interest. Employment injury benefits comprise the necessary medical, surgical, pharmaceutical, and hospital care, daily allowances in case of temporary incapacity to work, pension or invalidity grants in case of total or partial incapacity, and survivors pensions and a burial grant in case of the death of the insured.

Working Conditions

Working conditions, particularly in the public service, are controlled by law, which generally follows the international standards prescribed by the International Labour Organisation. Conditions are generally agreed upon by contract between employer and worker and vary widely in different private industries. The Labor Code specifies general conditions of private sector employment, such as hours of work and leave entitlement.

180

Private sector labor contracts concluded for a fixed term cannot exceed 2 years for Rwandan citizens or 3 years for foreigners; the contract period is limited to 1 year for a married worker who is separated from his family. If a contract is for more than 3 months or necessitates the employee moving from his normal place of residence, the contract must be approved by the labor inspectorate in the prefecture where the worker was recruited.

According to the Labor Code, no worker can be dismissed by his employer except for legitimate reasons, which the employer must substantiate if challenged. Employment contracts for an unspecified period of time may be terminated at any time by either party giving notice. Contracts for a fixed term cannot be terminated by only one party before they are due to expire, except for reasons specified in the contract itself or for serious misconduct. Account must be taken of a worker's skills, seniority, and family responsibilities before he is released because of a work force reduction.

Working hours vary widely with the type of work done, but the legal workweek for full-time employees is 48 hours. One rest day a week, normally Sunday, is compulsory. The rate for overtime work is 25 percent of the daily salary for the first 2 hours and 50 percent for overtime exceeding 2 hours. Wages are paid daily, weekly, bimonthly, or monthly, depending on the nature of the employment contract.

Labor Organization and Relations

The Labor Code states that all workers are free to establish and to join trade unions and that employers may form occupational associations; it provides for the conclusion of binding labor-management agreements regarding conditions of work and employment. Within individual organizations, the code makes provision for the election of workers' representatives who main task, in addition to sitting on the Labor Advisory Board, is to submit to the employer any individual or collective grievances concerning conditions of work, protection of workers, application of collective agreements, occupational classification, and wage rates. In early 1969, however, there were no known labor unions or employers' associations; it was not known whether employees' representatives had been elected in any firms.

The Labor Code lays down two different procedures for the settlement of labor disputes, depending on whether they are individual or collective. Labor tribunals, established by special legislation which also defines their operation, deal exclusively with individual disputes between a worker and his employer relating to the employment contract. All collective disputes must be referred immediately to the prefectural labor inspectorate for settlement. If conciliation fails, a report to that effect must be forwarded to the minister responsible for labor affairs, who then decides whether to submit the dispute to arbitration. If an arbitration board is convened, it must give its ruling within 15 days of the date on which the dispute was referred to it. If no appeal is lodged by either side, the ruling is put into immediate effect; if an appeal is made to the minister responsible for labor affairs, he refers the matter back to a differently constituted arbitration board.

Provided that 4 days' notice is given, strikes and lockouts are legal if the minister has decided not to submit a dispute to the arbitration procedure or if the arbitration board gives a ruling that is opposed by either of the parties concerned. Strikes and lockouts are prohibited before the existing conciliation machinery has been exhausted; however, the code makes no provision for sanctions in the case of an illegal strike or lockout.

CHAPTER 10
THE ARMED FORCES, PUBLIC ORDER, INTERNAL SECURITY AND SAFETY

In early 1969 the military and police forces consisted of the National Guard, with more than 2,500 men, and the National Police, with approximately 1,200 personnel. Both forces were under the direct close supervision of the Minister of Police and National Guard, who reported directly to President Grégoire Kayibanda, the constitutionally designated head of the Armed Forces. Because of the centralized authority, the Police and National Guard may be utilized to augment and support each other in coping with internal or external threats to national security.

The Guard was established 2 years before independence and obtained its combat experience by repelling several small invasions in 1963 and 1964 by Tutsi who had fled from the country earlier. From this experience the Guard gained a confidence in its ability to handle future emergencies. There are legislative provisions for compulsory military service, but the number of qualified volunteers for enlistment has consistently exceeded requirements.

The Guard is dependent on foreign sources, mostly Belgian, for military equipment. Belgian Army officers and noncommissioned officers (NCO's) perform training, technical, and advisory functions, thus maintaining adherence to Belgian military procedures and concepts.

The Police are responsible for law enforcement. Aside from the records of infrequent judicial actions published in the *Official Journal of Rwanda,* little data concerning crime or the incidence of crime were available in early 1969. Serious crime and problems of lawlessness have not constituted a national problem. A formal court structure exists for the disposition of criminal cases, but the overwhelming majority of cases are adjudicated in accordance with customary law in local ad hoc courts (see Political and Governmental Systems, ch. 6).

HISTORICAL DEVELOPMENT

During the more than 40 years of Belgian rule, the Administrating Authority utilized detachments of the Belgian Congo police force (Force Publique) to maintain law and order. The force had

Belgian officers and Congolese troops. In 1959, as part of the preparation for Congo independence in 1960, the Belgians recruited 35 Rwandans into the force as the initial step in the establishment of the Rwanda National Guard (Garde National). After the additional recruitment of 70 Rwandans, it was planned to recruit 140 more each succeeding year until a total of 1,300 had been trained. In addition, a few Rwandans were selected for training at the Royal Military School in Belgium and the NCO school at Luluabourg in the Belgian Congo.

When it became evident that independence would be achieved, more than 50 Belgian officers and NCO's were assigned to organize and train the new Guard. The low educational level and a general lack of mechanical and technical skills among the potential recruits required extensive screening in the initial selection program. French was designated as the official language for the Guard, although fewer than 10 percent of the population spoke French. Training objectives were to develop a number of competent platoon commanders and to impart to the platoons basic infantry skills. By independence in 1962, small National Guard detachments were stationed in all prefectures (administrative divisions).

By late 1963 the Guard had about 950 troops and several Rwandan officers, but Belgian advisers were attached to most units. During late 1963 and early 1964, the Guard successfully repelled a number of poorly organized but potentially dangerous invasion attempts by Tutsi from their refugee areas in Burundi and Rwanda. These were the last serious Tutsi efforts to reclaim power.

RELATIONS OF THE MILITARY TO THE PEOPLE AND THE GOVERNMENT

The decisive defeats of the Tutsi stimulated the development of an espirt de corps in the Guard and increased its prestige and popularity. The Guard, almost exclusively Hutu in both the ranks and the officer corps, shares the general public's loyalty to and respect for President Kayibanda and willingness to support his government.

A military career as either an officer or an enlisted man offers financial benefits and security attainable in few civilian occupations. In addition, while on active duty, military men receive technical and general training, which prepares them for civilian occupations upon retirement.

ORGANIZATION, TRAINING, AND MOBILIZATION

In early 1969 the Minister of Police and National Guard, Lieutenant Colonel Juvenal Habyarimana, also was Chief of Staff of the National Guard with headquarters at Kigali. The General Staff included a Secretary General; Chiefs of Personnel, Intelligence, Operations, and Materiel Sections; and a Belgian Aviation Adviser. Among support facilities were a National Guard Officers' School at Kigali, a Non-Commissioned Officers' School at Butare, and the Kigali Logistical Base. A small Belgian Aviation unit provided maintenance and supply functions.

In early 1969 rifle companies were stationed at Gako, Butare, Cyangugu, Gisenyi, and Kibungo. Platoons were rotated to Kagitumba, Nyagetare, Bugarama, and Nshili, and independent rifle platoons were garrisoned at Byumba, Gitarama, Kibuye, Nyanza, and Ruhengeri. A Kanombe-based Intervention Group with three companies and one support company constituted a standby reserve force capable of deploying to augment the border-based units. Police detachments could be utilized to reinforce the National Guard units, and reserve units could also be mobilized under Presidential decree.

Initial enlistment in the National Guard is for 4 years. Volunteers must be bachelors and must remain single until they are either eligible for reenlistment or have been promoted to commissioned or warrant officer status. Enlistments may be extended during periods of hostilities or upon declarations of national emergencies. Exceptionally qualified NCO's and technical specialists are screened for career enlistment contracts upon the completion of their second reenlistment period.

Candidates for officer training must possess a superior school diploma (education beyond the 9 years of primary and middle schools), pass the written entrance examination, and favorably impress the candidate selection board. Candidates must also pass both oral and written French-language entrance requirements. The annual officer candidate classes are limited to fewer than 20 members, which results in the selection of only the best qualified applicants. Candidates qualified but not selected for the class beginning on August 1, 1967, were offered the opportunity to enter the National Police School at Ruhengeri for training in a career as police officers.

Construction of a new paracommando training facility was begun in September 1967 near the Mt. Karisimbi area, just north of the midpoint on the Ruhengeri-Gisenyi road. Upon completion, the facility will increase the in-country training capabilities and reduce the need for foreign training programs.

At the schools to produce competent infantry personnel training is conducted almost exclusively by Belgian military advisers. A small number of exceptionally qualified men are sent to Belgium for advanced or specialist courses. Pilot aptitude tests were administered in late 1968 to select one candidate for pilot training in Belgium.

Until 1967 the NCO school at Butare had accepted candidates from the enlisted ranks, but in that year, from among elementary school graduating classes throughout the country, Guard officers sought civilian applicants for training, stressing the economic benefits of a military career.

The National Guard has a standby reserve mobilization program that may be implemented by Presidential decree. Structured on a prefectural basis, the program is applicable to each prefecture. A partial mobilization of the Butare and Gikongoro prefectural reserves was ordered by President Kayibanda on November 22, 1966, but the force was deactivated in February 1967.

SECURITY FORCES AND THE NATIONAL ECONOMY

In 1963 the total expenditures for the National Guard and the National Police constituted about 20 percent of the national budget. In 1966, 35 percent of the budget was expended on the security forces, but in 1968 expenditures decreased to 23.3 percent (see table 25).

PUBLIC ORDER AND INTERNAL SECURITY

The only threats to public order since independence have come from the attempted invasions of the country by Tutsi refugees and the related danger of an uprising, in support of an invasion attempt, among Tutsi still residing in Rwanda.

National Police

The primary mission of the Police is the maintenance of law and order, which includes protecting public property, enforcing traffic regulations, supervising border checkpoints, maintaining public order, quelling riots, staffing prisons, and maintaining order during court sessions.

A Director General commands operations under the direction of the Minister of Police and National Guard. A few foreign police advisers assist the Director General and his headquarters staff. Most of the 1,200-man force is assigned to the 10 prefectural administrations. Although responsible to Police headquarters for matters of discipline, promotion, training, and general policy, the prefectural detachments receive their operating instructions from the prefect and his assistants.

The National Police School is located in a former Belgian medical training center at Ruhengeri. Some qualified candidates for

Table 25. *Ordinary (Recurrent) Expenditures for Security Forces of Rwanda,*
1963–68
(in millions of Rwandan francs[1])

Year	Total budget	Defense	
		Amount	Percent
1963............................	547.6	111.9	20.4
1964............................	659.6	166.2	25.2
1965............................	837.2	220.5	26.3
1966............................	1,321.9	462.8	35.0
1967[2]........................	1,375.3	378.7	27.5
1968[2]........................	1,382.6	322.0	23.3

[1] For 1963–65, 1 Rwandan franc equals approximately U.S.$0.02; for 1966–68, 1 Rwandan franc equals approximately U.S.$0.01.
[2] Provisional.

Source: Adapted from Rwanda, Ministère de la Coopération Internationale et du Plan, *Etude de Développement-Plan Intérimaire d'Urgence,* I, p. 240; "Le marché du Rwanda," *Marchés Tropicaux et Mediterranéens,* No. 1145, Octobre 21, 1967, p. 2760; and "Un budget équilibre pour 1968," *Rwanda Carrefour d'Afrqiue,* No. 75, Febvier 1968, p. 11.

the National Guard Officers School who are rejected annually because of quota restrictions are given the opportunity to pursue police careers by accepting appointment to the National Police School. The objective is to upgrade the caliber of police applicants.

Civilian and police applicants with the educational qualifications required for a particular rank may take a written examination for a position within that rank. Candidates must obtain at least 50-percent scores on the written test to be eligible for acceptance. A 6-month course for enlisted personnel usually includes training and basic lectures on court procedures, traffic regulations, drill, manual of arms, weapons, self-defense, first aid, administration, and functions of police detachments. A similar curriculum is taught in the course for officers, with additional emphasis on police administration. Limited Belgian, West German, and French support, mostly consisting of basic training programs, has been obtained for the school. A few Police personnel have been sent abroad for advanced courses.

In 1969 equipment, facilities, and logistical support for the Police ranged from poor to fair. Weapons were mostly of Belgian origin. Vehicles and maintenance support were furnished by a consolidated motor pool in Kigali, and communications equipment and facilities were inadequate.

There is a small but adequate in-country facility for the manufacture and repair of police uniforms, which are made from a gray twill fabric purchased from Belgian sources. Upon enlistment a recruit is issued one dress, one service, and one fatigue uniform. An additional set is provided each year the individual remains on active duty. Headwear includes an overseas-style cap; a dress cap with wide brim; and a helmet liner, often painted white for guard and parade functions.

Communal Police

The authority to recruit, suspend, and dismiss communal police personnel is exercised by the communal mayor. Each communal police force is commanded by a *brigadier* (sergeant), who is appointed by the mayor. The communal police are responsible for implementing the provisions of communal laws, regulations, and ordinances, and their functions include maintenance of public order, safeguarding public and communal property, overseeing the public market area, apprehension of violators, and execution of court judgments.

The maximum size of each communal police force is fixed at 1 policeman per 1,000 inhabitants residing in the commune. Under conditions of widespread public disorders, the mayor can appeal to the prefect for additional police units. The prefect is authorized to assign units of the National Police to assist the communal police force. When National Police units are thus assigned, all logistical support and funding requirements are provided by the central Government.

INCIDENCE OF CRIME

Before independence the Central Directorate of the Judicial Police in Bujumbura, Burundi, maintained the central police records for both Rwanda and Burundi.

The shortage of personnel trained in administration, documentation, identification, statistics, and maintenance of central police archives was acute in 1962. Organizational experience in collecting and circularizing of criminal data traditionally has been the function of Belgian civil servants. The Government requested and obtained Belgian advisers to recruit and train the necessary personnel. In 1969 most police supervisory positions were staffed with Rwandans, but Belgian advisers continued to provide assistance. A few foreign personnel, designated as "technical assistance agents" are integrated into police units.

CONTROL OF FIREARMS

The possession of any type of firearm is subject to permits issued by the Ministry of Interior. Permits are renewable annually, and a yearly tax of 100 francs ($1.00) per weapon is assessed. The Minister of Interior can order at any time a nationwide investory of firearms, ammunition, and spare parts and, under special circumstances, he may revoke all permits and require that all weapons, ammunition, and spare parts be surrendered at public depots for storage.

Possession of firearms and equipment defined as war or forbidden weapons is limited to agents of the State. Violation of the statutes is punishable by a maximum fine of 5,000 francs ($50) or 1 year of criminal servitude, but persons found guilty of trafficking in sophisticated weapons in areas where military operations are underway may be sentenced to 10 years' imprisonment.

It is unlawful to carry a loaded weapon or to discharge a firearm within five-eighths of a mile (one kilometer) of a residential area. Firearms may not be carried into public market areas, banks, establishment serving alcholic beverages, and public meetings. A citizen holding a firearm permit who plans to leave the country for a period in excess of 2 months must comply with the provisions of the gun control law before a passport is granted. He must file a declaration of intent to export his firearm, produce a bill of sale from an authorized buyer, or deposit the weapon in a public depot. The importation of firearms by foreigners is permitted, but such weapons are registered by serial number in the individual's travel visa.

BIBLIOGRAPHY

RECOMMENDED FURTHER READING

Association Européenne de Sociétés d'Etudes pour le Développement. *Etude Globale de Développement du Ruanda et du Burundi.* Brussels: n. pub., 1961.

Belgium. Ministère des colonies. *The Handbook of the Ruanda-Urundi Ten Year Plan.* Brussels: De Visscher, 1952.

"Le café, base de l'économie rwandaise," *Rwanda Carrefour d'Afrique* (Kigali), No. 78, Mai-Juin 1968, 4–8.

Caldwell, John C., and Okonjo, Chukuka (eds.). *The Population of Tropical Africa.* New York: Columbia University Press, 1968.

d'Hertefelt, Marcel. "The Rwanda of Rwanda." Pages 405–440 in J. Gibbs (ed.), *Peoples of Africa.* New York: Holt, Rinehart & Winston, 1965.

——, et al. *Ethnographic Survey of Africa, Central Africa, Part XIV: Les Anciens Royaumes de la Zone Interlacustre Méridionale (Rwanda, Burundi, Buha).* London: International African Institute, 1962.

International Labour Office. *Rwanda 1: An Act to establish a Labour Code. Dated 28 February 1967.* (Legislative Series 1967–Rwa. 1) Geneva: I.L.O., 1968.

Kagame, Alexis. *La Philosophie Bantu-Rwandaise de l'Etre.* (Classe des Sciences Morales et Politiques Memoire, XII, No. 1.) Brussels: Académie Royale de Science Coloniale, 1951.

Legum, Colin (ed.). *Africa: A Handbook to the Continent.* New York: Praeger, 1967.

Lemarchand, René. "Political Instability in Africa: The Case of Rwanda and Burundi," *Civilisations* (Brussels), XVI, No. 3, 1966, 307–335.

Leurquin, Philippe P. "Agricultural Change in Ruanda-Urundi: 1945–1960," *Food Research Institute Studies,* IV, No. 1, 1963, 39–89.

Louis, William Roger. *Ruanda-Urundi 1884–1914.* Oxford: Clarendon Press, 1963.

Maquet, Jacques J. *The Premise of Inequality in Ruanda; A Study of Political Relations in a Central African Kingdom.* London: Oxford University Press, 1961.

"Le marché du Rwanda," *Marchés Tropicaux et Mediterranéens* (Paris), No. 1145, Octobre 21, 1967, 2747–2790.

May, Jacques M. *The Ecology of Malnutrition in Middle Africa.* (Studies in Medical Geography, V) New York: Hafner, 1965.

Mountjoy, Alan B., and Embleton, Clifford. *Africa, A New Geographical Survey.* New York: Praeger, 1967.

Nkundabagenzi, F. *Rwanda Politique 1958–1960.* Brussels: Centre de Recherche et d'Information Socio-Politiques, 1961.

Pauwels, Marcel. "Clan and Family Relationships in Rwanda," *Annali Lateranensi* (Vatican), XXIX, 1965, 258–324.

"Productions agricoles du Rwanda," *Rwanda Carrefour d'Afrique* (Kigali), No. 43, Avril 1965, 17–19; No. 44, Mai 1965, 13–14; No. 45, Juin 1965, 8–12.

Pro Mundi Vita. *Ruanda: Strength and Weakness of the Christian Centre of Africa.* Brussels: Pro Mundi Vita, 1963.

Rawson, David P. "The Role of the United Nations in the Political Development of Ruanda-Urundi." (Unpublished Ph.D. Dissertation, The American University, School of International Service, 1966.)

"Rwanda." Pages 231–236 in *The Worldmark Encyclopedia of the Nations: Africa,* II. New York: Harper & Row, 1967.

"Le Rwanda économique," *Rwanda Carrefour d'Afrique* (Kigali), No. 66–67, Mai-Juin 1967, 2–8.

Rwanda. Ministère de l'Agriculture et de l'Elevage. *Produits Agricoles d'Exportation.* Kigali: n. pub., 1966.

_____. Ministère de la Coopération Internationale et du Plan. *Etude de Développement-Plan Intérimaire d'Urgence.* 4 vols. Kigali: Imprimerie du Gouvernement, 1967.

_____. Ministry of International Cooperation and Planning. External Documentation. *Invest in Rwanda.* Kigali: Ministry of Cooperation and Planning, 1967.

Sebasoni, Servilien. "Condition humaine et tradition rwandaise," *Civilisations* (Brussels), XVI, No. 1, 1966, 97–108.

United Nations. Secretariat. *Study of Population, Land Utilization, and Land System in Ruanda-Urundi.* (T/AC.36/L.60) New York: 1957.

U.S. Department of State. The Geographer. Office of Research in Economics and Science. Bureau of Intelligence and Research. *International Boundary Study, Burundi-Rwanda Boundary.* Washington: Department of State, No. 72, June 1, 1966.

_____. The Geographer. Office of Research in Economic and Science. Bureau of Intelligence and Research. *International Boundary Study, Congo (Leopoldville)-Rwanda Boundary.* Washington: Department of State, No. 52, June 15, 1965.

U.S. Department of State. The Geographer. Office of Research in Economics and Science. Bureau of Intelligence and Research. *International Boundary Study, Rwanda-Tanzania Boundary.* Washington: Department of State, No. 69, May 2, 1966.

_____. The Geographer. Office of Research in Economics and Science. Bureau of Intelligence and Research. *International Boundary Study, Rwanda-Uganda Boundary.* Washington: Department of State, No. 54, July 1, 1965.

Vansina, Jan. *L'Evolution du Royaume Rwanda dès Origines à 1900* (XXVI). Brussels: Académie Royale des Sciences d'Outre-Mer, Classe des Sciences Morales et Politiques, 1962.

Wagoner, Fred. "A Study in Nation Building in Africa." (Unpublished Ph. D. Dissertation, The American University, School of International Service, 1968.)

OTHER SOURCES USED

"Accord de coopération avec la Chine (Taipei)" *Rwanda Carrefour d'Afrique* (Kigali), No. 56–57, Juillet-Août 1966, 6.

Adamantidis, D. *Monographie Pastorale du Ruanda-Urundi.* Brussels: Ministère des Colonies, 1956.

Albert, Ethel M. "Socio-Political Organization and Receptivity to Change: Some Differences Between Ruanda and Urundi," *Southwestern Journal of Anthropology,* XVI, No. 1, 1966, 46–74.

Annuario Pontificio. Vatican: n.pub., 1968.

"Apercu sur le régime foncier au Rwanda," *Rwanda Carrefour d'Afrique* (Kigali), No. 65, Avril 1965, 4–6.

Arnoux, A. "Le divination au Ruanda," *Anthropos* (Fribourg), XII–XIII, 1917–1918, 1–57.

"Autour du budget 1967," *Rwanda Carrefour d'Afrique* (Kigali), No. 62, Janvier 1967, 10–11.

Beaver, Stanley H., and Stamp, Dudley. *A Regional Geography, Part II, Africa.* (8th ed.) London: Longmans, Green, 1964.

Belgium. *Ruanda-Urundi: Economy.* I and II. Brussels: Belgian Congo and Ruanda-Urundi Information and Public Relations Office, 1960.

_____. *Ruanda-Urundi: Geography and History.* Brussels: Belgian Congo and Ruanda-Urundi Information and Public Relations Office, 1960.

_____. *Ruanda-Urundi: Social Achievements.* Brussels: Belgian Congo and Ruanda-Urundi Information and Public Relations Office, 1960.

_____. Ministère des Colonies. *L'Agriculture au Congo Belge et au Ruanda-Urundi de 1948 à 1952.* Brussels: Ministère des

Colonies et du Gouvernement Général du Congo Belge, Services de l'Agriculture, 1954.

Belgium Office de la Coopération au Développement. *Vade Mecum de la Coopération au Développement*. (3d ed.) Brussels: n.pub., 1967.

———. Office de Tourisme du Congo Belge et du Ruanda-Urundi. *Traveller's Guide to the Belgian Congo and Ru:nda-Urundi*. (2d ed.) Brussels: n.pub., 1956.

Brandel, Rose. "Types of Melodic Movement in Central Africa," *Ethnomusicology*, VI, No. 2, 1962, 75–87.

Brass, William C., et al. *The Demography of Tropical Africa*. Princeton: Princeton University Press, 1968.

"Budget 1965 équilibre aux deux-tiers," *Rwanda Carrefour d'Afrique* (Kigali), No. 54–55, Mai-Juin 1966, 11.

"Un budget équilibre pour 1968," *Rwanda Carrefour d'Afrique* (Kigali), No. 75, Fevrier 1968, 10–11.

Bureau Central d'Etude pour les Equipements d'Outre-Mer. *Etudes des Transports au Rwanda* 2 vols. Paris: n.pub., 1964.

Bureau International du Travail. *Rapport au Gouvernement de la République du Rwanda sur les Conditions de Développement du Mouvement Coopératif au Rwanda*. (OIT/TAP/Rwanda/R.1) Geneva: n.pub., 1963.

———. *Rapport sur les Salaires au Ruanda-Urundi*. (OIT/TF/Ruanda-Urundi/R.1) Geneva: n.pub., 1961.

Bushaijija, Stanislaus. *Le Mariage Coutumier au Rwanda*. Namur, Belgium: n.pub., 1966.

Codere, Helen. "Power in Ruanda," *Anthropologica* (Ottawa), IV, No. 1, 1962, 45–85.

"Comment tirer davantage de notre capital bananier," *Rwanda Carrefour d'Afrique* (Kigali), No. 48, Septembre–Octobre 1965, 15–16.

"Un commerce extérieur à équilibrer," *Rwanda Carrefour d'Afrique* (Kigali), No. 49, Novembre 1965, 12–13.

"Constitution of Rwanda." Pages 675–692 in Amos J. Peaslee (ed.), *Constitutions of Nations, Volume I—Africa*. (Rev. 3d ed.) The Hague: Martinus Nijhoff, 1965.

"Coopération belgo-rwandaise," *Rwanda Carrefour d'Afrique* (Kigali), No. 73, Decembre 1967, 2–3.

"La coopération 'TRAFIPRO' nous parle," *Rwanda Carrefour d'Afrique* (Kigali), No. 40, Janvier 1965, 5–6; No. 41, Fevrier 1965, 9–10.

Cordwell, Justin M. "African Art." Pages 28–48 in William R. Bascom and Melville J. Herskovits (eds.) *Continuity and Change in African Culture*. Chicago: University of Chicago Press, 1959.

Coupez, A. *Grammaire Rwanda Simplifiée*. Usumbura: Service de l'Information. 1961.

Coxill, H. W., and Grubb, Kenneth (eds.). *World Christian Handbook*. London: Lutterworth Press, 1968.

Czekanowski, Jan. *Investigations in the Area between the Nile and the Congo*. (Trans., Frieda Schutze). New Haven: Human Relations Area Files, 1960.

de Blij, Harm. *A Geography of Subsaharam Africa*. Chicago: Rand McNally, 1964.

Delhove, Georges. *Diagnostic d'Ensemble de Base Préalable a la Mise en Oeuvre d'une Politique de Commerce Extérieur*. (Rapport No. 1, Contexte Général d'une Direction Politique de Commerce Exterieur.) Kigali: Ministère des Finances et du Commerce Extérieur, 1964.

de Meyer, Roger. *Introducing the Belgium Conao and Ruanda-Urundi*. Brussels: Office de Publicité, 1958.

"Une démographie aziatique en Afrique," *Rwanda Carrefour d'Afrique* (Kigali), No. 80, Août 1968, 6–9.

"Démonstration agricole chinoise," *Rwanda Carrefour d'Afrique* (Kigali), No. 68, Juillet 1967, 9–11.

Derkinderen, G. *Atlas du Congo Belge et du Ruanda-Urundi*. Paris: Elsevier, 1956.

d'Hertefelt, Marcel. "Myth and Political Acculturation in Rwanda." Pages 114–135 in A. Dubb (ed.), Myth in Modern Africa. Lusaka: Rahodes-Livingstone Institute, 1960.

"Dix mille hectares de théiers," *Rwanda Carrefour d'Afrique*, No. 52–53, Mars-Avril 1966, 8.

DuFays, P. Felix. "Pages d'epopée africain." In René Weverbergh, *Jours Troublé*. Brussels: Libraire Coloniale, 1928.

Dumont, Rene. "Décolonisation et développement agricole au centre-est de l'Afrique, (Kigali), le Rwanda-Urundi," *Tiers-Monde* (Paris) I, No. 4, 1960, 421–445.

Foy, Felician (ed.). *National Catholic Almanac*. Garden City: Doubleday, 1968.

Frost, J. M. (ed.). *World Radio TV Handbook*, 1968. Hellerup: World-Radio Television Handbook Company, 1968.

Gildea, Ray Y., and Taylor, Alice. "Rwanda and Burundi," *Focus*, XIII, No. 6. Washington: The American Geographical Society, 1963.

Gourou, P. *La Densité de la Population du Ruanda-Urundi*. Brussels: Institut Royal Colonial Belge, 1953.

Gusinde, Martin. "Pygmies and Pygmoids: Twides of Tropical Africa," *Anthropological Quarterly*, XXVIII, No. 1, 1955, 3–46.

Hailey, Lord. *An African Survey*. (Rev. ed.) New York: Oxford University Press, 1957.

Hance, William A. *A Geography of Modern Africa.* New York: Columbia University Press, 1964.

Harroy, J. P., *et al. Le Ruanda-Urundi: Ses Ressources Naturelles, ses Populations.* Brussels: Les Naturalistes Belges, 1956.

Hattori, Masaya. "Ruwanda Ginkososai Nikki" (The Diary of the Director General of the National Bank of Rwanda), *Chuo Koron,* October 1967, 198–209. (Translated by U.S. Department of the Army, Washington: November 1968.)

International Monetary Fund. *International Financial Statistics,* XXII, No. 3, 1969, 264–265.

"Investissements et coopération," *Rwanda Carrefour d'Afrique* (Kigali), No. 66–67, Mai-Juin 1967, 22–26.

Johnston, B. F. *The Staple Food Economies of Western Tropical Africa.* Stanford: Stanford University Press, 1958.

Hiernaux, Jean. "Racial Properties of the Natives of Ruanda-Urundi," *Anthropos* (Fribourg), L, 1955, 967.

Kayibanda, Grégoire. *Discours Prononcés par Son Excellence M. G. Kayibanda, Président de la République Rwandaise.* Kigali: Service de l'Information, 1964.

"Kayibanda insiste sur l'émanicipation du peuple," *Rwanda Carrefour d'Afrique* (Kigali), No. 79, Juillet 1968, 5–7.

"Kigali, capitale naissante," *Rwanda Carrefour d'Afrique* (Kigali), No. 70, Septembre 1967, 4–11.

"Labour Code in Rwanda," *International Labour Review,* XCVII, No. 2, 1968, 299–301.

Lemarchand, René. "Revolutionary Phenomena in Stratified Societies: Rwanda and Zanzibar," *Civilisations* (Brussels), XVIII, No. 1, 1968, 16–51.

Leurquin, Philippe P. "Economie de subsistance et alimentation au Ruanda-Urundi: quelques cas conrets," *Zaïre* (Brussels), XII, No. 1, 1958, 16–28.

——. "L'évolution des prix agricoles au Ruanda-Urundi, exemple de marché non intégré," *Bulletin de Institut de Recherches Economiques et Sociales* (Louvain), XXIII, No. 6, 1957, 395–463.

——. *Le Niveau de Vie des Populations Rurales du Ruanda-Urundi.* (Publications de l'Université Lovanium de Léopoldville 6) Louvain: Institut de Recherches Economiques et Sociales, 1960.

——. "Le vie économique du paysan ruanda. L'exemple de Karama, Nyaruguru," *Zaïre* (Brussels), XI, No. 1, 1957, 41–67.

Loupias, P. "Tradition et légende des Batutsi sur la création du monde et leur établissement au Ruanda," *Anthropos* (Fribourg), III, No. 1, 1908, 1–13.

196

Maquet, Jacques J. "La participation de la classe paysanne au mouvement d'indépendence du Rwanda," *Cahiers d'Etudes Africaines* (Rijswijk), IX, No. 16, 1964, 552–568.

_____. "Le problème de la domination Tutsi," *Zaïre* (Brussels), VI, No. 10, 1952, 111–116.

_____. and Naigisiki, X. "Les droits fonciers dans le Ruanda ancien," *Zaïre* (Brussels), XI, No. 4, 1957, 339–360.

_____. *Ruanda. Essai Photographique sur une Société Africaine en Transition.* Brussels: Elsevier, 1957.

Merriam, Alan P. "African Music." Pages 49–86 in William R. Bascom and Melville J. Herskovits (ed.), *Continuity and Change in African Culture.* Chicago: University of Chicago Press, 1959.

_____. "African Music Reexamined in Light of New Material from the Belgian Congo and Ruanda-Urundi," *Zaïre* (Brussels), VII, No. 3, 1953, 244–253.

_____, and Merriam, Barbara W. "Banyaruanda Proverbs," *Journal of American Folklore*, LXVII, 1954, 267–284.

Miracle, Marvin P. *Agriculture in the Congo Basin: Tradition and Change in African Rural Economics.* Madison: University of Wisconsin Press, 1967.

Moes, John E. "Foreign Exchange Policy and Economic Union in Central Africa," *Economic Development and Cultural Change*, XIV, No. 4, 1966, 471–483.

Mulago, V. "L'union vitale bantu où le principe de cohesion de la communaté chez les Bashi, les Banyarwanda et les Barundi," *Annali Lateranensi* (Vatican), XX, 1956, 61–263.

Murdock, G. *Africa: Its People and Their Culture History.* New York: McGraw-Hill, 1959.

"New Social Security Legislation in Rwanda and Burundi," *International Labour Review*, LXXXVII, No. 5, 1963, 485–489.

"Nos ressources énergetiques," *Rwanda Carrefour d'Afrique* (Kigali), No. 59, Octobre 1966, 7.

"Notes of the Month," *U.N. Chronicle*, III, No. 10, 1966, 70–71.

_____. *U.N. Chronicle*, IV, No. 11, 1967, 34–46.

"Nouvelle législation sur l'exportation du café du Rwanda," *Rwanda Carrefour d'Afrique* (Kigali), No. 43, Avril 1965, 12–13.

"Où en est la coopération avec la CEE?," *Rwanda Carrefour d'Afrique* (Kigali), No. 59, Octobre 1966, 9–10.

"Où en sont les salaries," *Rwanda Carrefour d'Afrique* (Kigali), No. 50, Decembre 1965-Janvier 1966, 10–11.

Oxford Regional Economic Atlas: Africa. Oxford: Clarendon, 1965.

Pauwels, Marcel. "Le culte de Nyabingi," *Anthropos* (Fribourg), XLVI, 1951, 337–357.

——. "Fiancée et jeune mariée au Ruanda," *Zaïre* (Brussels), V, 1951, 115–135.

——. "Inheritance in Rwanda," *Annali Lateranensi* (Vatican), XXVIII, 1964, 50–107.

——. "Jeux et divertissements au Rwanda," *Annali Lateranensi* (Vatican), XXIV, 1960, 219–363.

——. "La magie au Ruanda," *Annali Lateranensi* (Vatican), XVII, 1953, 83–155.

——. "Le pacte du sang au Ruanda," *Annali Lateranensi* (Vatican), XXII, 1958, 9–40.

——. "Usages fenebre au Ruanda," *Anthropos* (Fribourg), XLVII, 1953, 30–43.

"Les paysannats au Rwanda," *Rwanda Carrefour d'Afrique* (Kigali), No. 46, Juillet 1965, 10–13; No. 47, Août 1965, 11–13.

"Perspectives de développement industriel," *Rwanda Carrefour d'Afrique* (Kigali), No. 81, Septembre-Octobre 1968, 5–7.

"Le plan rwandaise préparera l'indépendence économique," *Rwanda Carrefour d'Afrique* (Kigali), No. 66–67, Mai-Juin 1967, 16–21.

Population and Vital Statistics Report (Series A), XX, No. 2, 1968, 8–9.

"Le Président de la République présente la reforme monétaire," *Rwanda Carrefour d'Afrique* (Kigali), No. 52–53, Mars-Avril 1966, 6–7, 15.

"Problèmes de développement," *Rwanda Carrefour d'Afrique* (Kigali), No. 79, Juillet 1968, 8–11.

"Quatre ans de coopération rwanda-belge," *Rwanda Carrefour d'Afrique* (Kigali), No. 63, Fevrier 1967, 7–8.

"Report on Rwanda," *Atlantic Monthly*, CCXIII, No. 6, 1964, 30–38.

"Les ressources animales du Rwanda," *Rwanda, Carrefour d'Afrique* (Kigali), No. 43, Avril 1965, 8–11; No. 44, Mai 1965, 7–11; No. 45, Juin 1965, 6–8.

"Le rôle des cadres administratifs et sociaux," *Rwanda Carrefour d'Afrique* (Kigali), No. 68, Juillet 1967, 4–8.

"Ruanda." Pages 250–253 in *Africa 1968*. Paris: Société Presse Africaine Associée, for Jeune Afrique, 1968.

Ruanda-Urundi. *Evolution Economique du Ruanda-Urundi de 1949 à 1955*. Usumbura: n.pub., 1956. (typescript).

Ruhashyankiko, N. "La codification du droit au Rwanda," *Revue Juridique du Rwanda et Burundi* (Bujumbura), VI, No. 2, 1966, 61–69.

"Rwanda." Pages 1144–1148 in *The Europa Year Book 1968*, II. London: Europa Publications, 1968.

_____. Pages 1384–1386 in *The Statesman's Year Book 1968–1969*. New York: St. Martin's Press, 1968.

Rwanda. "Le Rwanda vous présente." (Secured from Embassy of the Republic of Rwanda, Washington, n.d.).

_____. Ministère de la Coopération Internationale et du Plan. Direction de l'Office Général des Statistiques. *Bulletin de Statistique*, No. 8, Janvier 1966.

_____. Ministère de la Coopération Internationale et du Plan. Direction de l'Office Général des Statistiques. *Bulletin de Statistique*, No. 9, Avril 1966.

_____. Ministère de la Coopération Internationale et du Plan. Direction de l'Office Général des Statistiques. *Bulletin de Statistique*, No. 10, Juillet 1966.

_____. Ministère de la Coopération Internationale et du Plan. Direction de l'Office Général des Statistiques. *Bulletin de Statistique*, No. 11, Octobre 1966.

_____. Ministère de la Coopération Internationale et du Plan. Direction de l'Office Général des Statistiques. *Bulletin de Statistique*, No. 12, Janvier 1967.

_____. Ministère de la Coopération Internationale et du Plan. Direction de l'Office Général des Statistiques. *Bulletin de Statistique*, No. 13, Avril 1967.

_____. Ministère de la Coopération Internationale et du Plan. Direction de l'Office Général des Statistiques. *Bulletin de Statistique*, No. 14, Juillet 1967.

_____. Ministère de la Coopération Internationale et du Plan. Direction de l'Office Général des Statistiques. *Bulletin de Statistique*, No. 15, Octobre 1967.

_____. Ministère de la Coopération Internationale et du Plan. Direction de l'Office Général des Statistiques. *Bulletin de Statistique*, No. 16, Janvier 1968.

_____. Ministère des Finances. Service des Douanes. *Tarif des Droits d'Entree*. Kigali: n.pub., 1966.

_____. Ministère des Postes, Telecommunications et Transports. *Kigali Telephone Directory, 1967*. Kigali: n.pub., 1967.

_____. Régie de Distributions d'Eau et d'Electricité du Rwanda. *Rapport et Bilan 1963*. Kigali: n.pub., 1964.

_____. Régie de Distributions d'Eau et d'Electricité du Rwanda. *Rapport et Bilan 1964*. Kigali: n.pub., 1965.

_____. Secrétariat d'Etat au Plan National de Développement. Direction de l'Office Général des Statistiques. *Bulletin de Statistique*, No. 17, Avril 1968.

"Rwanda." Secrétariat d'Etat au Plan National de Développement. Direction de l'Office of Général des Statistiques. *Bulletin de Statistique*, No. 18, Juillet 1968.

"Le sacre paien, le sacre chretien," *Rwanda Carrefour d'Afrique* (Kigali), No. 76, Mars 1968, 8–11; No. 77, Avril 1968, 6–8.

Sasnett, Martena, and Sepmeyer, Inez. *Educational Systems of Africa*. Berkeley and Los Angeles: University of California Press, 1966.

Schumacher, A. "Au Ruanda: considerations sur la nature de l'homme," *Zaïre* (Brussels), III, No. 3, 1949, 257–278.

Schumacher, P. "La phonetique du Kinyarwanda," *Anthropos* (Fribourg), XVI/XVII, 1921/22, 326–341; XVIII/XIX, 1923/24, 688–699.

"Les sciences agronomiques au Rwanda," *Rwanda Carrefour d'Afrique* (Kigali), No. 58, Septembre 1966, 13–14.

Segal, Aaron. *Massacre in Rwanda*. (Fabian Research Series 240) London: Fabian Society, 1964.

———. "Rwanda: The Underlying Causes," *Africa Report*, IX, No. 4, 1964, 3–8.

"La situation de la caféiculture au Rwanda," *Rwanda Carrefour d'Afrique* (Kigali), No. 40, Janvier 1965, 4–5.

"Speech Made by President Kayibanda on the Occasion of the Graduation of the 6th Group of Officers of the National Army," *Information Bulletin of the Embassy of the Republic of Rwanda* (Washington), No. 8, March-April 1967, 1–4.

Stamp, L. Dudley. *Africa: A Study in Tropical Development*. New York: John Wiley and Sons, 1964.

"Tour d'horizon du l'économie rwandaise," *Rwanda Carrefour d'Afrique* (Kigali), No. 47, Août 1965, 14–15.

"Le tourisme pour aprés-demain . . . ou dès aujourd'hui?," *Rwanda Carrefour d'Afrique* (Kigali), No. 75, Fevrier 1968, 6–9.

"La tranche prioritaire du plan quinquennal," *Rwanda Carrefour d'Afrique* (Kigali), No. 75, Fevrier 1968, 6–9.

Trewartha, Glen, and Zelinsky, Wilbur. "The Population Geography of Belgian Africa," *Annals of the Association of American Geographers*, XLIV, No. 2, 1954, 163–193.

United Nations. Department of Social Affairs. Population Division. *The Population of Ruanda-Urundi*. New York: 1953.

———. General Assembly. *Interim Report of the United Nations Commission for Ruanda-Urundi*. (A/4856) New York: 1961.

———. Trusteeship Council. Visiting Mission to Trust Territories in East Africa, 1948. *Report on Ruanda-Urundi*. (T/217) New York: 1950.

United Nations. Trusteeship Council. Visiting Mission to Trust Territories in East Africa, 1951. *Report on Ruanda-Urundi*. (T/1031) New York: 1952.

——. Trusteeship Council. Visiting Mission to Trust Territories in East Africa, 1954. *Report on Ruanda-Urundi*. (T/1168) New York: 1955.

——. Trusteeship Council. Visiting Mission to Trust Territories in East Africa, 1957. *Report on Ruanda-Urundi*. (T/1402) New York: 1958.

——. Trusteeship Council. Visiting Mission to Trust Territories in East Africa, 1960. *Report on Ruanda-Urundi*. (T/1551) New York: 1960.

U. S. Department of Commerce. Office of Technical Services. Joint Publications Research Service (Washington). The following publications are JPRS translations from foreign sources:

"Brief Survey of Various Faculties at Rwanda National University," by Simon Cyaga, in *Le Diapason* (The Tuning Fork), Butare, II, No. 5, April 8, 1967. (JPRS: 41,006, *Translations on Africa*, No. 563, 1967.)

"Data on Education in Rwanda Released," *Umunyamuryango TRAFIPRO* (The Cooperative Member), Kabgayi, No. 32, October 31, 1967. (JPRS: 44,220, *Translations on Africa*, No. 681, 1968.)

"EDF Projects in Rwanda," *Rwanda Carrefour d'Afrique*, (African Crossroads), Kigali, No. 71, October 1967. (JPRS: 44,252, *Translations on Africa*, No. 682, 1968.)

"Facts on the Rwandan Ministry of Agriculture and Husbandry," *Umunyamuryango TRAFIPRO* (The Cooperative Member), Kabgayi, No. 8, March 31, 1966. (JPRS: 36,172, *Translations on Africa*, No. 387, 1966.

"FED Aid to Rwanda," by Louis C. D. Joos, in *Umunyamuryango TRAFIPRO* (The Cooperative Member), Kabgayi, No. 36, February 29, 1968. (JPRS: 45,498, *Translations on Africa*, No. 714, 1968.)

"First Pyrethrine Factory," *Umunyamuryango TRAFIPRO* (The Cooperative Member), Kabgayi, No. 32, October 31, 1967. (JPRS: 44,382, *Translations on Africa*, No. 684, 1968.)

"German Investments in Rwanda," *Umunyamuryango TRAFIPRO* (The Cooperative Member), Kabgayi, No. 28, June 30, 1967. (JPRS: 42,342, *Translations on Africa*, No. 383, 1966.)

"A Glance at Cooperatives in Ruanda," *Umunyamuryango TRAFIPRO* (The Cooperative Member), Kabgayi, No. 8, March 31, 1966. (JPRS: 35,938, *Translations on Africa*, No. 383, 1966.)

"Law Concerning the Rwandan Electoral System," *Journal Officiel de la Republique Rwandaise* (Official Journal of the Republic of Rwanda), Kigali, VI, No. 19, October 1, 1967. (JPRS: 43,599, *Translations on Africa*, No. 663, 1967.)

"Law Setting Up Rwandan Development Bank," *Journal Officiel de la Republique Rwandaise* (Official Journal of the Republic of Rwanda), Kigali, VI, No. 16, August 15, 1967. (JPRS: 43,573, *Translations on Africa*, No. 662, 1967.)

"Minister of Commerce, Mining and Industry Outlines Regulations for Selling Coffee in Rwanda," *Umunyamuryango TRAFIPRO* (The Cooperative Member), Kabgayi, No. 28, June 30, 1967. (JPRS: 42,342, *Translations on Africa*, No. 623, 1967.)

"Ministerial Decree No. 6/20/020 Dated 5 May 1967 on the Implementation of the Law Dated 28 February 1967 Governing the Conditions of Employing Foreigners Under the Labor Code," *Journal Officiel de la Republique Rwandaise* (Official Journal of the Republic of Rwanda), Kigali, VI, No. 20, October 15, 1967. (JPRS: 43,964, *Translations on Africa*, No. 675, 1968.)

"Problems of Rwandan Education Reviewed," *Umunyamuryango TRAFIPRO* (The Cooperative Member), Kabgayi, No. 33, November 30, 1968. (JPRS: 47,356, *Translations on Africa* No. 763, 1969.)

"Pros and Cons of Return of Rwandan Refugees," by Jean-Maire Mbaguta, in *Remarques Africaines* (African Remarks), Brussels, May 1967. (JPRS: 41,416, *Translations on Africa*, No. 586, 1967.)

"Reflections on the Conditions and Prospects for Economic Development in Rwanda," by Marcel Ch. Heimo, in *Geneve-Afrique* (Geneva-Africa), Geneva, VII, No. 1, 1968, 7–29. (JPRS: 46,465, *Translations on Africa*, No. 736, 1968.)

"Rwanda Ordinary Budget for Fiscal Year 1967," *Journal Officiel de la Republique Rwandaise* (Official Journal of the Republic of Rwanda), Kigali, VI, No. 3, February 1, 1967. (JPRS: 41, 373, *Translations on Africa*, No. 583, 1967.)

"Rwanda Presents Interim Development Plan to European Development Fund Officials," *Umunyamuryango TRAFIPRO* (The Cooperative Member), Kabgayi, No. 26, April 24, 1967. (JPRS: 41,362, *Translations on Africa*, No. 582, 1967.)

"Rwandan Development Budget for 1967," *Journal Officiel de la Republique Rwandaise* (Official Journal of the Republic of Rwanda), Kigali, VI, No. 9, May 1, 1967. (JPRS: 43,495, *Translations on Africa*, No. 660, 1967.)

"Statistics on Swiss-Organized Rwandese Cooperative Members," *Umunyamuryango TRAFIPRO* (The Cooperative Member), Kabgayi, No. 26, April 24, 1967. (JPRS: 41,362 *Translations on Africa*, No. 582, 1967.)

"Taiwan Rice Experts Start Pilot Project in Rwanda," *Umunyamuryango TRAFIPRO* (The Cooperative Member), Kabgayi, No. 26, April 24, 1967. (JPRS: 41,362 *Translations on Africa*, No. 582, 1967.)

"TRAFIPRO Director Discusses Cooperative's Use of Ugandan Trucks," by F. Friedly, in *Umunyamuryango TRAFIPRO* (The Cooperative Member), Kabgayi No. 35, January 28, 1968. (JPRS: 45,498, *Translations on Africo* No. 714, 1968.)

U.S. Department of Labor. Bureau of International Labor Affairs. Bureau of Labor Statistics. *Directory of Labor Organizations, Africa*, II. (Rev. ed.) Washington: GPO, 1966.

U.S. Department of State. Bureau of Public Affairs. *Background Notes, Rwanda.* (No. 7916) Washington: Department of State, 1967.

_____. Foreign Service Institute. *Kirundi.* (Basic Course Series) Washington: GPO, n.d.

United States Information Agency. Office of Policy and Research. Research Service. *Communications Data Book for Africa.* Washington: USIA, 1966.

Vanhove, J. *Essay on the Common Law of Rwanda.* (Trans., Dorothy Crawford.) New Haven: Human Relations Area Files, 1961.

van Tichelen, H. E. "Problèmes du développement économique du Ruanda-Urundi," *Zaïre* (Brussels), XI, 5, 1957, 451–474.

"Vers un code de travail," *Rwanda Carrefour d'Afrique*, No. 49, Novembre 1965, 10–11.

Webster, John B. "The Political Development of Rwanda and Burundi." (Syracuse University, Maxwell Graduate School of Citizenship and Public Affairs, Program of Eastern African Studies, Occasional Paper No. 16.) Syracuse: Program of Eastern African Studies, 1966.

Weeks, George. "The Armies of Africa," *Africa Report*, IX, No. 1, 1964, 4–10.

Wiedner, Donald. *A History of Africa South of the Sahara.* New York: Random House, 1962.

Wood, David. *The Armed Forces of African States.* (Adelphi Papers No. 27) London: Institute of Strategic Studies, 1966.

(Various issues of the following periodicals were also used in the preparation of these chapters: *Africa Confidential* [London], September 1968; *Africa Report* [Washington], from January

1964 to December 1968; *Africa Research Bulletin: Economic, Financial, and Technical Series* [London], from January 1964 to December 1968; *Africa Research Bulletin: Political, Social, and Cultural Series* [London], from January 1966 to December 1968; *Economist Intelligence Unit Quarterly Economic Review: Congo, Rwanda, Burundi* [London], from March 1966 to December 1968; *International Commerce* [Washington], from January 1966 to December 1968; *International Financial News Survey* [Washington], from January 1964 to December 1968; *Keesing's Contemporary Archives* [London], from January 1962 to December 1968; *New York Times,* September 1968; *Uganda Argus* [Kampala], September 1968.)

GLOSSARY

communes—Lowest administrative subdivision of which there were 141 in 1969. Administered by an elected mayor and council.

gross domestic product—Value of total production originating within national borders. Calculated before deduction of depreciation of fixed assets. Monetary gross domestic product excludes value of subsistence production.

Mwami—Title of the traditional Tutsi king of Rwanda. Plural, Bami. Monarchy abolished as a result of 1961 election.

PARMEHUTU—(Parti du mouvement de l'emancipation Hutu; Party of the Hutu Emancipation Movement.) Political party formed in 1959 with the goal of ending Tutsi rule. After the overthrow of the Tutsi monarchy, PARMEHUTU, under leadership of Grégoire Kayibanda, governed the country and, in 1969, was only active party.

paysannats—Planned agricultural settlements established by Government to increase agricultural production and to promote resettlement from densely to thinly populated areas.

prefecture—Major administrative division of which there were 10 in 1969. Administered by a prefect who is Presidential appointee.

RF—Rwandan franc, the unit of currency. Until devaluation in April 1966, equivalent to approximately U.S.$0.02; after devaluation, U.S.$0.01.

Before April 1966		*After April 1966*	
RF1	—U.S.$0.02	RF1	—U.S.$0.01
RF50	—U.S.$1	RF100	—U.S.$1
RF100	—U.S.$2	RF1,000	—U.S.$10
RF1,000	—U.S.$20	RF1,000,000	—U.S.$10,000
RF1,000,000	—U.S.$20,000	RF1,000,000,000	—U.S.$10,000,000
RF1,000,000,000	—U.S.$20,000,000		

ubuhake—Patron-client relationship between the Tutsi and the Hutu by which the Hutu obtained use of Tutsi cattle and rendered services to the owner in return. Formally abolished by Hutu Government.

umusozi—Hill. Social and economic division of the districts, comprised of a neighborhood formed by a hill, the surrounding valleys, and the families living within.

INDEX

Ababanda clan: 58
Abacyaba clan: 58
Abagesera clan: 57
Abaha clan: 58
Abakono clan: 58, 68
Abaniakarama clan: 58
Abanyaginya clan: 7, 45, 57
Abashambo clan: 58
Abasigaba clan: 57
Abasinga clan: 57
Abatira clan: 58
Abatsoba clan: 58
Abega clan: 45, 57
abortion: 60
Agence Maritime Internationale
    (AMI): *See* International Maritime Agency
Agency for International Development: 119
agricultural settlements: *See paysarnats*
agriculture (*see also* crops, livestock): 14, 26, 133, 137, 144–50
airlines and airports: 38, 127
Akanyaru River: 33
Albert National Park: 36, 128
amulets: 68
ancestral spirits: 45, 64, 66
Anglican churches: 73 (table 7)
arabica coffee: 111, 154
Arabs: 50, 52, 102
arts and crafts: 104–5, 170
Asian population: 50, 65
Association for the Social Betterment of the Masses: 18, 19, 20, 22, 23, 24
Association Internationale de Développement Rural Outre-Mer (AIDR): *See* International Association for Overseas Rural Development
Association pour la promotion sociale de la masse (APROSOMA): *See* Association for the Social Betterment of the Masses
Astrida: *See* Butare

Bagaragaza Thadée: 89
balance of payments: 119, 121 (table 14)
balance of trade: 109
bananas: 39, 105, 151, 152
Bank of Kigali: 129

banking and credit: 128–33
Banque Centrale du Congo Belge et du Ruanda-Urundi: *See* Central Bank of the Belgian Congo and Ruanda-Urundi
Banque d'Emission du Rwanda et du Burundi (BERB): *See* Issuing Bank of Rwanda and Burundi
Banque Nationale du Rwanda (BNR: *See* National Bank of Rwanda
Bantu language: *See Kinyarwanda* language
Baptists: 73 (table 7)
barley: 157, 160
Base River: 33
Bashara clan: 67
basket weaving: 104, 105
beer: 61, 79, 151
Belfeld Mission: 71
Belgian population: 12, 50, 85
Belgium: 10, 13, 23, 42, 69; source of aid. 92, 117, 148; trade with, 115, 116
beryl: 170, 171, 172 (table 23)
Bethel Missionary Society: 71
bicycles: 126
Birgirumwami, Aloys: 72
birth rate: 48, 59
Biruruma River: 33
blood brotherhood: 56–57
Bralifwa brewery: 168, 173
bridewealth: 45, 58, 60, 61, 62, 79
budget, national: 86, 134–38, 140; education, 97; health programs, 26; security forces, 186, 187
Burgesera-Mayaga region: 147
Bujumbura: 31, 38
Burton, Richard (explorer): 9
Burundi: 7, 10, 13, 89; trade with, 115, 116, 126
Butare Parish: 72
Butare Prefecture: 32, 40, 49 (table 5), 52, 127; agriculture, 146, 153; industry, 172, 173; university, 101
Butera, Sixte: 52
Byumba Prefecture: 32, 49 (table 5), 172; agriculture, 146, 159, 160, 167

Caisse d'Epargne du Rwanda (CER): *See* Rwandan Savings Bank
Canada: 118
cassava: 151, 152

207

Kibuye Prefecture: 32, 49 (table 5), 172; agriculture, 146, 153

Kigali Prefecture: 32, 129; agriculture, 146, 153, 154; airport, 117, 127; industry, 166, 173; population, 25, 39, 49 (table 5); press, 94

Kigeri IV, Mwami: 8

Kigeri V Ndahindurwa, Mwami: 19, 21

Kigwa: 7

kinship systems, 44, 45, 57–58

Kinyamateka: 94

Kinyarwanda language: 2, 43, 47–48, 63; press, 94; used in schools, 95, 98

Kirundi language: 47

Kivu, Lake: 25, 26, 27, 37, 127, 128, 164

Korea: 91

kraal: 54

kwashiorkor: 26, 41

Labor Code: 179

labor force: 166, 173–75

lakes: 164

land tenure system (*see also ubuhake*): 75, 150, 163

land use: 144–47; pastureland, 36, 163

languages (*see also* English language, French language, Kinyarwanda language): 47–48

legumes: 151, 152

libraries: 94

life expectancy: 49

literacy rate: 2

lithium ore: 171, 172 (table 23)

livestock (*see also* cattle): raising, 160, 162; diseases, 30, 161

local governments: 32

Luhwa River: 31

Lukarara River: 33

lulunga: 103

Lyangombe: 61

magico-religious practitioners: 67

maize: 151, 152

Manifesto of the Bahutu: 17

manufacturing: 165–70

Marist Brothers: 70

marriage: 45, 57, 63

Mbonyumutwa, Dominique: 23

medical care: 26, 42, 68, 180

men (*see also* children, women): 48 (table 4), 174; ideal man, 78; status, 55, 60

methane gas: 37, 166, 171, 173

Mibambwe I Mutabazi, Mwami: 7

Micombero, Michel: 90

migration: 50, 51, 58, 176, 177

milk: 161, 168

millet: 151, 152

minerals: 37, 114, 170

mining: 170–71

missionaries (*see also* Protestant churches, Roman Catholic Church): 26, 42

Missionaries of Africa: *See* White Fathers

Mobutu, Joseph: 90

Mugesera, Lake: 164

Muhazi, Lake: 164

Mukungwa River: 33

Mulindi: 167

Murura hydroelectric plant: 171, 172

music (*see also* drums): 102

Musinga, Mwami: 13

Mutara III Rudahigwa: 14, 19

Mutara Big Game Hunting Reserve: 128

mutual aid societies: 58

Mututsi: 7

Mwogo River: 33

mythology: 7

nagana: 30, 148, 161

Naigiziki, S.: 104

National Assembly: 82

National Bank of Rwanda: 128

National Guard: 137, 184–86

National Park of the Volcanoes: 36, 128

national parks: 29, 36, 37, 128

National Pedagogical Institute: 102

National Police: 186

National Water and Electricity Distributing Company: 172, 173

Ndahindurwa, Jean-Baptiste: *See* Kigeri V, Mwami

Netherlands: 116

Nikwigize, Phocas: 72

Nkundabagacenzi, Fidele: 91

Ntaruka: 171, 172

Nyabarongo River: 33, 154

Nyabiingi: 67

Nyabisindu: 52, 168, 172

Nyabugogo River: 33

Nyampundu: 7

Nyanza: 8, 50

Nyundo Diocese: 72

occupational prestige: 76

Office of Industrial Corps of Rwanda (OCIR): 125, 155, 158
oral literature and tradition: 7, 76, 103
Organization of African Unity: 91

Pakistan: 91; Pakistanis, 50, 52
Parc National des Volcans: *See* National Park of the Volcanoes
Party of the Hutu Emancipation Movement (PARMEHUTU): 2, 3, 19, 20, 22, 23, 24, 82
patron-client relationship: *See ubuhake*
paysannats: 58, 117, 147, 150, 153, 159, 160
peanuts: 152, 153, **168**
pensions: 180
Pentecostal churches: 73 **(table 7)**
pharmaceuticals: 169
pigs: 161, 162
Plan Intérimaire d'Urgence: *See* Interim Emergency Plan
police: 137, 183, 186, 188
police courts: 88
political parties (*see also* Party of the Hutu Emancipation Movement): 19, 22, 82
polygyny: 55, 75
population: 11, 43; densities, 29, 49
population control: 52
Portugal: 91
post office: 38; postal savings, 134
potatoes: 151, 152
power: 171–73
prefectures (*see also* names of individual prefectures): 32; employment, 174, 175; land use, 146, 149; population, 49, 146; prefects, 85
Presbyterian churches: 73 (table 7)
president: 83
press: 18, 94
primary education: 95–99
Protestant churches: denominations, 73 (table 7); missionary activity, 10, 71
proverbs: 76–77, 104
provinces: *See* prefectures
public health: 42, 137
Public Law 480 (U.S.): *See* Food for Peace
public schools: 95
pygmies: 6, 45
pyrethrum: 125, 156, 157, 159; ex-

ports, 110, 111, 112 (table 11), 115, 167

radio: 38, 93–94, 169; broadcasts, 44, 48
Radio Diffusion République Ruandaise: 93
railroads: 26, 38
rainfall: 27, 32, 34
rainmaking: 67
Rassemblement Démocratique Ruandaise (RADER): *See* Rwanda Democratic Rally
refugees: 20, 51, 89, 90
Régie de Distribution d'Eau et d'Electricité du Pays (REGIDESO): *See* National Water and Electricity Distributing Company
religion: *See* chapter 5 and Roman Catholic Church resettlement programs: 27, 30, 40, 51
retail trade: 123
Reweru, Lake: 164
rice: 152, 153
rituals and cults: 66
rivers (*see also* waterways): 27, 38
road network: 26, 31, 37–38, 125
Roman Catholic Church: cooperative, 124; mission activities, 10, 54, 69–70, 167, 169, 170, 179; parishes, 71, 72; youth societies, 58
Ruganzu I Bwimba, Mwami: 7
Rugwero, Lake: 35
Ruhengeri Diocese: 72
Ruhengeri Prefecture: 32, 36; agriculture, 146, 159; airfield, 127; police school, 186; population, 40, 49, 166
Ruhondo, Lake: 164
Rumira, Lake: 164
rural areas: 39, 49
Ruzizi River: 27, 31, 32
Rwanda Carrefour d'Afrique: 48, 94
Rwanda Democratic Rally: 19, 22
Rwanda National Union Party: 19, 20, 22
Rwandan Savings Bank: 133
Rwasibo, Jean-Baptiste: 23
Ryangombe: 45, 66

Sabinio, Mt.: 32
Sake, Lake: 164
savings: 133–34
scholarships: 117
schools: 71; Koranic, 73; Roman

211

Catholic missions, 3, 14, 54, 69, 95
secondary education: 3, 96, 97, 99–100; vocational training, 101, 179
Seventh Day Adventists: 73 (table 7)
sheep: 161, 162
Sibomana, Joseph: 72
snakes: 37
social security: 180
social services: 138
soils (*see also* erosion) : 27, 35–36
sons, status of: 55
sorghum: 151, 152, 153
soul: 64
soybeans: 153
Speke, John Hanning: 9
Stanley, Henry Morton: 9
strikes and lockouts: 182
sugarcane: 153
Sunday: 181
Supreme Court: 83, 87–88
Swahili: 48
swamps and marshes: 29, 158
sweet potatoes: 151, 152
Switzerland: 118

taboos: 56, 62; food, 41, 59, 68
Tanganyika: *See* Tanzania
Tanzania: 30, 90, 126
taxes: 130, 135, 139, 140
tea: 156, 157, 158–59; exports, 110, 111, 112 (table 11), 167
teacher training: 96, 99, 100
telephone system: 38
Telli, Diallo: 91
textiles: 112, 113, 168
tilapia: 164
tin ore: 170, 171, 172 (table 23) ; exports, 110, 111, 112 (table 11), 115, 122
tobacco: 168
totem: 57
tourism: 127–28, 137
Trade School of Kicukiro: 101
trade unions: 181
TRAFIPRO: *See* Travail, Fidèlité, Progrès
transportation (*see also* road network) : 37–38, 112, 113, 125–27
Travail, Fidèlité, Progrès: 124
tsetse fly: 30, 40, 148, 163
tungsten: 170, 171, 172 (table 23)

Tutsi (ethnic group) : 1, 6, 11, 12, 74; basis of rule, 8–9; clans, 57; music, 102; population, 43, 46–47; refugees, 20, 184
Twa (ethnic group) : 1, 6, 43, 45–46, 102
twins: 59

Ubuhake: 6, 13, 16, 44, 73–74
ubwoko: *See* kinship systems
Uganda: 90, 177; trade, 115, 116, 126
unemployment and underemployment: 176
Union nationale runandaise (UNAR) : *See* Rwanda National Union Party
United Kingdom: 116
United Nations: 91; Trusteeship Council missions, 15–16, 21; aid, 118, 167
United States: aid, 118; trade, 115, 116
Université Lovanian: 96
Université Nationale du Rwanda: 101, 117
Université Officielle: 96
urban areas: 52
Urundi: *See* Burundi

vegetation: 35–36
Vice President: 83
Victoria, Lake: 33
virginity: 62
Virunga Mountains: 26, 27, 128
vocational schools: 101
volcanoes: 27, 128

wages: 144, 166, 174, 179–80
Wahu Island: 35
warthogs: 40
waterways: 26, 127
wheat: 152
White Fathers: 10, 69
wildlife: 29, 37, 128
witches: 68
women (*see also* taboos): 48 (table 4) ; ideal woman, 78; status, 54, 55, 63, 64
wood products: 114

Yuhi IV Gahindiro, Mwami: 8
Yuhi V Musinga, Mwami: 69

Published Country Studies

(Area Handbook Series)

550–65	Afghanistan		550–151	Honduras
550–98	Albania		550–165	Hungary
550–44	Algeria		550–21	India
550–50	Angola		550–154	Indian Ocean
550–73	Argentina		550–39	Indonesia
550–169	Australia		550–68	Iran
550–176	Austria		550–31	Iraq
550–175	Bangladesh		550–25	Israel
550–170	Belgium		550–182	Italy
550–66	Bolivia		550–69	Ivory Coast
550–20	Brazil		550–177	Jamaica
550–168	Bulgaria		550–30	Japan
550–61	Burma		550–34	Jordan
550–83	Burundi		550–56	Kenya
550–50	Cambodia		550–81	Korea, North
550–177	Cameroon		550–41	Korea, South
550–159	Chad		550–58	Laos
550–77	Chile		550–24	Lebanon
550–60	China		550–38	Liberia
550–63	China, Republic of		550–85	Libya
550–26	Colombia		550–172	Malawi
550–91	Congo		550–45	Malaysia
550–90	Costa Rica		550–161	Mauritania
550–152	Cuba		550–79	Mexico
550–22	Cyprus		550–76	Mongolia
550–158	Czechoslovakia		550–49	Morocco
550–54	Dominican Republic		550–64	Mozambique
550–52	Ecuador		550–35	Nepal, Bhutan and Sikkim
550–43	Egypt		550–88	Nicaragua
550–150	El Salvador		550–157	Nigeria
550–28	Ethiopia		550–94	Oceania
550–167	Finland		550–48	Pakistan
550–155	Germany, East		550–46	Panama
550–173	Germany, Fed. Rep. of		550–156	Paraguay
550–153	Ghana		550–185	Persian Gulf States
550–87	Greece		550–42	Peru
550–78	Guatemala		550–72	Philippines
550–174	Guinea		550–162	Poland
550–82	Guyana		550–181	Portugal
550–164	Haiti		550–160	Romania

550–84	Rwanda	550–89	Tunisia
550–51	Saudi Arabia	550–80	Turkey
550–70	Senegal	550–74	Uganda
550–180	Sierra Leone	550–97	Uruguay
550–184	Singapore	550–71	Venezuela
550–86	Somalia	550–57	Vietnam, North
550–93	South Africa	550–55	Vietnam, South
550–95	Soviet Union	550–183	Yemens, The
550–179	Spain	550–99	Yugoslavia
550–96	Sri Lanka (Ceylon)	550–67	Zaïre
550–27	Sudan	550–75	Zambia
550–47	Syria	550–171	Zimbabwe
550–62	Tanzania		
550–53	Thailand		
550–178	Trinidad and Tobago		

☆U.S. GOVERNMENT PRINTING OFFICE: 1986 0-490-994